T5-ARO-501

Notes of a Guilty Bystander

Books by Robert Sylvester

Dream Street	(1946)
Rough Sketch	(1948)
The Second Oldest Profession	(1950)
Indian Summer	(1952)
No Cover Charge	(1954)
The Big Boodle	(1956)
Tropical Paradise	(1960)
Notes Of a Guilty Bystander	(1970)

Notes of a Guilty Bystander

by

Robert Sylvester

PRENTICE-HALL, INC., Englewood Cliffs, N.J.

Notes of a Guilty Bystander
by Robert Sylvester

© 1970 by Robert Sylvester

All rights reserved. No part of this book may be
reproduced in any form or by any means, except for
the inclusion of brief quotations in a review, without
permission in writing from the publisher.

ISBN 0-13-624932-9

Library of Congress Catalog Card Number: 75-110670

Printed in the United States of America   *T*

Prentice-Hall International, Inc., London
Prentice-Hall of Australia, Pty. Ltd., Sydney
Prentice-Hall of Canada, Ltd., Toronto
Prentice-Hall of India Private Ltd., New Delhi
Prentice-Hall of Japan, Inc., Tokyo

For Jane and Karin, who are
too young to remember any of this

AUTHOR'S NOTE

In the memories that make up this book, no attempt has been made to separate the current living from the recent or long dead. To have identified everybody chronicled over so many years as "the late" whoever, might have made the book so long that it would have scared off my editor and/or publisher. Things change fast these days, so fast that there have been major upheavals between the time the book was written and the date of its publication. Moore's historied restaurant, for instance, was turned over to a new operator by the last of the Moore family. One continues to hear talk that such places as Sardi's and Shor's will "franchise the operation" or otherwise undergo metamorphosis. Who or what will still be a part of the scene by the time this is a book in your hands deponent knoweth not. What *is* the important thing, the author hopes, is that everybody and every place discussed was very much alive and active indeed when the incidents and anecdotes concerning them were happening back in those wonderful and, for once, "late" years.

CONTENTS

contents

Notes of a Guilty Bystander

What Time Is It? Where Am I?

TIME, CLAIMS THE OLD ADAGE, is a thief, and memory is a liar. Not in my case. In my case time is a sneak. In my case memory is a magpie. For me time didn't pass—it sneaked by when I wasn't looking. Time would stand stock still and then, next time I looked at the clock, it was five years later. As for my memory, it should be ashamed of itself. All the important things are stored there somewhere, but my memory dismisses them and instead keeps bringing back the frivolous, the frolicsome and the foolish. It is probable that a competent psychiatrist would decide that my memory has a built-in leak. Anything important was heavy enough to leak out. The froth stayed where it was put.

It is almost forty years since I started working on New York newspapers, and where am I? At no place that calls for pointing with pride. Still a working newspaper stiff like all working newspaper stiffs. A mugg, as *Variety*, the show biz bible, calls its serfs. A newspaper stiff is never part of anything—he is just *around* things. He is just as important as what he wrote yesterday and—alas!—not only does nobody remember what he wrote yesterday, but if they do remember they think somebody else wrote it somewhere else.

1

Until reasonably recent years all newspapermen, with a few glowing exceptions such as William Randolph Hearst, Arthur Brisbane, Walter Winchell and a few political pundits, were unidentified men. A newspaperman at work was "the man from the *Globe*," or whoever. In certain circles, of course, this might be amended to "the gentleman from *The Times*." Now everybody, including the kid just promoted from the mailroom, is a personal expert on any subject and is qualified to sign his full name to his highly opinionated version of deathless prose concerning a sewer break, senile delinquency, the rise in the incipiency of whatever. Ad infinitum, ad nauseum and Ad Wolgast.

This is somehow amusing to me because so many news stories, big and small, concern unidentified men (smallest stories) and unidentifiable men (biggest stories). And this, in turn, somehow reminds me of the classic of the cub reporter who was firmly told twice by his city editor that he simply had to bring in more facts with his stories. On his third try he made it.

"The bodies of three nude men, all Jews, were recovered from the East River yesterday," he dutifully wrote.

To any man who has achieved any authentic success in any other field, the "name" newspaperman must indeed take a position somewhere between cretin and character. Red Smith, the sportswriter, once summed it up best.

"Newspapermen," said Red, "are the most underpaid and overprivileged people in the world."

So expect no personal memoirs of the wordly great in the pages that follow. Look not for intimate glimpses I viewed by virtue of being a newspaperman and thus on the *inside* of events and coincidences effecting the history of our world. Many times I have been near enough to reach out and touch greatness. There has been plenty of adventure; the wings of romance and mystery have brushed close. Yet, looking back, all I seem to remember—indeed, all I *want* to remember—are the laughs, the color, the atmosphere of what I am sure any analytical critic would agree has been a fairly wasted life.

I once talked with Winston Churchill (before his comeback to greatness) but can't remember what he said, much less any epigram or glowing phrase he made. But I can draw a picture of those funny shoes Beatrice Lillie used to wear in her lady's maid sketch. I spent three and a half years in World War II, and what I remember most vividly was the war-is-hell that went on when somebody stole six hundred cases of Officer Club whisky on Pelelieu. I crawled through the Depression with millions of others and am not ashamed to say I would try it all over again if it would again also be an era of a Kid Chocolate in the prize ring, a Frank Frisch or Dizzy Dean in baseball, a Ken Strong playing for the football Giants or Frank Fay doing a monologue at the Palace.

I talked many times with Cuba's Fulgencio Batista, one of the earlier so-called dictators, and what I remember about him was his obsession with the life and times of Abraham Lincoln. I have shaken hands with two Presidents, an ex-king and a reigning prince, and have had my ears bruised by a stadium full of self-made heroes, kingmakers, experts, great names and every other tiresome variety of big shot. All faces and figures of same have faded from a weak mind.

My racket, at times, also brought me into close contact with disaster. In my racket your nose gets to recognize the smell of a fired policeman's revolver and the unforgettable aroma of human bodies broiled in a tenement fire. Drowned bodies don't smell worse. They look worse.

Yet once the horror of disaster has faded, as horror decently insists on doing, there inevitably remains at least one single, small sidebar, closely connected with disaster, which insists upon being perversely amusing.

The *Andrea Doria*, sunk in collision, its beauty now rusting on the Nantucket shoals, was a major disaster. Yet whenever that disaster comes to mind, I also think of poor Captain Piero Calamai, the master of the doomed ship. He was brought ashore, dazed and in shock, and the newspapermen clamored at him—what happened? "What happened?"

"Somebody sinka my ship," said the captain.

My memory is not only a magpie, it is also a clown.

What, I often wonder, are the innermost thoughts and conclusions of other, perhaps more serious folk. I once asked a man who should know, the late Dr. Foster Kennedy, a pioneer in the fields of mental disorder, psychiatry and just plain human behavior. He had diagnosed a friend's illness, and after a conference with him I remarked that he looked tired. He admitted that he was. He had been listening to his patients' innermost thoughts all day long, and it sometimes got wearing.

"I sometimes wish," said this man who spent his life prying into the secrets of strange brains, "that people would show a little more 18th Century reticence."

That doubtless applies to this book and its author. For half of my newspaper life my work has kept me in the fields of show business, sports, Broadway (when we had one), nightclubs (ditto), racetracks, amusement parks, hoodlums, footpads and cutpurses, and the mentally lame, halt and blind. Any life must have its share of pain and disappointment. To hell with the pain and disappointment. The doctors don't know it yet, but the human heart is made of sponge rubber. Whatever hurt it has to soak up it can squeeze out again, given a little time. The only trouble is, of course, that time is the only enemy that gets stronger as it goes along.

The image of the newspaperman in the public mind, partly due to literature, the stage and the moom pitchers, is that of a sloppy looking character with a pint of booze sticking out of one pocket and a highly literate magazine crushed into another. Probably half right, at the least. Even today the newspaper reporter does not have the aplomb, the gravity, the clothes, or the hairdo of the TV news reporter. Boozewise, however, he is still right in there trying.

Which reminds me of the first time I came into personal contact with the publishing colossus, William Randolph Hearst. I was sitting alone in the early morning gloom of the old New York *American* city desk, when the fabled figure loomed up at my elbow. I almost swallowed my cigar.

He asked me where the managing editor was. I stuttered that he had just gone to dinner. He asked for the news editor. I stammered that he was not back from dinner. I found an excuse for the city editor, for the assistant managing editor, for all the lost and strayed who should have been exhibiting industry at their posts. Mr. Hearst heaved a sigh.

"For a man who doesn't drink," he complained in his high voice, "I suffer more from acute alcoholism than anybody I know."

For many more years I worked for another great and unpredictable publisher, the late Joseph Medill Patterson. As I write this I am a columnist. I got to be a columnist by replacing another columnist who, in turn, had replaced still another. This is a line of direct succession that goes back to the time our first columnist, Mark Hellinger, left for greener pastures. At that time the editors of our little paper, annoyed at building a columnist only to see him take off for where the bigger money was, had a bright idea.

Let's copyright a byline, they decided, have anybody and everybody on the staff contribute anything they can, edit the contributions into a column, run them under the fictitious byline and pay everybody pro rata for what was used of their contributory efforts. This sparkler was taken, hats in hand, to Mr. Patterson. He listened and considered.

"No," he decided at last. "We will ruin one man at a time."

So here I am, being ruined one man at a time.

A silly, wasted, useless life.

Know something? I wouldn't have changed a minute of it.

A Walk in the Shades

THE OTHER DAY I BETOOK myself to try and amble, as best I could remember, the first walk I made on the surface of New York City back in the summer of 1928. Silly? Of course. Sentimental? I like to think so. Anyway, I went to Grand Central, where the New England trains still pull in, came out and turned west on 42d Street. I had only to go a block before I had a memory. On that summer day in 1928, all dressed up in my campus finery, I must have been what the con men call a real mark. My suit was almost white and of a heavy, hairy material. It was called an "ice cream" suit. The buttons were of leather, and in shape and size resembled sliced golf balls. In my right hand I clutched that long-forgotten traveler's emblem, the Gladstone Bag.

I made Madison Avenue, in all my innocence. There I didn't need a nonexistent traffic light to halt me. I was stopped by a sinister "Pss-s-s-st." I turned. A rather frightened looking fellow beckoned me. I walked over. He looked furtively up and down the street.

"You're not a cop, are you?" he demanded.

I hastened to reassure him. He walked me over to the window of a (then) Schulte's cigar store. From his pocket he drew some object, wholly concealed in his fist, and cut a long, deep scratch in the plate glass window of the cigar store.

"Y'gotta admit that only a real diamond could do that," he said flatly. I agreed. We made a deal. I bought the "stolen diamond" for eight dollars. I was on my way, one of the smart boys.

At Sixth Avenue, determined to see the whole metropolis in the weekend I had before looking for work, I paused to ask directions of a fellow standing in the summer warm outside his store. I asked him how I could get to the Bronx Zoo.

"You gonna walk?" he asked. I said I was. He pointed uptown. "Just keep going," he advised, "you can't miss it."

Not too long after this, however, I somehow got blocked off by a big park and denied myself the Bronx Zoo as an adventure until the morrow. It was time for lunch, and I knew just where to have lunch on my limited budget. All through my childhood I had read the comic strip "Bringing Up Father," and every time Jiggs' harridan wife, Maggie, chased him out of the house, he went to Dinty Moore's for corned beef and cabbage. This would, of course, be just the right economical eatery for me. The telephone book showed no Dinty Moore's (and indeed there has never been one so listed), but it did show a Moore's. I asked a cop if the West 46th Street Moore's was Dinty's. He said sure, of course.

I forget what the hamburger sandwich cost. I remember with pain that the pot of coffee cost fifty cents. I had never heard of a place this side of hell that charged more than a nickel for a cuppa cawfee. Indeed, to go back to an early joke: "Where I came from there wasn't a man who could *lift* fifty cents worth of coffee."

So the other day I went into Moore's again and Anna Moore, the last of the family, asked what on earth was I doing in there at that time of day. What to answer? To answer that I was going over to see who was standing around in front of the Palace Theatre while the big vaudeville show went on inside? Miss Moore would have told me to stop betting race horses and see a good, reliable doctor. So I said nothing and went over to the Palace, at 47th Street and Seventh Avenue, and tried to remember some of the things said and quoted in the great days of vaudeville.

In my early days around newspapers and Broadway, the openings at the Palace were artistic events of high importance. On the stage were the chosen greats of the week. But on the sidewalk in front of the theatre gathered the outcasts. They were outcasts because E. F. Albee, who ruled variety with an iron hand in a mailed glove, had put them on the blacklist. So they stood outside, available to fill in for any possible disaster, explaining that they were "at liberty" or just resting. These were the regulars. The late Fred Allen was a Palace sidewalk star. So was the late, stuttering comic, Joe Frisco. So were a host of others.

I remembered one premiere afternoon when Frisco, at harsh odds with the Albee empire, moodily watched workmen who for some reason were tearing up West 47th Street near the corner. Somebody asked Joe—who will ever know now whether his stutter was uncontrolled or professional?—what all the digging was about.

"Albee's b-b-b-boy lost his b-b-ball," explained Joe.

From the Palace I walked down and east, past the Lambs, that home-away-from-home of the actors, great and small, in other years. It was in the Lambs club that the great humorist Ring Lardner, brooding in his cups, was forced to listen to a diatribe by the actor George Broadhurst. Broadhurst was bitterly complaining that another member had said that the next time he saw George, he intended to pee on him.

"What would you do, Ring?" demanded Broadhurst, "if somebody threatened to pee on you?"

"Keep moving," mumbled Lardner.

The Broadhurst Theatre was for some reason named for this hero.

Another active member of the Lambs in my day was John McGraw, immortal in baseball history, the greatest Giant of all baseball Giants. Mr. McGraw was, indeed, so active at the Lambs that he was finally asked to cease and desist being a member after he activated his ready fists upon another member. I have recently wondered if there is something in reincarnation, after all. Surely Vince Lombardi of the Washington Redskins pro football team (formerly of the Green Bay Packers) is John McGraw all over again.

"Show me a good loser," once growled John (Vince Lombardi?) McGraw, "and I'll show you a yellow son of a bitch."

I walked up Sixth Avenue and stopped at 52d Street, in my day referred to only as Swing Street and not only because of the music that nightly reached us all so easily and cheaply. Swing Street was the block of West 52d between Sixth and Fifth Avenues. God only knows how many gopher-hole and rabbit-warren nightclubs flowered and/or festered there.

Originally the block was a stretch of prim, brownstone homes occupied by a fading but solid society. Even before Repeal and the "legit" nightclubs, one or two of the old guard still held the ramparts. Standing cheek by jowl with the speaks and blind pigs, these last bastions of an older social order all had uniform white-on-blue metal signs that read: "This Is a Private Residence. Do Not Ring Bell." Everybody with half a skinful rang the bells anyway.

I paused at the corner of Sixth Avenue and 52d Street alongside a big bank (there is the side of a big bank on almost any corner in New York today). Where the side of this bank is was once the site of Jack Osterman's Lido Club. Jack was on the vaudeville blacklist, too, and had opened a small cellar nightclub. It didn't exactly shake up the town. One night Jack came to work and found there was some city repair being done to the sidewalk in front of his club. For safety, the police had blocked off the torn-up space with those wooden sawhorses. Jack gazed at them morosely.

"Business isn't bad enough," he sighed, "so now they're putting hurdles in front of the joint."

Further west on Broadway, the apple peddlers have long since departed. But when the Great Depression lay like a blight upon the land, every corner would have a man with an apple box upended, a few apples spread atop the upright end, offered for a nickel apiece. On the box would be scrawled on a piece of paper or cardboard, "Unemployed."

"I ate an unemployed apple yesterday," explained a chorus girl who had missed a show, "and today it started to work."

Turning downtown at Seventh Avenue, I passed the site of the original Lindy's restaurant and delicatessen. In my day this was the public office of all the bookmakers and big-time gamblers in town. Arnold Rothstein, one of the earliest and most publicized underworld figures, left his corner table at this Lindy's (before the bigger one was added at Broadway and 51st Street) to meet his fatal bullets during a card game at the old Park Central Hotel.

The gamblers picked at their food inside the restaurant or stood staring in stone-faced groups on the sidewalk. They had a sort of uniform in those days. It was a heavy blue overcoat with a velvet collar, plus a snap-brim felt hat and highly shined shoes. There is nobody like a professional gambler or a bookmaker for wariness. They must think hard before they dare tell the time of day. I remember the great ballroom dancer, Tony DeMarco, stopping to shake hands with an old acquaintance in one of these nightly groups, and then asking a little too insistently how the plunger was doing.

"About the same," was the reply. Tony laughed.

"About the same," he repeated. "About the same as what?"

One of these stalwarts was the late Nicholas Dandolas, the fabled Nick the Greek. It was reliably reported that the Greek would gamble on anything, and he is supposed to have once stood in front of Lindy's and bet a contemporary a thousand dollars a shot on whether the license numbers of the cars that turned into the block from the cross street would end in an even or odd number.

Nothing fazed the Greek. It is a fact that he could win or lose hundreds of thousands of dollars in those financially stricken days in a matter of straight hours or days. Win or lose, he never turned a hair nor lost his even disposition. It was always suspected that he was the "play" man for a syndicate of Greeks, most Greeks—like most Chinese—being inveterate gamblers.

I once asked Nick a professional question. I asked him outright if all gambling casinos are crooked. He thought for a moment.

"Well, let's put it this way," he said at last. "Let's just say that they are never helpless."

Further down Broadway was the cellar nightclub that opened, in the long ago past, with an act called Clayton, Jackson and (Jimmy) Durante. The club was called the Silver Slipper. On opening night a party of very hard hoodlums, numbering about a dozen, strode in. The new owner turned an uninteresting shade of gray. He saw his new investment being taken over before he had a chance to cheat the first customer. However, it developed the hoods were there on a purely social call. They were there to "drop a few" (dollars) and show good fellowship. The head hood called the owner to the table.

"How much did this joint cost to open?" he demanded.

"About $18,000," said the owner nervously. The head hood imperiously beckoned the headwaiter.

"Bring $18,000 worth of champagne," he ordered.

Around a corner off Broadway in the middle 40s was the only one of Texas Guinan's several speakeasies that I personally remember, and I cannot remember what she called it. The place was upstairs. Texas' famous cry of "Hello, sucker!" rang through the smog of tobacco smoke, and her pretty chorines danced merrily, or at least bounced about merrily. She gave out those little wooden mallets with which customers would bang on tables or glassware to make noises indicating applause. I once saw one of the highly social Goulds, the one who was some sort of a squash or court tennis amateur champ, sitting there with his little mallet in his big fist. The chorus girls would throw small cotton balls at him, and with the head of the little wooden mallet he would bat them straight back.

What should have been one of the most romantic of Broadway stories played out its script here. A rich young fellow from Princeton was smitten with one of the chorus girls and would rush up to Guinan's every night after classes. The chorus girl—you know, the one with the heart of gold, like in the old movies—either from indifference or fear of family reprisal, refused to have anything to do with him unless he kept up his studies.

So night after night, while she cavorted on the dance floor, he sat in Texas' office, pored over his books, and wrote his papers. He would take his girl home and, somewhat after dawn, race his sports car back to Princeton in time for his first class. I do not know when he slept. Possibly during chapel.

It would be a nice ending to this story to say that he married the girl, they now have grown children, and are still happy. Alas, she married somebody else and so did he.

I went on and about, uptown, and repassed the original Lindy's restaurant. Leo Lindemann wanted no table in his place more than twenty waiter-paces from the kitchen. He was a restaurateur who was interested in his customers. There aren't many like him left.

Further uptown, on Central Park West, there was a dry-out sanatorium for local drunks called Doctor Towne's. May still be there, for all I know. Anyway, the late Jimmy Ryan was finally persuaded by his sister Billie to take the waters there. Jimmy demurred. First he wanted literature. So sister got him all the brochures that showed the Central Park view with its bridle paths and lakes and whatnots. So James agreed to go. But first he went to Abercrombie and Fitch and outfitted himself with fishing tackle, saddles, riding equipment and other sporting clothes. After all, our James wasn't going to the country just to be a disgrace to his loving family!

And thence to the decayed apartment buildings and stale hotels on Broadway in the 70s. This was where every kid migrated in the tough days. If you were from Alabama you lived in a house young Alabamans had discovered; if you were from Maine, ditto.

And you would encounter the most unusual people. You would, for example, possibly meet the chap who got up almost at dawn to board the commuter trains, after first entraining to some hour-away suburban station, with his card-playing partner. They had a gimmick. They would engage some legit Wall Streeters in a card game for several days before they lowered the boom. It was hard work. So was the work of the fellow who pushed queer one-dollar bills. He had to circulate all over town, with only one counterfeit bill in his pocket, all the rest legit, so that if anybody called for the bluecoats he could honestly show that all the rest of his pocket money was as good or better than the pocket money we have today.

Hard work? You bet. Harder than making an honest buck.

Almost opposite Lindy's is a playhouse that was once the bright shining jewel of the living theatre in New York. Since almost the turn of the century this theatre had the same treasurer. In those days a theatre box office treasurer's salary was $99 per week. After thirty-odd years of handling tickets for the biggest hits on Broadway, this treasurer cashed in his ticket stubs. He left an estate of over $3 million.

The Broadway boys, hearing this, nodded in approval. "He saved," they explained.

I turned the Seventh Avenue corner and walked uptown past a hotel barbershop. It was into this barber shop, one morning, that Albert Anastasia, overlord of Murder Incorporated, came for his daily shave. The barber draped his face with a hot towel. Into the shop, also, came two gentlemen with hand guns. They not only parted Albert's hair, but also parted his skull. He was Dead On Arrival, as the official saying has it.

There was nothing particularly original and nothing amusing about this routine rubout. But I always chuckle when I think of it, because to this day Frank Costello, the retired Gray Eminence of the underworld, always dates certain occurrences as happening "since Albert's accident."

Walking further west, I passed the site of the early jazz club called Kelly's Stables. During its brief but popular period it had an act of six singers and dancers, three of whom went on to fame and thus had best be left anonymous. In those days marijuana was not the national issue it is today, and the fumes of "grass" or "weed" assaulted the nostrils in and around almost any music enclave. The stars of Kelly's Stables used to go out in the back alley and cool off with some sticks of tea.

One night the traffic cop who used to tie his horse in the alley while he went about his theatre-hour street duties faced the owner with a new order: "Those guys have got to stop blowing that smoke in my horse's face," he ordered sternly. "It makes him so hungry he fights me all the way back to the barn."

All was not fun and games during the Depression. At one point public funds were so low that the Child's restaurant chain offered "All You Can Eat for 60 Cents." We ate all we could and went back for seconds. Lots of times we couldn't afford a radio, or the radio we could afford was in hock, so we would join the other small crowds that always assembled in warm weather outside some radio store. Inside the owner would turn up the volume of the house set and, on the sidewalk, we would laugh free at Amos 'n' Andy.

If we had enough loot we could take our date to the real theatre for small money. A man named Joe LeBlang took over a Times Square cellar drugstore called Gray's and turned it into a cut-rate theatre ticket agency.

As curtain time neared, all shows—hits or flops—that had unsold tickets rushed them over to LeBlang. He put them on sale for what he could get. Otherwise we entertained ourselves with passes to shows, ball games and prizefights. These passes called for the holder to pay so many pennies for this tax, so many pennies for that tax and the balance for "service charge." The total was always fifty cents, whether for baseball game or prizefight. Then there were the GO—General Organization—tickets that went to companies and schools and clubs that would buy them in quantity.

Benny Friedman, quarterback of the old football Giants, remembers that once the Giants had to sell 12,000 fifty-cent GO tickets to be sure they had the guarantee for the visiting Green Bay Packers.

The financial turn for the better came, I suppose, with the repeal of Prohibition. Everything somehow looked brighter from that moment on, although at first—and for some months—the only legal drink we could get was "three-two beer." This was beer with an alcoholic content not to exceed 3.2 percent. We didn't like it much. We waited for the real stuff. Today we are getting the "real" stuff. Domestic beer nowadays has an alcoholic content of about 3.4 percent, or at best 4 percent. So many things have changed since those days—but not everything.

MOONLIGHT*

Through the 1930s and, indeed, until well after World War II, college football was indeed a big weekly event in New York as well as elsewhere. Fordham and New York University and even, occasionally, Columbia would have standout teams. The old Polo Grounds and Yankee Stadium saw some titanic Saturday gridiron battles, and when the local attraction wasn't up to snuff, many of us would take the short auto or train trip to New Haven or Princeton to watch the still-glamorous Ivy League teams. The Yale Bowl has always been my favorite football stadium, partly because I covered many games there and, even more importantly, because veteran sportswriters were still, in my day, talking about the grand opening of the huge saucer back in late November 1914.

The Bowl opened for "the Game," the annual heroic confrontation with hated Harvard. In its first stages the Bowl could seat 80,000 persons. This, of course, was considered idiotic. Loud were the anguished howls that the big, sunken, concrete dish would prove the "White Elephant" of all time and bankrupt the halls of higher learning. These dire groans had no effect on the premiere audience, which numbered the full 80,000.

As is typical of late fall in that section of New England, it was a bitterly cold day. At half time approximately 80,000 half frozen persons made for the men's rooms and the ladies' rooms. You

---

* Moonlight: Newspaper jargon for little squibs of news that are set in type and placed on galleys (trays) that can be lifted at anytime for any page to fit into small spaces left at the bottom of newspaper columns. They can remain unused until they grow "type lice." For instance:

Rainfall Up

Albany, N.Y. The Weather Bureau announced today that the annual mean rainfall throughout the state was 4.7 inches during 1970. This was 0.6 inches above the rainfall for 1969.

That piece of moonlight will not grow "type lice" until the annual mean rainfall for 1970 is announced.

enter and exit the Bowl through long, dank, ground-level tunnels. The crowd spilled through the tunnels, looking right and left for rest rooms. The mobs spilled outside the big structure, still looking.

No rest rooms. None for men, none for women. Somebody had goofed. There were 80,000 football fans with bladders swollen harder than real footballs and no place to go.

Luckily, neighboring grounds were underdeveloped acres in that year. Surrounding the bowl stretched fields of second- and third-growth trees. Also bushes. The 80,000 football fans took their cramps into the bushes and trees. On the double.

And that is why, for years and years, to veteran sportswriters the Yale Bowl was always known as Willow Run.

The Funny Phony

IT IS DOUBTFUL THAT THERE IS A single veteran newspaper reporter, writer, editor or publisher who hasn't, at least once in his career, had that peculiar sinking feeling that comes when it is borne in upon this recipient that he has been stuck with a phony story. It is a part of a newspaperman's education. The phony story—"plant" as it is known to the trade—is one reason all publications hire large staffs of lawyers, one of whom is always looking over a writer's shoulder to stave off the libelous, the slipshod or the careless treatment of fact or fancy.

Often, when a newspaperman is thus professionally impaled, some sort of a defense can be thrown up. Testimony can be gathered to semisupport the blooper. Arguments and threats, promises and wheedling, are brought to bear. A "folo" story can be run that, it is hoped, will take the paper and the writer off the hook. At worst, a public apology must be made, whether or not the false story was submitted and used in the best of faith.

Like most of us, I have had to eat the crow of retraction on various occasions. But once, and only once, it was a pleasure. This time the phony I fell for was not only funny in the beginning but got funnier as it kept getting exposed. It was the story of the cuckolded truck driver. In sequence, it went like this:

First, one of my editors, who lives in a fancy Connecticut suburb where anything wild can and does happen, came into the office all agiggle and said a wonderfully hilarious thing had happened up in his lecherous part of the world. It seems a fellow who drove one of those huge, ready-mix, revolving concrete trucks had taken out his daily load this day and his route to the construction site happened to be past his own home. There, in the driveway of his own nest, a big, convertible Cadillac was parked. Now this truck driver for some time had been suspicious that his boss had designs on his wife. The license number on the Caddy was clearly identifiable as his boss's car. Proof was at hand.

So what did Our Hero do? Why, he backed his concrete mixer truck up the driveway, put it to work, and dumped part of his load of wet concrete into the back seat of the open convertible. Then he went about his business, leaving the concrete to harden on its own time.

That was the story in the beginning. Then the corrections began to come in.

"You got the story wrong," said a friend just back from Florida. "It happened in Miami and the car was a big Oldsmobile. I saw it. Well, I didn't really see it, but I was told by guys in the garage where they hauled the Olds. They said it was a fantastic sight."

Next the mail began to bring clippings from towns in upstate New York, in Jersey, Pennsylvania, Ohio and points west. Each paper had picked up my original and detailed it with one minor differential: In each paper the incident had happened "in a small town nearby."

Things got even more giddy in the city of Binghamton, N. Y. Only one real estate operator there was building in the suburbs, and now all his friends were leering in his presence and innocently asking what type of new car he planned to buy. This fellow, of course, happened to own a Caddy convertible.

He had to go to the *Binghamton Press* and get them to publish a story and pictures showing that there was no concrete in the back seat of his car and that, furthermore, he didn't even have in his employ any truck drivers with wife trouble. In two nearby towns, immediately following this shall we say concrete defense, a lawyer and a businessman who owned Caddy convertibles also signed statements and had them printed as paid newspaper advertisements.

Meanwhile, the bigger Florida papers were busy checking tips that this garage or that garage had the real star car of the story. Photographers were sent scurrying around trying to find and photograph same. Meanwhile, the clippings kept coming in, now being mailed all the way from the West Coast. A good detective would have noted that the story always popped up anew in cities where my column was syndicated, or in nearby cities. Interested readers kept sending these clips. They didn't do this to show me that the story must have been a phony. No, indeed. Just to prove that I had my locations and facts wrong.

There were various sidebars to the funny phony. A contractor in Pennsylvania took ads and radio spot announcements that said, simply: "No! No! A thousand times no! Not me. No concrete in my car. It isn't even a Caddy. It isn't even a convertible."

So then my syndicate and one of the wire services launched a thorough search to find out the facts, if any. This research indicated that the incident had happened in about fifty different places. It always took place "in a nearby town." Nobody had ever seen the car, nor could professional search find it or any garage that had towed it away. No Caddy convertible registrations, of suggested place and vintage, had been returned with notation that the car had been destroyed. No truck driver came forward to take his bow.

So finally I printed the entire history of the gag anecdote and admitted that it had just been a funny phony. If anybody had any pictorial proof, I suggested, please forward same. I thought that such a deposition had put away the funny phony for good.

Alas, no! A couple of weeks went by and I had forgotten the whole affair. And then the photographs started to arrive.

The first one was a standard, glossy, newspaper-type photo of a policeman standing by the front seat of a car. The front seat was filled with what looked to be congealed concrete. The back of this picture had a stamped notice that it was the property of a Pennsylvania daily paper. By this time my radar was working a little better. I felt there was something wrong with the shot. In the first place, the cop shouldn't be looking so amused. Second place, it was the *front* seat of this car and the original story plainly identified the *back* seat.

So I called the Pennsylvania paper and, sure enough, they laughed fit to kill and admitted they had gone to a junkyard and filled up an old red jalopy just so they could keep the phony going and cause some more talk and rumor.

Sometimes I don't know what the newspaper business is coming to.

And the thing isn't over yet. Every now and then the whole yarn pops up again, but now it is always accompanied by "pictorial evidence." The photographs submitted have that gray overtone indicating they are copies pulled not off a negative but off another photo. Looking closely at most of them, it can be seen that the car is inevitably a beat-up old heap, is indubitably parked in a junkyard and is by no means a shiny new Cadillac. Also, the car in the picture is invariably surrounded by a full quota of grinning, happy witnesses.

This is the only phony story in my career that bids fair not to die of its own anemia. And because of this fact, I keep wondering how it originated. Maybe I am as gullible as all the other people who have heard the story. Did it really happen somewhere? Was all evidence carefully and shamefully destroyed? If it happened, would any of the principals ever admit it?

Possibly the story did originate with the driver of a concrete-mix truck. Somehow I can see him in his favorite saloon, a shell of beer in his hand, a scowl on his face because he has just left home in a huff. To his bored friends he is berating the Little Woman whom he suspects of cheating with some rich slob in town. A slob who drives a sporty car.

"If I ever catch them," I seem to hear him telling his bored pals, "you know what I'll do? I'll drive my truck right over and fill up that chariot with all that concrete I sweat over all day long just to have money to spend on her."

Maybe that's all that happened.

But I have to wish that somebody, somewhere, could convince me that it *did* happen. It ought to have.

A Large Case of Murder

IT MIGHT NEVER HAVE HAPPENED if the Dutchman's speakeasy had been open that night. It might not have happened if a prizefighter named Ruby Goldstein hadn't felt like a glass of beer after an easy two-round knockout. Probably it couldn't have happened if one of the leading players wasn't unique even in the legends of gangland. But it happened, and when it was all over there were five—and probably seven, possibly ten—people dead. One thing that hot Friday, July 13, 1929, proved conclusively was that you could be murdered just for being in a nightclub. But away with philosophy. Let us turn to the historical facts.

On that Friday night at the old Rockaway Beach Arena, a fast, mercurial welterweight named Ruby Goldstein—"the Jewel of the Ghetto"—polished off a long forgotten "opponent" in two rounds. Despite his quick victory, Ruby's manager noted that the Jewel seemed a little stale and listless in going about his appointed task. The manager advised his charge to stop off at the Dutchman's, a speakeasy near the Manhattan end of the 59th Street bridge, and have a few beers. Then, as now, a few beers were considered better than tranquilizers for nervous tension and general ennui.

Ruby stopped at the Dutchman's but found it closed, for one reason or another. So he continued across town with a couple of admirers to a place just north of 54th Street where, at 1721 Broadway, a small electric sign said merely: Hotsy Totsy Club. The trio parked their car—yes, it was possible in those uncluttered times—and climbed the stairs to the Hotsy Totsy.

The Broadway Hotsy Totsy was the third edition of a speakeasy that had been forced to shift around here and there, but had always remained in the same neighborhood. There are ancient nightclubbers with livers that have withstood the ravages of time who contend that the Hotsy Totsy was the first nightclub, as we think of nightclubs. It was the first "cafe type" operation to become popular and famous. It got "we of the theatre," us of the press and them of the underworld. The place had cost an original investment of $1,000 and was now paying $100 a month rent for its upstairs quarters. And just a few nights previously, a single waiter had collected $1,200 in tips from a heavy spender with a broken nose.

As you entered the club, the big cabaret room was at the rear of the building. To the left as you came in was the smaller bar. Ruby and his pals turned left and entered the bar. Both bar and main room were crowded. The fighter, tired and tense, had his beers. Around three o'clock Ruby finished his last beer and announced his intention of going home to bed.

It was only then, he later remembered, that he became aware that he was the focal point of a growing argument.

As a man who was used to strife of various sorts, Goldstein quickly gulped down his beer and left with his friends. What he had heard of the heating-up argument revealed to him that the bone of contention was whether or not Ruby Goldstein, the Jewel of the Ghetto, could box-fight wonderfully or whether he was a yellow this and that. He was the unwilling object of attention, of that he was sure. On other matters he was later to find his memory at odds with police and other witnesses.

For instance, Goldstein remembered that all parties involved in the argument were seated at the same table. Other and more official versions disagree. At any rate, the disagreement soon had all protagonists on their feet. A short peace was effected, which then left two debaters at the bar and three others still at the table. Then, as so often happens with such physical flash fires, tempers exploded again, and soon guns were exploding also. The argument ended with two men on the floor, one dead and one dying. Many customers left without paying their tabs.

In the next forty-eight hours only a few basic facts were sorted out. Police Commissioner Grover Whalen announced that the original dead man was one Simon "Sammy" Walker. The man who had died soon thereafter was one William "Red" Cassidy. Red's brother, Peter, was in a hospital with blackjack bumps on his head. Some twenty-four bullets had been fired and were dug out of walls and furniture—not to mention bodies. More facts were soon revealed.

It was discovered that the nominal owner of the Hotsy Totsy was a character named Hymie Cohen. More questioning soon brought to light the presence in the bar, at the time of the shooting, of fabled Jack "Legs" Diamond, and with Diamond was a very hard specimen named Charles Green, alias Entratta. And somewhere nearby had also been a hardshell known in rugged circles as Tough George Heaghney. People who encourage such names as Tough George are, in the normal course of events, often called upon to prove their title is deserved.

There were three bullets in the dead Walker. There were four slugs in the dead Cassidy. Cassidy's lead mine came from a .38 calibre revolver, and the metal in Walker was of the .32 calibre variety. The police announced with assurance that the victims had been killed by two different revolvers, doubtless in two different hands. The other gentlemen in the contretemps seemed to have successfully dodged the remaining seventeen bullets. Another basic fact was established. Diamond and Green had quarreled over Goldstein with the Cassidy-Walker-Heaghney entente. The police were under the command of Inspector Edward Mulrooney, later to become an outstanding Police Commissioner and still later a national figure in crime fighting.

On the face of it, Mulrooney had an open-and-shut case. Even the surviving Peter Cassidy was ready to admit, "We were drunk as often we can be [sic] and we were all drunk that night and ready for a fight or a frolic." Other witnesses corroborated.

Later some of these witnesses were to regret that they had volunteered.

It was such an open-and-shut case, at the beginning, that on the second day the press was inclined to slough it off as just another hoodlum rumpus. On the third day the shootings were back among the truss ads, as veteran newspapermen used to say. Both newspapers and police would have shown a great deal more interest if they could have foreseen the activities that were to follow. Before the case was over, veteran cops and reporters were in agreement that at least seven men were ultimately murdered, and, in all likelihood, another two men and a girl. To repeat, all were killed for being in a nightclub in 1929.

So the police went about the routine business of picking up Mr. Diamond and Mr. Green. This chore was expected to be relatively easy. It soon proved to be extremely difficult and, after that, apparently impossible. The most trustworthy stool pigeons were suddenly very naive and ignorant of current events. One even went to jail because he refused to admit that he had ever heard of a Jack or Legs Diamond.

At this point we must pause for a short character and personality sketch of Mr. Diamond, since he was, in his day, one of the most unbelievable figures in the history of Public Enemies.

He was born in Philadelphia, and as both boy and adult he was tall, skinny and gangling. He had a rather handsome face and wore conservative clothes. Historians claim he earned the "Legs" tag because as a boy robber "he could run like a package thief." Diamond always claimed he earned the sobriquet because he was such a fine ballroom dancer.

He was in New York at eighteen, trying his hand at violence and crime. He soon did a short bit for burglary. He was drafted in World War I and sent home as completely useless military material. He finally did three years in an Army disciplinary barracks for breaking every rule he could find, including physical attack on an officer. Released, he became a protege of "Pretty Louis" Amberg and, later, Jacob "Little Augie" Orgen, both lower East Side terrorists. Later he earned higher status when he became body-guard for the legendary Arnold Rothstein.

In August 1929 John Thomas Diamond was thirty-four years old and had partly earned his later title of "the Clay Pigeon of the Underworld." His entire career, which lasted until two years after the Hotsy Totsy murders, was something of a fiasco—whether Diamond's or society's is debatable. He was arrested twenty-six times for various and sundry lawbreaking, and he beat every rap except the early burglary one. More important was the variety and violence of the assaults he also beat.

He was riddled with bullets and shotgun pellets on no less than seven separate occasions. In a 1924 brawl an unidentified opponent shot him in head and foot. Next he took two more slugs in 1927 when ill-wishers cut down Little Augie, who was walking with his "bodyguard" Diamond. Three years later, peacefully asleep in his hotel room, three strangers pumped three more bullets into him. On a later occasion he caught a slug in his ribs in Harlem. He accepted unwillingly a few more shotgun pellets in his old downtown haunts. Only seven months after the hotel shooting, he was ambushed near Cairo, N.Y.—eighty-one shotgun pellets that time.

He survived everything after tiresome hospitalization. Between receiving bullets, the Pigeon managed to dodge or outwit or outblast other volleys and ambushes. When he broke with Rothstein—then an acknowledged rackets liege and the man who is supposed to have engineered the Black Sox baseball scandal—after mutual charges of double crossing, Rothstein dispatched two "hit" men to take vengeance on Diamond's tubercular brother, Eddie, in a Denver hospital. It was a mistake.

Diamond was devoted to his brother, almost hysterically so. He somehow learned of Rothstein's treachery. The assigned gorillas were apprehended by police. Ultimately freed, they didn't live long enough for a repeat assignment. One was found murdered, bea the evidence of heavy-handed torture. Two months later second suffered the same fate. Just to make the point clear, thr more Rothstein strong-arms were burned off.

Ever the businessman, Mr. Rothstein made a treaty.

Diamond's trigger-quick madness kept him from ever reaching the gangland stature of Owney Madden or Big Bill Dwyer of his own era or, later, Louis Lepke Buchalter or the diplomatic Frank Costello. Never a ganglord, he was dangerous and powerful enough to operate with the nervous approval of the big boys. This was the man who calmly walked out of the Hotsy Totsy Club after the shooting and simply, quietly and completely disappeared.

The disappearance, which all in authority figured to be temporary, did not slow the investigation. Mulrooney could use the time to build and bolster his case by collating all testimony from all available witnesses until the Pigeon was flushed from his cote. Mulrooney began to collect witnesses.

And then strange and frightening things began to happen.

The most important witness was Thomas Ribler. As bar cashier at the club, sitting on a high stool, Ribler obviously had an unobstructed view of all nearby proceedings. He was not at home when detectives called for him. "He came home last night," his mother told police, "changed his clothes and said he was going to the beach. He hasn't come home yet."

He still hasn't come home yet, forty-one years later. Police Commissioner Whalen worriedly admitted to the press that "secret sources" had furnished information as to Ribler's rubout "so that he can't testify against Diamond." A week later Whalen was making another worried admission. He said the police had reason to believe, from "confidential sources," that a waiter at the Hotsy Totsy bar, known to the cops only as Volst, had also been murdered. For the same reason.

By now the reportorial pack was snapping at Whalen's heels. What witnesses did he have? What evidence? What was happening in this investigation and pursuit of two murderers? Whalen first assured everybody that the cops were "making progress." But somebody was apparently making even more progress, because a few days later Whalen made another depressing admission.

"A man unknown to us until yesterday," the Commissioner had to admit, "was found murdered near Bordentown, N.J., three weeks ago. Yesterday he was positively identified as William Pelgast, bartender at the Hotsy Totsy on the night of the murders."

Only a week or so later there was further gory news. "We are convinced," said Whalen, "that Hymie Cohen, one of our most important wanted witnesses, has been murdered to seal his lips." And only two days later Whalen was again admitting that a man named Herman Henry had been shot and killed in Philadelphia, and friends of the dead man had told Philadelphia police that Herman had described to them the shooting at the nightclub.

Of all the victims so far, Hymie Cohen was best known to the Broadway mob. He was an intimate of actors, showgirls and big shots of the upper and lower worlds. More perversely, Cohen was thought to have been a partner of Diamond's in the club, was Diamond's favorite court jester, and it was agreed that Diamond had more or less sponsored him on Broadway. This shook up hard-guy philosophy. Surely, they whispered, Legs had nothing to fear from Hymie. Why, it was Hymie who had ordered the band to play its loudest during the pistol contretemps. Why would a guy even as tough as Legs kill a pal?

Pal or no pal, the amiable Cohen had a premonition of his fate. He had told the late Broadway columnist Mark Hellinger: "Just wait and see. One day Hymie Cohen will just disappear. Wait and see." The boys at Hellinger's table laughed at Hymie's macabre humor.

Cohen, of course, knew something his listeners didn't. Cohen knew Cohen was a drug addict. And so, of course, did his pal Legs. A hoodlum who was still around just a few years ago remembered both. "If Cohen had been picked up for questioning," this stalwart pointed out, "it would have taken the police about an hour to discover he was on junk. All they had to do was ice him away with no junk until he broke. He was loyal to Legs, all right, but no junkie can stay right in the head when they take that needle away from him. Legs knew it. Hymie knew it. Hymie had to go. We heard, though, that at least Legs made it easy for Hymie when he turned him off."

The heat on the Hotsy Totsy investigation was such that all ace sleuths were pulled off another case, that of the murdered Frankie Marlowe, a semi-big-time hood who was getting extra headlines because it had been learned that he was an associate of the still missing Judge Crater and possibly a key witness to the judge's disappearance. Two dead victims and five "possibles" made a bigger case than one hood and one missing judge. Everybody in law enforcement was looking for Diamond and Green.

But nobody knew nothing, as the saying has it, and continued to know nothing about the murders of one Archie Senville and a man named George Miller near Newark, N.J. Police did say that their "information" connected Senville and Miller with the Diamond-Green-Cassidy axis. And soon there was further frustration. Nobody, but nobody, could find Gracie Carroll. Gracie had been the hatcheck girl at the bloodied nightclub.

Miss Carroll simply just up and disappeared—whether willingly or painfully we have yet to discover. Some veteran cops dismissed Miss Carroll as a victim. "Murdering a woman always causes a lot of hell," these cops opined. "Both Diamond and Green would remember the heat when Vivian Gordon and Dot King were killed.

They could just as easy have scared her half to death and sent her into hiding. And even made it worth her while."

Nonetheless, Miss Carroll is still among the missing. The futile weeks stretched into futile months. The sum total of what the cops had in hand was one (1) doubtful witness and considerable evidence—seven or even ten murders notwithstanding—that the Hotsy Totsy brawl had been just a drunken shoot-out that everybody still alive would now like to forget.

The one available witness, safely jailed for his own protection, was a club employee named Thomas Merola. This worthy was either a singing waiter, who thus might have been wandering around the bar during the unpleasantness, or a violinist in Hymie Cohen's loud-playing orchestra. Either way, the cops thought it best to keep Merola in the jug for his own protection. Merola thought otherwise, and so did his lawyers, doctors and psychiatrists.

The latter argued steadily and steadfastly that Merola's brain was being undermined by his incarceration and persecution. Also, confinement kept him away from his loving wife. The District Attorney argued otherwise. It was better for Merola's brain, the D.A. contested, to be addled by boredom than altered by bullets that might end the brain's function.

More and more doctors examined the brain and mental anguish of Thomas Merola, violinist and/or singing waiter. Meanwhile, nobody was coming up with either Diamond or Green. Such a state of affairs caused Commissioner Whalen to make a public statement of alarm.

"Gangdom is in control of nightclubs," he stated. "All decent people will shun such places."

Fat chance.

Five months after the shooting, the case had faded from the front pages. The year 1929 ran out its declining weeks. Even such witnesses as were still cooperating with the police must have been almost as irritating as informative. One after another they swore on their tarnished honor that Diamond, Green, the Cassidys and Walker were engaged in no power struggle or internecine underworld war. Nobody was much further ahead in the apprehension of the suspects, the cause of the shooting, the fate and whereabouts of missing key witnesses than they had been only a few days after the rumpus.

And then, in January 1930, Charlie Green either surrendered in Chicago or was arrested there. He was hurriedly brought back to New York and stood trial for murder in February.

It was obvious from the first day of the trial that the state had neither witnesses nor any solid case against him. Nobody knew nothing, as usual. Green was acquitted.

Exactly one month to the day later, Jack "Legs" Diamond, accompanied by legal counsel, walked into the West 47th Street police precinct with the casual statement: "I hear you want me. I'm here to surrender."

Long questioning brought the police no more information than they had at hand. Diamond was speedily brought to trail. The District Attorney took his best hold, but to small avail. About the only witness the D.A. could offer was Thomas Merola. You remember Tom—the one whose head was or was not addled by being cooped up in a place of detention.

"I was dozing on the bandstand," testified the addled or unaddled Merola. "I didn't see anything. I didn't hear anything, either." The District Attorney admitted somewhat sadly that "at least five important witnesses are unavailable."

The verdict of acquittal was then directed. Mr. Diamond walked out of court a free man—free to rejoin such pals and associates as the equally free Mr. Green. Both acquittals left some questions that a modern criminologist might find intriguing. Why, in either or both trials, did Peter Cassidy, brother of the dead William and himself wounded in the fray, never appear? Where was Tough George Heaghney? Why, only a few years later when a newspaper sought to re-create the entire story, were there no records of the case in the District Attorney's files?

Although theoretically free men, Messrs. Diamond and Green were face to face with other disciplinary measures: the heavy justice of their own masters. Somebody in command—presumably the disgusted Owney Madden, at that time the hard and sensible boss of New York's illegal industries—plainly told Diamond that his troublesome presence was no longer wanted or needed in the bright-light district. Mr. Diamond wisely went abroad, had further trouble with immigration authorities and came home to settle in Acra, in upstate New York, where he suspectedly had a booze business.

Mr. Green was less fortunate. Never a glamour hoodlum, and

from all accounts merely a relentless hard guy, he had been on parole on the night of the Hotsy Totsy bloodbath. He was sent back to Sing Sing to do what the cons call "short time"—in his case, two and a half years remaining on a seven-year sentence for armed robbery.

Upstate, Diamond's willful character appeared uncurbed. He was tried and acquitted for kidnaping and torture. As stated, he was punctured by shotgun pellets. He was convicted of bootlegging and sentenced to four years in a Federal pen. He was out on appeal the night a final period was put to his life of violence.

He got very drunk on the night of Dec. 18, 1931, only two and a half years after the nightclub imbroglio. It was a bad night for him to get drunk, because person or persons unknown were watching him. He went back to his rooming house and collapsed on his bed. He did not see or hear his visitor or visitors.

The autopsy showed that he had been held down on the bed while somebody put a gun to the front of his head and fired once. Then they put the gun to the back of his head and fired once. Then they put the gun to the side of his head and fired once.

This time he was quite dead.

Charles Green, alias Entratta, lasted only a few weeks more. Released from prison, he went back to New York and opened a "bottling works" on the West Side. He was either bottling the wrong goods or bottling the right goods in the wrong neighborhood. In the spring of 1932, party or parties unknown entered the plant and shot off the whole top of his head.

There was to be a further tragic—and much more startling—epilogue to Diamond's life story. On June 30, 1933, a year and a half after Diamond's murder, another party or parties unknown visited the thirty-three-year-old Mrs. Alice Schiffer Diamond, widow of the racketeer, in her Ocean Avenue, Brooklyn, apartment. Mrs. Diamond was at her kitchen table drinking coffee. Her visitor placed a .38 calibre pistol to her temple and fired once. For her, once was enough.

The killers of Diamond, Green and Mrs. Diamond are possibly still at large. At least, they were never apprehended. Nor, technically, were the killers of Walker and Cassidy, or the killers of the five—or seven, or ten?—persons whose only need for being killed was that they just happened to be in a Broadway nightclub when something unusual happened.

The old Hotsy Totsy Club has long gone the way of so many of its kind. Several years ago, passing the site, I looked up and saw that it was (at that time) a table tennis parlor. I went up and talked with the son of the landlord of the building. He called his father, but Dad couldn't remember any Hotsy Totsy Club either. Now even the table tennis parlor has disappeared and, in the modern surge of new construction, so has the entire old building.

Grover Whalen's advice that decent people should shun night-clubs hardly made a deep impression on even the most decent. In 1929—as even now, alas!—decent people had a poor ear for good advice.

The Faithful Heart

WHEN THE HARLEM NIGHTCLUBS were the mecca of all stay-up-lates and thrived on the downtown white trade, various hoodlum consortiums controlled the big ones and always used a "clean" manager—no police record—to front the joint as "owner." One of these owners was a man we will call Herman. He was married with a full family, but he had two obsessive hobbies—horse racing and a girl friend we will call Mabel.

The Harlem fad gradually wore itself out, the hoodlum operators were cut down or jailed, repeal brought the final crusher, and Harlem was through as a big-time entertainment area. Things with Herman went from bad to worse. He had no place in the new dawn of "straight" nightclubs, and there came times when he had no money to play the horses, much less hang another bangle on Mabel.

One day he collected an old debt, the tidy sum of $550. Hoorah! Off went Herman and Mabel to the racetrack.

Playing his usual system, he started with a $100 bet and, when that lost, cut back to tens and twenties. Nothing worked. The last race was his only escape route. He had $200 left. He studied his charts and his figures. He asked advice. He got more and more excited. His face flushed and his breathing quickened.

"Herman, remember your heart condition," the solicitous, loving Mabel warned him.

So the race started and more blood rushed to Herman's neck and face as his heart beat faster. Herman had bet his last $200 on a horse that was on the board at 20 to 1. As the field came around the turn, there was Herman's long shot running eyeball to eyeball with the even-money favorite. They ran like that, stride for stride. Herman could scarcely breathe at all now.

They went over the finish line, still nostril to nostril.

The lights came up on the board: PHOTO.

Herman's heart just gave out, and he fell down dead in a grandstand aisle. The faithful Mabel quickly knew what to do. She flung herself upon Herman's body, screaming and yelling for a doctor, for an ambulance. She paid no heed to the cries of "Give him air." Her arms were about the prone body, her hands now here, now there.

Finally Herman was removed, a sheet over his head. Mabel turned her back and stared at the odds board. The number of the winner went up. Herman's ticket was worth over $4,000. Mabel quickly took Herman's ticket, which she had removed from his pocket as he lay on the cold cement, and cashed it in.

Then she went home and within a few days bought a small saloon in midtown that she called Mabel's. I rode past it in a cab recently, and Mabel's is still there after twenty-odd years. I don't know whether Mabel is or not.

Days in the Sun

IT IS AN ORDINARILY UGLY LOOK-
ing housing development today, as is the other one in Brooklyn,
but once it was a big part of our lives. For some reason it was
called the Polo Grounds, although no polo was played there within
memory. It housed National League baseball as played by the
Giants and National League football as played by the Giants. The
one in Brooklyn was called Ebbets Field and, of course, we New
York Giants' addicts ridiculed and despised the inmates of that
place.

All of us Giant diehards who usually suffered through the long
seasons knew that across the Harlem River was a team called the
New York Yankees, which won almost all the time and never
seemed to run out of a perennial string of brilliant new youngsters,
one of whom was always on hand and ready to replace any fading
veteran. Possibly the trouble with the Yankees, for us, was that
stadium. Yes, we could recognize Lou Gehrig because of his square
ass, and we could spot Babe Ruth because it was impossible *not* to
identify him. But to this day we do not know what Bob Meusel
looked like or Earl Combs or Eddie Lopat or dozens of others.
Everything has always been too anonymous at Yankee Stadium.

The fabled John McGraw did not turn loose the reins of his
baseball Giants until the early 1930s. By that time he was old and
ill and overly pugnacious. I only met him one or two times.

"His trouble was that he knew everything there was to know about the game of baseball," says one of the last of the old sportswriters who knew him well. "So he could manage and run a baseball operation with only about half of his attention. With the other half he tried to run a Havana racetrack or get into real estate or try to beat Wall Street or whatever. That's where he always stubbed his toes."

The game between McGraw's Giants and "Uncle" Wilbert Robinson's Brooklyn Dodgers always brought emotional fever to patriots on both sides. The Dodgers—or "Them Bums" as our side long ago christened them—had some colorful players indeed. There was Babe Herman, a hard-hitting outfielder who one day somehow turned a three-base smash into a triple play when two other base runners couldn't make up their minds which way they should run. There was Uncle Robbie himself, the Brooklyn manager for what seemed forever. Once he announced that the next man who made a bonehead play would be automatically fined $100, a solid sum in those days.

So Uncle Robbie then sat down, made out his lineup and sent it out to the umpire. Then, as the game was about to start, he changed his mind. He sent a different batter to the plate without notifying the umpire of the lineup change. Automatic out. We never discovered whether Robbie fined himself the hundred bucks.

There was another day when, the rivalry with the Giants being what it was, Ebbets Field put some ropes in the outfield and let the overflow crowd stand out there behind the ropes. Came a late inning and the Dodgers got two men on base. The next batter hit a hard smash that rolled into the standing crowd.

A Giant outfielder went into that insanely partisan mob after the ball. That was his mistake.

Our boy leaped into the surging bodies. He disappeared. First his hat came flying out. Then one of his shoes. Then his glove. Finally he came out himself, propelled like a bum being thrown out of a saloon. Only then did somebody throw out the ball. All Dodger base runners had scored, of course.

But the funniest memory of the Old Dodgers happened else-where—in Philadelphia's old Shibe Park, to be explicit. On this great occasion a chap named Hack Wilson was playing right field for Brooklyn. Hack was built exactly like a fire hydrant, and he was no stranger to alcoholic beverages. In fact, on this day he was suffering one of the most monumental hangovers in baseball history.

Now, on the pitching mound, if memory still serves, was a hero named Walter "Boom Boom" Beck. At the moment, Walter was living up to his nickname.

Ever since the game started, Philly batters had walked up to the plate and hit a ball over Hack Wilson's head, or out of his reach, and Old Hack had spent these early innings puffing, panting and sweating in unending chase. Many of these hard hits were bouncing off the old Shibe Park outfield fence which—and keep this in mind—in those days was covered with tin advertising signs. These base hits would make a sharp "ping" each time a ball caromed off the tin signs.

So now the Brooklyn manager strode to the mound to remove Beck and bring in a pitcher more finely tuned to the day's labors. The trouble was that "Boom Boom" didn't want to leave the game. He refused to hand over the baseball. Finally, surrendering in part to his fuehrer's orders, Boom Boom whirled and, with all his strength, threw the ball into right field.

Meanwhile Old Hack, grateful for the brief respite, had leaned over and placed his hands on his knees. His head hung in weariness. He was paying no attention to the contretemps on the mound, so he did not see Beck throw the ball into his territory.

But he heard it "ping" off the tin signs. He immediately got into motion, retrieved the baseball *and threw it to second base!*

No, I do not remember any funny or ridiculous stories about our beloved baseball Giants. They were too beautiful to be funny. Naturally. The Brooklyns got their nickname because they were "The Trolley Dodgers."

There was another team in the Polo Grounds that also ensnared our hearts—the football Giants. Ah, what memories of Benny Friedman and Cal Hubbard and Mel Hein and Ken Strong and Ward Cuff and Tuffy Leemans and all those other old heroes! Further, although built for McGraw's baseball titans, the Polo Grounds was an oval with one end open and, being longer than a round stadium, was ideal for football.

Professional football came to the old stadium in the mid-1920s with Red Grange and the Chicago Bears against the first Giants. I was not there—alas!—but the new game had made the big town. Pro football of sorts had been struggling for some years before that date. There are many legends about the Providence Steamrollers, the Canton Bulldogs and all the other early crusaders who played the pigskin game more for fun than for the small money that came out of it.

I wish, having watched the game since the earliest 1930s and Ken Strong's Stapleton (Staten Island) Stapes, that I could have known, for instance, Theodore Nesser and his five sons. They were all original "professional" football players. They all worked for the Pennsylvania Railroad and theoretically played for the railroad line's own team, the Panhandle A.C. But when better money offers came along, the Nessers were inclined to scatter. Since each of them, as a railroad employee, had a railroad pass, each could entrain for any team that offered some loot.

Thus, on any given Sunday in the football strongholds of the Midwest, one might see Pop Nesser playing with two of his sons against three of his sons, or all the Nessers playing on separate teams. Or all together. It depended on where the best offer happened to be. Team loyalty was like that, then.

The early pro game also produced such colorful figures as "Blondy" Wallace who, after a suspicious ending in an important game, was eased out of the sport and was next heard of in the national press as "the King of the Bootleggers," headquartered in Atlantic City.

Even in the 1930s the pro game was something of a scramble. Ken Strong, later to be a Giants hero, remembers that in Stapleton, where he started the pro game after his all-American college career, most of the enthusiasts stood along the sidelines because there were insufficient seats in the stands. Once, tackled and under a mass of bodies, Ken became infuriated when somebody kept hitting him on the head.

"I got up and looked to slug somebody," he remembers, "and discovered that it was a little old lady who was using her umbrella to try to beat to death the guys who had tackled me. Those were the days."

In the early days of the Giants, people like Jules Glaenzer, who for years ran the American end of the great Cartier's jewelry firm, became fascinated with Sundays at the Polo Grounds. Glaenzer ended up by staking out some six full boxes for himself and friends. When Giants tickets became as valuable as Cartier jewels, Glaenzer could still host six boxes full of Sunday friends.

In those days and, indeed, until his death not too many years ago, the Giants team doctor was Dr. Francis Sweeney, who also may have been their most rabid fan. Once Strong had his face ground into a clay field, and when he got to his feet, a long strip of flesh hung like a string from between his eyebrows. Dr. Sweeney ran out on the field. "No sense stitching that," he proclaimed, whipping out his scissors and cutting off the string of flesh.

On another occasion, kneading Frank Gifford's wrenched knee and looking over his shoulder at the progress of the game, he saw the hated opponents complete a long pass. Dr. Sweeney swore loudly. And, in anger, he also gave Gifford's knee a yank that put Giff out of action for four weeks instead of two. And then there was the time both Strong and Ward Cuff were injured in Washington. Sweeney, being the good doctor he was, insisted that he take them to St. Elizabeth's Hospital in New York, the official sick bay for the team.

"I had an injured back," Strong recalls, "and Cuff had a hurt leg. We got to New York and took a cab, and one of us decided it would be nice to stop in a favorite saloon to ease our pain. We did. Then Doc Sweeney remembered a favorite bartender near the hospital. We stopped there. We stopped other places. The end result was that when we got to the hospital, me with the hurt back and Cuffy with the bad leg had to help our doctor up the steps."

Sweeney was no clown, however. In the 1938 championship game against the Bears, the Polo Grounds' field became covered with ice. At half time the good Doctor Sweeney had his inspiration.

Sweeney was also team doctor for Manhattan College sports teams and, as such, had keys to the gym. He sent messengers rushing to the college gym. The runners brought back every pair of rubber-soled basketball sneakers that could be found. In a pair of sneakers that didn't quite fit but didn't slide on ice, Strong single-handedly beat the Big Bad Bears in the second half.

As pro football has taken over as *the* big TV sport, as athletes now get staggering bonuses and contracts just to agree to play the game, the more relaxed attitude of the early times fades from memory. But there will always be with us such philosophers as Emlen Tunnell, now a Giants coach but once the greatest of our pass defenders.

On the occasion best remembered, the late Steve Owen, for over a generation the Giants top coach, told Tunnell in the pregame dressing room that his assignment was to make sure that Elroy "Crazy Legs" Hirsch of the Los Angeles Rams did not, under any conditions, get "behind" Tunnell—that is, outrun him.

So Em kept right on Hirsch's behind for almost all the game, crowding him and jostling him and keeping him safely "inside" for short gains. But near the end, Hirsch did put his crazy legs to their full potential and did get behind Tunnell and did score a touchdown. In the dressing room Coach Owen was furious.

"I told you not to let Hirsch get behind you!" he screamed. Tunnell wiped off his sweaty face.

"Coach," he said tiredly, "Hirsch is paid $18,000 a year. I'm paid $8,000 a year. He is *supposed* to get behind me!"

When I read about the bonuses and promises and salaries paid to the Joe Namaths and O. J. Simpsons and the other college superstars just to show up at training camp, with "no-cut" clauses all over the contract, lawyers and tax experts in advisory attendance and the cameras hanging on the superstar's every word, I have to remember back to the early days.

Veterans recall that a lineman or any other unglamorous star was lucky to play the game for $100 a Sunday. Also, for that kind of money, with the old leather helmets that had no face guards, he was a sure shot to lose all his front teeth. And further, he had to pay a dentist out of his own pocket to make him some new teeth.

The F-F-Funny F-F-Fellow

HE WAS BORN LOUIS WILSON Josephs in Rock Island, Ill., in 1891, but from 1918 until his death in 1958 he was known to show business, a host of imitators and an army of quoters as Joe Frisco. You have to have reached a mellow age to remember when the Frisco dance—derby, tilted at sharp angle, long cigar slanted upward from the corner of the mouth—was as common a vaudeville routine as the Charleston was to become. There was a period when all witty sayings were credited to the late Dorothy Parker. Before the Parker period, the most quoted jokes were Frisco jokes. And in his last years, when he had become a legend, the Frisco jokes were repeated again and again in show business circles.

I am in contention with Peter Lind Hayes as to which of us should be Frisco's official Boswell. Pete was closer to him because Frisco worked on and off for years at Pete's mother's Grace Hayes Lodge out in California. But I'm older than Pete and remember Frisco in his earlier stages. Actually, Frisco could probably use two biographers.

He was the fastest natural wit in the history of comedy, and it is the rare comedian who will argue this.

It was always argued among the hip set as to whether Frisco's stutter was natural or a planned affectation to make his timing more effective. Asked why he moved from Rock Island to Dubuque at an early age, he claimed, "Because my bookmaker was g-g-giving me a b-b-bad morning line." Told that Dubuque was an unlikely city for a man who stuttered, he admitted, "Yes, b-b-but who wanted to move to V-V-Vladivostok?" Years later, almost at the end of the line, he was living in a scrubby hotel in Hollywood where the clientele was mostly former vaudevillians on the downbeat. Joe sneaked an old pal into his room and bedded him down on the floor.

"Mr. Frisco," the hotel manager said firmly on the phone one day, "if you have an extra guest in your room it will be one dollar a day extra."

"All right," agreed Joe, "b-b-but send up another B-B-Bible."

In his later years he worked in Bing Crosby films and was the pet of other Hollywood stars. He kept himself going and, as long as there was a racetrack nearby, he was happy enough. He apparently had mixed feelings about Southern California, though.

"This is the only p-p-place in the world," he once told us, "where you c-c-can fall asleep under a rose b-b-bush in full bloom and freeze to death before m-m-morning."

When he wasn't doing small roles in the films, he was appearing (or wasn't) at Grace Hayes' Lodge. He was fired with regularity and rehired just as regularly. He could infuriate Miss Hayes and her partner, Charlie Foy, but they simply couldn't stay that way.

Once Gary Cooper appeared at the lodge and Joe showed him around the place. First stop was Miss Hayes's dressing room, where she sat before her mirror putting on makeup. On her dressing table was the usual assortment of lotions, powders, astringents, makeup and perfumes.

"Look at all the stuff she uses," Joe told Cooper, "j-j-just to look f-f-forty-five." Fired.

On another occasion Charlie Foy bought a twenty-eight-pound turkey so that the Chef could cook up a nice, friendly Thanksgiving dinner for the staff. Somebody stole the turkey. Foy was furious. He gathered all employees and gave them a tirade on the dastardly thief who would steal a twenty-eight-pound Thanksgiving turkey. He somehow kept stressing the twenty-eight pounds.

"If you think I t-t-took it," Frisco finally suggested wearily, "weigh m-m-me." Fired again.

One night Joe arrived for his stint to find a customer out on the floor singing classical songs in a ringing voice. Joe listened a minute and then told Grace Hayes to hire the chap.

"Are you mad?" Grace demanded. "That's Lawrence Tibbett."

"So change his n-n-name," advised Joe, "and then p-p-put him in the show."

When Grace's son, Peter Lind Hayes, took off for New York and his own comedy career, Joe had some advice for his favorite fan. Pete was booked to do his act on the enormous stage of the vast Roxy Theatre, one of the long-disappeared Broadway movie and stage spectacle palaces.

"Never get c-c-caught in the middle of that stage," was Joe's advice, "without b-b-bread and water."

During World War II a submarine sailor took a girl to the lodge. In the style of submariners of the day, this youth sported a full, flowing beard. "That's a g-g-good sign," Joe opined. "Lincoln's b-b-boy has joined the Navy."

The lodge attracted many former vaudevillians, and one night a midget who had played on many variety bills with Frisco came over to the latter's table to say hello. The midget's head came just above the tablecloth.

"Who ordered J-J-John the B-B-Baptist?" Frisco demanded.

It was sometime later that he had trouble with his teeth and finally had two entire new sets of choppers inserted. The new teeth gave him a smile that made him look like Ingrid Bergman, friends insisted.

"I c-c-can't understand it," Joe told them. "My dentist had the c-c-coroner send over at least f-f-fifty plates."

Behind the bar the lodge had a mounted deer head on the wall to aid the place's outdoorsy atmosphere. Frisco would look at this deer head in wonderment.

"He m-m-must have been c-c-coming pretty fast," he would decide, "to g-g-go right through that wall."

In his younger days his gab and his dancing got him co-star billing in several hit Broadway musicals, and even the colorful Florenz Ziegfeld finally hired him for a specialty in *The Ziegfeld Follies.*

At the end of his act, Frisco would tilt the derby, stick the cigar in the corner of his mouth, put his hands in his pockets, hike up his pants and start the Frisco dance. At the end of his dance, opening night, he ostentatiously dropped a half dollar on the stage. The audience roared and soon began throwing coins and bills up at him, all of which Joe retrieved. It was a funny piece of business but it drove Ziegfeld wild. The meticulous arbiter of American beauty was somehow antipathetic to patrons turning his gilded temple of art into a corner saloon.

Once the old Forrest Hotel had a Western Union office down the block and Joe sent for a Western Union messenger. We were there in the lobby when the kid arrived, and we all held our breath when the kid took the message. The kid stuttered worse than Frisco. Joe looked at him sternly.

"G-G-Go back to the office," he ordered, "and t-t-tell them to send me a straight m-m-man."

In those days Abe Lyman's orchestra was practically the house band in any new, big nightclub, and was the standard attraction at many hotel ballrooms. Frisco lived in the same West Side hotel where the Lyman band was playing. One night he came into the lobby and there was a big blown-up photo of Lyman with the notice that the Lyman orchestra was the attraction at the hotel's main public room. Around the photo, because it was in the wee hours, the cleaning women had shoved about twenty of the lobby's brass spittoons.

"Abe's g-g-got a great b-b-band," Joe admitted to a friend, pointing at the photo and the spittoons, "b-b-but I'll never believe he won all those c-c-cups."

In his forty-odd years as a stage and screen star, Joe never left the country except for a single trip on a cruise boat to Nassau. He reported on it upon return. He said when the ship hauled up the gangplank it was about twelve blocks long and had linked rails. "I thought they had Fifth Avenue in chains," he admitted. Later he and his pal, Frank Farnum, went on deck and gazed at the ocean sliding by.

"Did you ever see so much water?" asked the equally uneasy Farnum.

"No," replied Joe, "and remember, you're only looking at the top of it."

At his death he had never been inside an airplane. He had his reason for not flying.

"Those things have no running b-b-boards," he explained.

Before he took off for Hollywood, when the living theatre was staggering under the Depression and vaudeville was gasping its last, Frisco found work hard to get. One reason was that he insisted on his "price," the same salary he had been paid in happier days. His price was $2,000 a week, a solid sum then, and he once firmly refused a week's work that would pay only $1,600.

"Joe," said his anguished agent, "do you realize that's more money than President Hoover gets?"

"Hoover hasn't m-m-made g-g-good yet," was Joe's firm reply.

Yet he would work Jack White's 18 Club, with Jackie Gleason, Frankie Hyers, Pat Harrington and the others of that mad mob, for a few dollars a night because he felt that the racetrack tips he got from the jockeys who congregated there were worth more than mere money.

White's was also a rendezvous for hecklers and customers who thought they could holler down the talent. Frisco invariably slaughtered them. Once Maxie Rosenbloom, then light-heavyweight champion, thought he could top Frisco's gags.

"Lay down," Frisco advised him. "More people will recognize you that way."

Another night Pie Traynor, the great third baseman of the Pittsburgh Pirates, was in the place and Jack White, an incurable baseball buff, nearly went hysterical introducing "the immortal third baseman."

"If he's so g-g-good," Joe demanded, "why isn't he playing f-f-first b-b-base?"

In another nightclub one night Frisco was eating a steak when a young comic on the floor began to make jokes at his expense. He finally dragged the microphone over to Joe's table and asked him if he liked the steak.

"I c-c-can't take you on an empty stomach," Joe said into the mike.

Once in California he turned his attention to his only love, the racetrack. Year by year the horses wiped out whatever earnings he made, big or small. With Crosby at a California track, he was questioned by an old lady in a wheelchair. She wanted to know what the "star" after a horse's name meant. All racetrack addicts know that this asterisk after a horse's name means that he is a superior mudder. But because the day was sunny and warm, Joe figured the little old lady was entitled to a more sentimental explanation.

"It m-m-means," he said kindly, "that the horse has a s-s-son in military service."

Jimmy Duffy, of the long-forgotten comedy vaudeville team of Duffy and Seeney, was a racetrack companion. One day they stood at the rail watching a tight finish that looked to the naked eye like a dead heat. The number four horse had Joe's money. It had come head and head to the final wire alongside the number one horse. (A true horse player never bothers with horse's names. It's the horse's number and what the number pays or doesn't pay.) Next to Frisco and Duffy a stranger turned and asked Joe if he had number four. Joe said yes. The stranger said he had number one but he thought four had won. Joe said he made it number one. It developed each had bet ten dollars.

"Tell you what," said the stranger. "If your horse wins you give me ten dollars and if my horse wins I give you ten. That way neither one of us can lose."

Joe thought it a thoroughly sensible business deal, but Duffy began to loudly point out flaws in the plan and advise Joe against the agreement. Joe turned on him.

"Listen," he ordered, "d-d-don't try and t-t-tout me on the photo."

Joe had his own nightclub in New York once, with a beautiful partner named Loretta McDermott. There were two playboy Canadian mining millionaires, Jack and Duncan McMartin, and Joe was a particular favorite of Jack's when the latter was in and on the town. One night a friend rushed in with the news that Abe Attell, the great featherweight prizefighter of olden days, then running a Broadway saloon, had been hit by a car while crossing the street. Abe was carted away with a badly shattered leg. Attell was then in his late sixties.

"It's a shame," Joe agreed. "They t-t-tell me he'll never f-f-fight again."

Joe got more and more mellow in his last years. He used to recall what his mother said the first time she saw him on the stage.

"Either he's crazy," was her opinion, "or the public is."

"And she was d-d-dead right t-t-too," Joe would conclude.

His last recorded witticism came shortly before the end. He sat in a Los Angeles steam bath and, through the mists, listened to two other gamblers bemoaning their recent losses. One, hidden by the clouds of steam, finally philosophized:

"Oh well, you can't take it with you."

"No," said Joe Frisco from his corner recess, "and you can't send it in advance, either."

DIRTY JOKE

Since his clientele included Oliver St. John Gogarty, Lord Dunsany, and the better writers for the smarter magazines, plus those creative young minds of the advertising business, it is little wonder that the late Tim Costello, of the saloon of the same name, was doubtless the most literate and erudite Third Avenue grog shop proprietor ever to lean over the sensible side of a bar.

But like most Irish (and, indeed, like so many of us) he was never so stricken with nostalgia as after the death of an old friend or customer. Thus, following the funeral of the writer John McNulty, Tim took a deep breath, took a tiny sip of his drink and let his thoughts wander back to better, younger days when he first came to the new country and got a job bartending over near the "cair bairns," which we all assumed to mean the old car barns in the then Irish stronghold of Tenth Avenue in midtown.

"One night," Tim started softly, "a little old lady in a little black dress and little black shoes and a funny little black hat staggered in, waltzed right up to me and told me to serve her a double rye whisky. I stared, gulped and finally said, Mother, we don't serve little old ladies here. Mother, you should run along home and to bed. She looked me square in the eye for a moment and then said loudly, 'Ah, go and fuck yourself.'"

Tim shuddered, remembering. And then, he said, one of the cair bairn boys at the bar spoke up and his tale went as follows, if my memory and Tim's memory can both be depended upon. I make no attempt to use the brogue, merely to repeat the cair bairn boy's memoir as Tim related it.

I haven't heard an old lady use that word since I was a young gossoon in London, said this cair bairn boy, still shocked. I had gone to London to make me a fortune and to add a little culture to me life, so I joined the Waltham Stowe Gossoon Brass Band. Now the Waltham Stowe Gossoon Brass Band did not have enough instruments, so we members divided up the Irish-English parts of Waltham Stowe and we set out to take up a collection that would enable us to buy instruments and proper music.

The first house I called at was built back from the street. It had a neat little lawn and the house was white. Also, at the sidewalk, there was a small white fence with a little swinging gate. I marched up onto the steps and rang the bell.

Well, a little old lady came to the door and she had one of those ear trumpets. I said that I was collecting donations for the Waltham Stowe Gossoon Brass Band. She said something like "Whah?" and fiddled with that old-fashioned ear horn. I explained again about the Waltham Stowe Gossoon Brass Band. She said she still couldn't hear and started twisting that ear tube again. I went at it again, pleading that a shilling or even a few pence would be of help.

Again she shook her head, showing that she still didn't make me out. So after one more appeal for the Waltham Stowe Gossoon Brass Band, I turned on me heel and started down the walk toward the fence. I was almost there when she called after me:

"Mind the gate!"

Discouraged as I was, and dealing with a stone-deaf old lady, I turned me head and said softly, "Ah, fuck the gate!"

And in a voice as clear as a bell, I heard her call, "And fuck the Waltham Stowe Gossoon Brass Band!"

City Dog

IF, IN RECENT TIMES, YOU HAVE sat in a taxi or in your car on a New York cross street and ground your teeth as the traffic light went from green to red to green to red to green again, and nothing on wheels ahead of you has moved an inch; if you have crawled up a main avenue bumper to tight bumper, with the trailer trucks, the buses and the shiny new Detroit models; if you are paying whatever the burglarious rate is at this writing for garage space somewhere near your home, then you are simply going to call me a liar for making the following deposition.

Deponent avers that there was a time in New York City when you could cross the street with just a casual glance both ways, that you could always find a street parking space in midtown Manhattan and even Times Square, that you could park on the street overnight near your abode, and that the public parks, now blitzkrieged by protest meeting, rallies, "happenings" (whatever they are), hippies and muggers, were virtually empty at all hours—except for the dog walkers.

There are still hordes of dogs and dog walkers in the city. Also dog *carriers*, a new breed of pet owner. The difference is that in an earlier day everybody had a *different* breed of dog. Probably more people own city dogs in New York today than ever before—but they are all poodles, to the casual eye.

During the Dark Depression I had a city dog for fifteen years. He was an oversized, big-boned black spaniel named Captain. Central Park was our Elysium. Our enemy was the patrolling park cop. Magistrates in the city had less violent crimes to contend with then than now, and every time Captain and I—or any of our dog army pals—lost a decision to a park cop with a book of tickets, we would have to come before a magistrate.

"A dog," these annoyed justices would inavariably proclaim, "has no business in the city. It is unfair to the dog and to other citizens. If you keep a dog in the city you must keep him on a leash. Two dollars."

Out two dollars, we would hurry right back to the Sheep Meadow in Central Park where at least a dozen other convicted dog miscreants would be running wild, leashless. The owners would gather around to hear if we had beat the stupid magistrate or lost the decision. Bitter threats would be uttered. We all knew each other. We saw each other sometimes twice a day in that vast meadow where dogs ran all-out until exhausted. Us two-leggers never knew each other's names. We would refer to "Champ's father" or "Spotty's mother," and an ancient actress who paraded nine wheezy canines of varied breeds was known simply as "the woman with all the dogs."

My Captain's black hair was flat and only slightly waved, without a white spot. Strangely, for a black dog he had soft brown eyes. The black hair grew thick around his mushroom feet and pointed upward, giving him the appearance of walking on his heels. He had the jaunty, preoccupied walk of a wise guy. He *was* a wise guy. And nobody knew it better than he.

Captain had decided when he was six months old that taxicabs were wonderful things, and had proceeded with low cunning to make fast friends in all the taxi lines at the Central Park South hotels near which he spent most of his life. (Note: Yes, there was an era when taxicabs lined up in front of hotels and *waited* for customers to appear.) If it was summer and the apartment door was open against the city heat, he would gallop downstairs on his own, climb into the first taxi whose driver called him by name, and ride out a couple of calls. An hour or so later the doorbell would ring, his master or mistress would call to him sharply that the fun was over, and upstairs he would come, nicely refreshed. He never once approached a strange taxicab driver.

Sometimes, partly to make him work for his pleasures or out of our own sheer laziness, we would tie a note to his collar reading "Two packs Chesterfields," or whatever, and just tell him "Go fetch!" He would clump downstairs again, into the gin mill on the ground floor, and a bartender or waiter would untie the note, put the cigarettes in a bag and put the bag in his mouth. He would come upstairs unhurriedly, reflecting on the true pleasures of a job well done and the importance of his residence at headquarters.

He could realistically be described as a real sophisticated and hip citizen. He shared midnight snacks with the hatcheck girls in most of the midtown nightclubs when his boss was at his newspaper chores. He was fed caviar on thin crackers at the cocktail bars. He saw most of the art exhibitions his bosses attended and, briefly, he was a ham actor in a Broadway play. If he visited a hotel room once he always remembered just where it was and preceded everybody down the halls and turnings.

Also, he had the veteran New Yorker's wary distrust of street traffic. I doubt if he stepped off a curb alone three times in his life. He would no sooner have thought of crossing a street except at somebody's heels than he would have jumped out the third story window of his pied-à-terre, from which he hung day and night like a tenement housewife.

He was contemptuous of all strangers and almost all other dogs, but there was nothing timid about him. Whenever insulted or challenged, he threw himself into battles against almost any animal smaller than an elephant. He hated Scottish terriers for some remote, atavistic reason, and although his breed was never made for warfare, he would enter battle with a Scotty as if joining a holy war. Large dogs he walked around cautiously, giving them a wide berth, pretending he didn't see them.

Like all city dogs he did his fighting strictly according to the code. It was all right for two dogs off the leash to fight, and all right for two dogs on the leash to try and fight. But a dog off the leash never fought a dog on a leash. It wasn't cricket. Dogs didn't fight in Central Park, either—possibly because they all knew each other, or possibly because, like pickpockets in Madison Square Garden, they had learned from bitter experience that discipline from boss or owner was swift and painful. He was always ill at ease with country dogs during his vacations from the big town. They would sidle up to him, tentatively offering fight or frolic, but he would brush them off. He had no time for yokels.

Although he had walked perfectly at heel since a puppy and was completely obedient even when excited, the whims and fancies of his owners never diverted him from any serious business that came to hand. Serious business to him, for instance, was the door of any drugstore or ham-and-eggery where he was favorably known. He would simply turn into the eatery, sit up in front of his favorite counterman and emit something that sounded like a pained yawn. The boys behind the counter would start throwing him bits of liverwurst or ham.

He would catch them in his mouth without ever going to four legs, although often forced to lunge dangerously. Every once in a while, just to keep him awake, a counterman would toss him a small piece of pickle. It would get halfway down his cavernous throat before he could reverse his laryngeal gears and spit it disgustedly out onto the floor.

Nobody could fool him about his food and nobody ever changed his tastes, either. He was part epicure and part glutton. Like many restaurant-trained eaters, he preferred to vary his diet between chophouse food and the highly flavored dishes of exotic origin. Vegetables, mashes, malts and other health-giving foods left him cold. During his early years we would surreptitiously mix green peas, spinach, string beans, carrots and other vitamin-laden goodies into his chopped meat. We soon gave up. It took him no more than five minutes to sort out all the greens and discard them around his dish on the kitchen floor.

He was a great one for sweets and olive oil, and he probably got more than was good for him. He would drink olive oil and water alternately, like a man drinking boilermakers. But whatever his own gluttony, he was irritated and impatient with the vices of others. He hated the sight and smell of whisky, possibly because of remembrance of the painful alcohol medications for his occasional ear cankers, and he acted among drunks in the manner of a man who has recently and successfully conquered the drunkard's curse. He was tolerant and uncomplaining, but bored stiff. And very, very superior.

He was a 100 percent city dog, but the things that had been born in his bloodline never completely atrophied. He would have made a splendid working dog. He never had enough of the park or the countryside even in the bitterest weather. The lawns, rocks, hills and bushes were an ever-absorbing book to him. He ran with his nose scraping the ground. He swam in the filthy ponds. He found, now and then, his particular kind of grass, and he carefully pulled the stalks one by one and chewed them thoughtfully.

Something in the dim recesses of his mind told him that he ought to chase any animal that looked like a squirrel. He flatted out his body and chased as hard as he could. It was obvious that he had no real motive in it. It was just something he knew he ought to do. The squirrels always made a tree yards ahead of him, and once they were up the tree he immediately lost interest and veered away on some other project.

Once, in the Shakespeare Gardens, he came suddenly face to face with a squirrel sitting on its haunches. He was almost as flabbergasted as the squirrel. They both froze and, for a long moment, stared at each other with eyes a foot apart. Then Captain uttered a low, seductive whine. The noise snapped the squirrel's nervous system back into gear and he scuttled up a tree.

It was almost as bad a turn as the time, in the country, when he had almost stepped on a rabbit that came out of a hedge. He jumped straight up in the air, that time. I always believed that his true vocation was flushing house flies. He would point a fly like a bird dog. If the fly came near enough he would lunge, snap and grab it in his mouth. He spit out the flies immediately, looking somewhat nauseated but satisfied with doing a disagreeable job as best he could.

His archenemy in Central Park, and the bane of all other dog walkers, was a big, new and eager policeman named Art McKeane. McKeane's dull assignment was to keep people off the grass, see that dogs were properly leashed, discourage the stealing of peanuts from the stands and other such corroding chores. Policemen had less to do in those innocent times. McKeane started his career with understandable bitterness. He handed out summonses right and left, but no man, no matter how strong and ambitious, could long weather the storms that galled McKeane.

"You idiotic, unhappy man," raged the woman with all the dogs as she took her umpteenth summons, "I have written the stupid mayor and that stupid Robert Moses. I am an old woman and I will live to see you in jail where you belong. Why aren't you somewhere chasing murderers?"

Ultimately, it was McKeane who surrendered. He bought a dog himself and this brought a new attitude. He would pretend not to see the dogs running free, but would blow his whistle wildly. Everybody would call in his animal and hook him up.

"Sorry, Captain," McKeane would have to mumble once in a while, "but I've got to give out *some* summonses. I gave Spotty one yesterday and Gypsy the day before. This week I also got Rusty and Kerry Patch. Too bad, but it's your turn."

Captain loved the country equally with the park, but he never got quite enough of the country to take it in easy stride. He went all out all the time. He came home with dead fish in his mouth and mud matted in his hair. And he could always find a too-big piece of driftwood that had to be dragged from where it was to where he knew it ought to have been in the first place. He would take to a heavy Long Island surf as confidently as he would jump into a millpond and seem surprised when the surf knocked his knockers. Back home in the city he always seemed pretty beat. He would lie tiredly in his corner, moaning and tossing and resting his battered bones. He would be almost too tired to eat. Almost.

We were never particularly awed by dogs who could do tricks, but Captain learned so easily, when any payoff seemed to be in the offing, that we taught him a few of the standard sit up, lie down, roll over, play dead routines. It was understood that the parties of each part were engaged in a business transaction and that he was not to be called upon to perform without a stipend. One dog biscuit was a stipend. Two dog biscuits were better.

After a few months all we had to do was shake the biscuit box and he would sit up, lie down, roll over and play dead in finger-snapping time. We tried to abandon the deal, but when he considered it to be biscuit time he would go through his act and then lay "dead," looking at us in pained betrayal.

I often wondered how large a human vocabulary he really understood. It must have been surprisingly comprehensive. Certain words spoken in certain tones would send him into a growling rage. Other words would produce other moods. He also had his own ideas about people. He knew accurately which were old friends of the family and which just happened to be temporarily around the house a lot. There was only one man that I remember he adamantly hated. This was a mendicant who roamed our territory as a one-man band, laden with various instruments that he blew, pounded, fingered, kicked and shook.

Long after the one-man band had disappeared around the corner, Captain's hair would still be upright on his neck and he would be grumbling and muttering curses to himself. The one-man band could spoil his whole evening.

He was past fifteen years of age when the tumors first became evident. He began to have trouble with his breathing, and to touch him in the wrong place would bring a whine of pain. For a while we tried carrying him up and down the stairs and letting him slowly cruise the fire hydrants and telephone poles. Even with a hassock in front of it, he couldn't climb up and lean out his favorite window. There were nights when he couldn't lie comfortably no matter how he tried.

The inevitable day came when I had to take him to a hospital for the last time. In the cab he managed to get his head out the open window. On the sidewalk in front of the animal hospital he stopped dead in his tracks. No animal hospital could fool that old nose, no matter how sick it was. I got him to the door, took off his lead and put it in his mouth.

"Carry it up, Cappie," I told him. "I know you want to go there under your own power." He took the folded lead in his mouth and laboriously followed me up the stairs. For some reason, I was glad the veterinarian was a young man. He insisted on lifting the dog himself and putting him in the box they used in those days. Captain turned his glazed eyes at me and stared a questioning moment. The young vet gently closed the box and turned on the motor.

Downstairs I stood on the sidewalk for several minutes. I had to get my face back in shape.

There'll Always Be a Village

NIGHT LIFE ON BROADWAY IN THE 1930s and early 1940s was roaring along at peak pitch, the "class" cafés of the East Side had attained their social summit and up in Harlem things jumped until dawn, or even next day. Downtown, the sector called Greenwich Village had what many entertainment epicures considered to be the most colorful and varied night life in the entire city. Today Broadway's night life has long been embalmed: Only El Morocco remains of the East Side old guard, and Harlem at night is an alien land to the downtown pleasure seeker. The Village is still having itself a ball. It has always been there, and it probably always will be. It seems like a fairly safe bet that when the last nighttime entertainment oasis disappears from New York, the millennium will be someplace in Greenwich Village.

How and why the Village flowered as an early area of arts, crafts and just plain entertainment are moot questions. Some historians hold that the opening of the Whitney Museum, just after World War I, brought the artists downtown to take advantage of cheap rentals and garret atmosphere. Another theory is that the neighborhood was populated almost entirely by Italians who were the first brave bootleggers and thus fathered the first speakeasies. For whatever motivating force, the downtown hegira was underway more than fifty years ago.

Although Eugene O'Neill, Theodore Dreiser and other giants of the legitimate theatre are popularly credited with bringing fame to the Village, the facts seem to indicate that what might be called the Provincetown Playhouse Group followed the downtown movement rather than created it. At any rate, all sorts of colorful if pecunious folk appeared on the territory. One of the earliest of these was a combination saxophonist and painter named Don Dickerman. His first rendezvous had a few pre-Prohibition whisky drinkers, but the main item was ordinary cider at twenty-five cents a glass.

This was the Pirate's Den. Through Prohibition and into the 1930s, Dickerman operated a whole string of Village boîtes, all the while painting (without notable success) and playing his sax (not very well). Above his original Pirate's Den cellar in Minetta Lane was a woman who called herself Romany Marie. She started with poetry readings during which the "guests" drank Turkish coffee. She didn't discover that she could sell hard booze until years later. Marie ultimately became a sort of historic landmark in the Village. As late as the early 1950s she was advertising in the Village papers for "a large room well situated." However old she must have been, some thirty-five years after her Village fame she was obviously willing to try again, possibly because, by the 1950s, poetry readings were once again a big kick in the Washington Square environs.

A Village original named Sam Schwartz had a place called the Liberal Club, originally at 137 McDougal Street, which by the early 1920s had such regulars as famed novelists Sinclair Lewis, Lucien Cary, Susan Glaspell and John Haynes Holmes. Schwartz ultimately came to the depressing decision that there was no money in arty talk or literary opinion. So he borrowed $185 and opened the Black Knight Club across the street—with booze as the attraction. It was an established oasis for many years.

One night Schwartz stood watching the usual newspapermen's card game at the Black Knight and soon decided that the only stranger at the table was double-dealing. Schwartz called him aside and told him sadly that it was rather useless to cheat newspapermen and/or writers, and would the stranger please decamp as of this moment.

"Would you give me twenty minutes?" asked the stranger. Not knowing what the fellow planned, Schwartz nevertheless agreed. The stranger returned to the card game and within twenty minutes neatly cheated himself out of all his winnings and, even more neatly, managed to lose back the right amounts to the right losers. He was the fabulous Jesse Fry, Jr., a card manipulator who had been cheating luxury steamship-riding millionaires and even European royalty for years, and was to continue doing so for many more years.

Fry became a great favorite with the Village set from that moment on. Until 1950, his last telegraphic contact with any old friend, Village veterans would get Fry's cables from the far ends of the earth. The cables would request either quick loans or would be money orders to repay old loans.

Schwartz, too, lived to be a human landmark. He was still managing clubs or restaurants as late as 1956, and was looking around for another good, cheap investment like the Black Knight. Alas, like Jesse Fry, he is heard from no more. Today's Village literateurs doubtless would not recognize his name.

From the Village's stone age through the Depression years, my own favorite Village impresarios were the Strunskys. I knew them only to say hello, but I wish I had known them well. In my early dotage, it is hard for memory to properly sort them out. There was, I think, a Morris, an Albert, a Max, a Hyman, a sister-in-law named Marscha and a sister named Lenore who married Ira Gershwin, the lyricist. The Strunskys were Village landlords en masse. They rented the cellars and the rooms for the dank Village clubs. They rented furniture for same. They rented apartments to the nightclub operators and rented beds, couches, tables, et cetera for same.

As landlords they left behind one indelible legend. For years and years any old or broken-down piece of furniture in a nightclub—be it a refrigerator, kitchen range or table—was known to any veteran Villager as "Strunsky period furniture." The Strunskys, possibly contaminated by the night types they dealt with, now and then would take a fling at running their own nightclub. At one of these, a cellar on West 8th Street called Three Steps Down, it was not uncommon to wander in and find a pianist named George Gershwin playing for his brother and his in-laws.

Not all Village operations were on such a marginal level. In the 1930s a man named Barney Gallant ran a series of Village spots and was probably more responsible than anybody else for bringing the rich and the social downtown. He had a personal following of celebrities not eclipsed by the more publicized uptown class joint operators. In deep Depression, his Studio Club could demand, and get, an unheard of $5 cover charge.

He had another claim to fame. He may have been a part of the first authentic Village nightclub. As early as 1911 a woman named Polly Holliday went into partnership with actor Frank Conroy and artist Harold Meltzer to open a bistro off Sheridan Square, that was to become the Greenwich Village Inn. They hired a chap named Barney Gallant as combination greeter, waiter and handyman around the place. He graduated to a headwaiter's jacket and later to his own series of cafés.

Others of the early operators improved their lot. Two fellows named Jack Kriendler and Charles Berns opened a small spot on Sixth Avenue and called it the Fronton. When the city decided to widen the avenue, they were forced out. They moved up, first to 48th Street and later to 21 West 52d Street, where Berns and Kriendler's brothers and heirs still run the fabled "21" Iron Gate, perhaps the classiest eatery in town.

Another favorite hangout of mine was Ben Collada's El Chico. It lasted from 1925 until 1964, a pretty fair stretch, and while it was a cellar place, it was no cellar joint. It introduced most of the later famous Latin American and Spanish artists, and the food, if you please, was cooked by a former chef to the king of Spain.

The chef was Juan Nieto. On this worthy's first day in the cellar at 80 Grove Street, he was baking an oven full of fancy cakes. On that afternoon, too, the great flamenco dancer Juan Martinez decided that he and his wife needed some rehearsal. The Martinezes stomped around the floor in fine flamenco pounding. In the kitchen, all of the former king of Spain's chef's cakes promptly collapsed in their pans. Swordplay was narrowly averted.

Spanish art lined the walls and Spanish grillwork separated the booths. Bulls' heads dedicated by one matador or another were prominently featured. The place became the mecca for the rich

South Americans, Cubans and Spaniards who were so prominent in night life throughout the pre-World War II era. One wonders whatever became of those coffee and sugar and tinplate zillionaires.

The rumba and the danson were first introduced at El Chico. The orchestra leader, Emil Coleman, and the composer Eliseo Grenet got their starts there. Flamenco music was introduced. This wailing type of song plucked at the homesick heartstrings of the Spaniards, but it left some of the drop-ins confused. These patrons were convinced that the gypsy singers were doing Jewish chants, and nightly Collada was asked what section of the Bronx some gitano came from.

What with union demands, skyrocketing Village rents and exploding entertainment and music costs, Collada gave up the ghost at El Chico in 1964. He is one of many. The day of the class saloon, anywhere, is over—particularly a place pointed at a specific audience.

Jazz music as we used to know it made its greatest contribution on the aforementioned Swing Street, but even that block owed something to Village pioneers. A man named Nick Rongetti had one of the earliest "sizzling steak" places on Seventh Avenue. Himself a boogie-woogie piano aficionado, Nick decided in 1925 that he could mix sizzling platters with jazz music. He imported many of the great New Orleans and Chicago jazzmen and Nick's jazz sessions ran on until his death in the early 1950s. He was possibly the first to offer Sunday afternoon jazz concerts.

Nick always had a relief pianist in the middle of the floor, to play between the band sessions, and beside the relief pianist was always a second piano. This was Nick's own, to be used when he wanted to join the hired hand or just play a little for his own amusement.

There came a night when the floor pianist was the redoubtable Willie "The Lion" Smith. The Lion sat down to the keys and started off on his rather delicate "Echoes of Spring." Before long he was confused by a boogie-woogie beat accompanying his composition. He looked over his shoulder to find the boss of the place volunteering his own background to The Lion's music.

The Lion said naught. At the end of his set he got up, retrieved his derby hat and umbrella and went out into the night. This was not unusual, as most of Nick's musicians spent all their free time at Julius' saloon across the street. The Lion, however, did not return when it was time for his next set. Ultimately a phone call came for Eddie Condon, the bandmaster. It was The Lion.

"Where the hell are you?" demanded Condon.

"I'm at 135th Street and Lexington Avenue," said The Lion firmly. "Tell that guy I'll make a deal with him. I won't help him cook steak and he won't help me play piano."

At this writing the dean of Village operators is Max Gordon, whose Village Vanguard is still thriving. The Vanguard has been on the same premises for more than thirty-six years, and Max has been up nights with one idea or another for forty. He is a small man who in his youth studied to be a lawyer. To keep at his studies, he found it necessary to work as a waiter and dishwasher in various Village night operations. The big dream in the Village in Max's primary time was to have the "better coffee house" with intellectual trimmings.

Gordon somehow put together $200 and opened his Village Fair on Sullivan Street. Poets such as Maxwell Bodenheim and Harry Kemp declaimed there nightly. Bodenheim once reached the pinnacle pay of $15 a week, but ultimately settled for seventy-five cents a poem or a free drink of booze. There was also the poet Gildea, who would read his epics in exchange for beverage, with the further proviso that somebody would walk him home. The playwright Clifford Odets was always ready to do his version of "The Face on the Barroom Floor," even though he drank sparingly when at all.

It wasn't that Gordon was exploiting these talents. The hard fact of the matter was that he didn't have much more money than they did. When the Village Fair folded, Gordon borrowed $60 from a shylock and bought the furnishings and scenic (?) effects from a woman who had operated a place called the White Elephant. The furniture consisted of some barrel tables and a large potbellied stove. It was the first Village Vanguard and Gordon was literally frozen out of it because, on cold nights, the big stove was inadequate. A year after opening he moved to his present location.

Repeal beer was legal on the new Vanguard's opening night. Max was busy selling same when a cop arrived. "Where's your license to sell beer?" demanded the law. "Look," said Max, "give me a while to sell some beer and I'll pay for a license." The cop did. Max did.

In this small cellar, which Max thinks is shaped like the Southern Cross and veterans contend has the exact symmetry of a coffin, many a fine talent was unearthed over the years. Harry Belafonte, Eartha Kitt, Judy Holliday, Pearl Bailey, Wally Cox and a whole slew of top jazz musicians and unsung entertainers readily point to it as the first step on their careers.

The Village in the 1920s and 1930s also had its own version of a Broadway cabaret. This was Jimmy Kelly's on Sullivan Street, in the same building where, unless things have changed recently, an Off-Broadway attraction called "The Fantasticks" has been playing for almost ten years. Kelly was an Italian by birth but thought Kelly a classier name for a nightclub impresario. He was also the son of the Tammany District leader. Thus, throughout Prohibition he was never seriously bothered by the law in reference to contents of his drinks.

There is one Village phenomenon, over the years, that had and has nothing to do with the myriad nightclub and coffeehouse operators. That phenomenon has been their public. Elsewhere in the city, amusement seekers have proven fickle indeed. They embrace this fad and then turn their collective back on it. Jazz spots drew the class and the mass and then withered. The rumba and the samba are forgotten. The "society bands" were demoted from bandstands to wedding parties and Bar Mitzvahs. Whatever the Village has to offer always seems to be attraction enough.

A true Greenwich Village patron must be born pointed toward Washington Square. Most of them have never been anywhere else, on their nights out for entertainment, except one place or other in the Village. They distrust anyplace that isn't there, although it should be clear to any observer that the Village has as many overpriced operations as any other sector of town. Once I talked to a young couple from New Jersey who related that they came to New York once or twice a week and never had been anywhere else but the Village. I asked if they had not even tried an uptown place.

"You think we're suckers?" demanded the husband.

The old neighborhood still goes along, a sort of island within an island. There are more coffeehouses than there were in the intellectual days, although the customers are different. The small saloons feature flamenco guitar, just as Ben Collada did. The folk singers and the protest singers may, for all one knows, have similar laments to those of the forgotten poets of yesteryear.

MOONLIGHT

Even before our peerless political leaders formed a strange entente to make it almost impossible for an honest citizen to bet on a crooked jockey or horse race, the gambling industry (oh yes, it was) in New York had its periodic harassments of greater or smaller acuity. In the days when you could dial a New York city phone number and get a huge bookmaking plant over in New Jersey, the runners and the bet-takers for all sports flourished on Broadway. Then, one day, came a temporary "heat" on gamblers that badly scorched them. They were chased from candy store to phone booth to men's room.

So I was somewhat surprised, one day, to find the bookie who handled my own mild bets on the escalator at Macy's department store.

"I been here three weeks," he related. "I take calls on the pay phone on one floor and call my office with the slips on a pay phone on a different floor. Tell you the truth, I'm changing my office tomorrow. It's not that the work here is so hard on my feet, but these escalators are so damned monotonous. I'm moving my office to one of the big Broadway movie houses. It's nice and dark in there and they got three pay phones in the lobby."

He shook his head sadly.

"Of course," he admitted, "it won't be as good as when I could work the Trans-Lux theatre. The Trans-Lux even has a news ticker in the lobby and I can get my results off it without ever showing my face on the street."

There was, or so we heard, an even more enterprising bookmaker who had to wait for the heat to cool. This fellow just moved over to the International Enclave. And where is the International Enclave? Why, it is that plaza in front of and around those two modern buildings that are engaged in something called United Nations. All UN property is completely beyond the legal reach of the New York police, government tax collectors and any other butinsky who would seek to harass a poor bookmaker. (One or more of same may still be there.)

Up at Eddie's Place

PERHAPS THE BEST WAY TO INTRO-
duce the history of the two-room apartment on the top floor of a
building at 156 West 48 Street, is to pretend that it never was
there. The things that went on there just couldn't happen. They
didn't. Of course not—but they could, and they did. I care not
whether you, dear reader, believe the following epitaph or not.
What follows is gospel. The characters involved are indeed
legendary, but most of them are also indeed still alive and able to
take the witness stand and testify to the truth of a gaudier, giddier
series of years.

The building that was just east of Seventh Avenue became firstly
famous for its sidewalk-level restaurant, Billy La Hiff's Tavern.
Above it were two floors for tenants. Since the restaurant was, in
the earliest 1930s, the favorite hangout for the sports and theatre
mob (it was named for a George M. Cohan play, *The Tavern*), its
upstairs tenants naturally drew some socially conscious folk—socially conscious as to sports and show biz, I mean. Early rent-payers
included, at one time or another, Jack Dempsey, Damon Runyon,
Walter Winchell, Toots Shor, Mark Hellinger, Jack Kearns, Ed
Sullivan and Bugs Baer, to name but a few. Upon the gentlemanly
La Hiff's death, matters took a new turn.

For a brief while the Tavern and the building were inherited by the fabled Billy Duffy. He was front man for the mob that promoted Primo Carnera into the world's heavyweight championship (and just as quickly promoted him out of it). Duffy was a chap who knew a lot about big-city mob operations but not much about running a restaurant. In his top floor apartment he "trained" prizefighters and also Great Dane dogs. There was much idle speculation about which were tougher, Duffy's fighters or his dogs. Some said Duffy handled nothing *but* dogs.

Ultimately, the ground floor restaurant also went to the dogs; one can't consider a series of lunatic operators (including Shor) as anything else. The restaurant finally became a commendable Italian eatery named Zucca's. Just to keep in character, a Zucca niece was later convicted as Axis Sally, Tokyo Rose's World War II counterpart in enemy radio propaganda. The mind boggles, to coin a cliché, over the choice of whether the upstairs apartments became more "commendable" or less so. At least they became more colorful. The color followed the arrival, in the late 1930s, of a little fellow named Eddie Jaffe. It was then that the legends and the tall stories began to hit the fanless windows.

Eddie took over the late Duffy's top floor "owner's" apartment, the only rental in the joint that could properly be termed to have two actual rooms. He was a press agent. He was, and is, a small, wiry man with a shock of wiry hair. Underneath the hair is an imagination that knows no bounds, great energy and a basic nature so kindly that, thinking over everybody who is left from this act, I cannot name a single person who puts the knock on him.

Do not ask me how or why it happened. But almost overnight Eddie's joint became the twenty-four-hour hangout for a clientele that ranged from broken down Broadway actors and entertainers to some very glamorous celebrities indeed. There was scarcely a night—or even an afternoon—when a drop-in could not find there a Hollywood star, a noted beauty, a few hustlers and even some solid businessmen. Also producers, politicians, policemen and a rare few honest working folk.

There was, of course, a reason. Not only was the small apartment a home-away-from-home for pretty young actresses and out-of-work chorus girls, but it was the ever-open resting place for stripteasers in the burlesque shows that were then multiple around town, plus any lonely or displaced female of whatever motivation.

They flocked to Eddie's because he never demanded anything from them and was always helpful. A rendezvous such as this becomes a matter of conversation anywhere. Eddie's place was soon an additional drop-in for any displaced or dispirited male with family problems or, even more likely, in town for a few nights with no place to go and no female companion to whom he could tell his troubles and expect spiritual (and ultimately physical) sympathy.

Romance flowered at Eddie's, although hardly ever for Eddie. In the midst of the gab, the raucous laughter, the tears and sometimes the hysteria, some pretty fantastic deals were launched in Eddie's pad, and others were brought to fruition there. At one time, we all remember, Eddie was trying to do publicity for a hillbilly guitarist and country singer who arrived on the scene about thirty years before a new generation discovered the guitar and country songs.

"Look," Eddie told this client, "you sing and play guitar and you are from Louisiana. Why don't you go down there, get up in front of those hicks, play your awful guitar, sing those songs, make a speech and run for governor. I can get you a lot of publicity and maybe a record contract."

This advice seemed like a sound idea to the homesick folk singer. It got him some publicity, all right. It also got him something more. It got him a career in politics and ultimately got him the governor's chair in Louisiana. His name was Jimmy Davis.

Meanwhile, such burlesque queens as Margie Hart were under Eddie's promotional wings, and so were some young stage folk who were on their way up. Other colorful chaps decided that the tiny apartments above the Italian restaurant were the ideal place to work and/or live. One of these was Nat Hiken, who used a tiny one-roomer "owned" by press agent Jack Tirman as a daytime office wherein to write his many radio and TV shows, which later included "Sergeant Bilko" and "Car 54, Where Are You?" Nat had his office on a sublease from Mr. Tirman, of whom more later. In the only other one-roomer on Eddie's top floor was Joe Russell, also of whom more later. One flight down was the domicile of a song plugger named Johnny Farrow and, as his neighbor, he had a chap named Irving Hoffman. Of Mr. Hoffman, friend of Presidents and hustlers, much more later. This was the tenancy of the dandy little building.

An actor named Marlon Brando launched his big-time career

from Eddie's pied-à-terre after a brief period of bunking in at the Nat Hiken-sublease-from-Jack-Tirman-one-roomer across the hall. Hiken, a gregarious fellow, never cared who slept on which chair, sofa or what floor space as long as they were out by the time he and his staff arrived to start work on the Milton Berle show, or Martha Raye show or whatever chore faced them. Brando was a natural to advance up the social scale to Eddie's house guest list.

"He was a difficult guest," Eddie remembers. "He would take off his dirty socks, borrow a pair of mine from the top drawer and leave his dirty ones in the same place—as a reminder for laundry service, I guess. He thought he was the next classical concert pianist and actually managed to pick out a few Gregorian chants on my broken down piano. He would insist that everybody listen to his one-finger solos as 'a little something I wrote myself this afternoon.'"

Brando hated Eddie's phone, which rang constantly. He would answer with the simple: "Mr. Jaffe's former apartment. Mr. Jaffe passed away this morning."

"It hardly mattered," Eddie remembers. "I once had a sort of survey made and found that 63 percent of the phone calls that came to that joint were not for me anyway." One must know Mr. Jaffe to understand why a Brando would fascinate him. Your historian hopes the incidents that follow will somehow explain all.

Of the two rooms in the Jaffe "owner's suite," Eddie's bedroom was sacrosanct until at least four in the afternoon when the Master arose to face "his day." But there was a large couch in the "office" room and it was available to anyone who did not interfere too strenuously with the staff. The staff consisted of two people (never the same two people for more than a week or so). One late afternoon, urged by uncontrollable romance, a famed movie star ran a girl up to Eddie's office, dismissed the staff and went at his favorite personal hobby. The movie star, atop the young beauty on the busted-spring couch, was just about at one of the great moments of his physical life when—enter Ruth Cosgrove.

Ruth was then a show business press agent and is now the long-time wife of Milton Berle. Miss Cosgrove is not a girl who is easily put off balance. She surveyed the scene on the couch, kept walking right through the room, stopped above the "engaged" couple and said loudly:

"John! Stop that immediately and give me your autograph."

More businesslike things were simultaneously happening at all times at Eddie's place. The singer Dorothy Dandridge met the musical director of *Carmen Jones* at Eddie's and landed a leading role in the film. Miss Dandridge, who died much too young, was always a Jaffe favorite.

"Even when she was famous and playing the Waldorf," Eddie remembers, "she would insist on coming to my joint after work and washing the dirty dishes. Indeed, we rarely had any other kind of dishes."

The rodeo cowboys were great favorites at Eddie's place. They came every year. They came, first, when a few of them were brought to the old home by a girl-about-town, and who did they meet there? None other than their hero John Wayne. The rodeo riders were so impressed that they escorted the Jaffe permanents and, of course, distinguished visitor Wayne over to Madison Square Garden and tried to teach all (including, a cynic is forced to suspect, Mr. Wayne) how to ride rough horses. In the ensuing years, Mr. Wayne was not always available. But some film star usually was. Always. It is a wonder that Mr. Brando was not the one to anticipate such starring vehicles as *The Cowboy and the Lady*.

Alas, all was not just fun and games. There were broken friendships, even implied treachery. Eddie once had to sue his number one client, and possibly his secret love, Margie Hart, for various accusations of default. Miss Hart stood firm against all claims that Eddie had created her—even though Jaffe had written H. L. Mencken and asked the author of *The American Language* to submit a real word for stripteaser. Mencken had obligingly answered with the title "ecdysiast," which Margie used for years. For a while Margie seemed strangely bitter. She even took it upon herself to advise another defendent in a Jaffe case. This chap happened to be a fattish fellow named Jackie Gleason, then on his early upbeat.

Nobody remembers what this lawsuit was all about, but it never seemed to bother Gleason. "Hello, Party of the First Part," he would holler at Jaffe, on street or in saloon. Gleason would then turn to whichever stooges were with him. "Jaffe hasn't got a case," he would say with conviction, "because I drank it last night."

"I'll win that case," Eddie always assured us with total equanimity. "That fat bum will never be able to get up at nine o'clock in the morning to defend himself."

Margie Hart, at the time another Party of the Second Part, encouraged Gleason. "He couldn't beat me," Margie would say, "and after all I'm only a frail girl." The writer of this historical note avoids comment on his pal Margie's self-appraisal.

Possibly none of the litigants—or even the kind of lawyers they all had in those days—could get up early enough for an actual appearance in court. At least, neither of these *sensational* lawsuits ever came before judge or jury. Any settlement must have been made in a back room. Not Jaffe's back room. Even a Jaffe back corner would have been too close for tipsters who would have run downstairs to phone Walter Winchell or Ed Sullivan or whoever could make most use of the shattering news.

Another enthusiastic in-and-outer at Eddie's was Harold Young, an executive assistant to Vice President Henry Wallace. Young prevailed upon Eddie and his mob to convince Walter Winchell, then a journalistic power, that Wallace couldn't possibly be a Communist because he had so many signed photographs of Catholic monsignors and bishops. The campaign worked and Young was properly appreciative. As for instance:

Any of the Jaffe-sponsored stripteasers, actresses, showgirls or just plain regulars could be officially photographed sitting in the Vice President's authoritatively identified official chair—the only condition being that the Veep was not sitting in the chair himself or, better, was safely out of the building. Better still, far out of town.

These were the glory days for Eddie's place. It was in the "office room" of the joint that Jimmy Hoffa's lawyers and lieutenants hatched the deal that edged Dave Beck out of the top spot in the Teamsters Union and edged Hoffa into same. Less important matters went on simultaneously. Julie Newmar, unknown then except as a tall and buxom showgirl, used the kitchen equipment in her campaign to turn on all Broadway—to health foods. In another corner, during the same shenanigans, Jaffe and advisors were advising a young man named Jackie Mason to keep studying to be a rabbi and stop trying to tell jokes because he had a horrible Jewish accent.

Coincidentally, the dancer Gwen Verdon met her first New York friends and employers; a girl named Eva Madrid invented over the house hot plate what she was convinced was a surefire bunion cure, and, on the free telephone, the fabulous eater Ken McSarin spurned an offer of $500 to eat forty eggs at the film theatre that was about to premiere a movie called *The Egg and I.* Kenny wanted twice the amount to so publicly expose his unique talents.

Most of the above were nighttime incidents, of course. In the daytime Eddie's place was a business office. I know it was because I once heard the patron himself so identify it under very trying circumstances.

On this occasion, a bright late afternoon of summer, the Master was still abed. Mr. Jaffe slugabedded it almost all day because he was up all night. He would awake around 4 P.M., be soothed by a visit from his psychiatrist, instructed by his Spanish teacher, put through physical torture by his yoga professor, make his calls to his stockbroker and, possibly, ask the young lady who had stayed over at his side to please leave since he had to start his day's work.

Not that "the office" wasn't functioning while the landlord prepared for his long, arduous day. His "staff" had been out in the office since early morning, doing their best to transcribe the rambling memoranda Eddie had yelped into a dictaphone hours earlier and which, at the time of invention, Jaffe had convinced himself made great newspaper fodder for one or more columnists or editors.

On this fateful day there was an important baseball game on the radio and, possibly, more fans at Eddie's place than in the stadium stands. The room was so filled with smoke that the haze seemed almost liquid. The shades had been pulled to darken the surroundings and make the game sound more dramatic.

The activity was typical. In one chair a girl nobody seemed to know was eating Chinese food from a paper plate that she ultimately dropped on the floor. A regular seated on the rug was stoking down a pastrami sandwich. Somebody else had finished a pizza and left the crusts and cardboard box on a typewriter desk. At a quick but informal glance, I managed to identify empty paper cups, empty beer cans, half of an uneaten coconut, four banana peels and a half-eaten slice of cheesecake. Eddie's brigade were late lunchers. None of these objects were anywhere near a scrap basket or garbage can. The timeless, interminable gin rummy game was also in full force in its usual corner.

There came a crucial moment in the ball game. I forget whether somebody got a hit or didn't. At the moment the door to the Master's bedroom opened and the Peerless Leader made his entrance for the day. He was a colorful sight wearing his sleeping clothes. Such costume consisted, from top to bottom, of a red felt fez that, for some forgotten reason, he always wore to bed in those days; a twenty-four-hour growth of beard; a maroon smoking jacket that reached exactly to his scrotum; and nothing else. He stood in the bedroom doorway in bare feet and surveyed us all, and the mess about us, with open disgust.

"Goddamn it!" he fairly screamed. "This is a *business office!*"

One of the most businesslike guests of the owner, to get to him finally, was Mr. Joseph Russell. Yes, now get to old Joe.

Joe Russell, if he had kept to his first trade, would today be the distinguished doyen of the Broadway press agents. His record goes back to the now forgotten cabarets such as the Hollywood and the Paradise, where all those pretty girls worked and wherein so many of them found other ways to work. However, with the Depression years of the mid-1930s, he abandoned flackery to enter what we all assumed to be "the export-import business." Nothing about it was crooked. Joe bought and sold hard-to-get-items more cheaply than they could be bought or sold elsewhere. He made many friends. He could get many things.

Once when the mystic Howard Hughes was flying some kind of publicity-motivated, transcontinental flights full of Hollywood and Broadway stars, a Hollywood luminary complained that the flight hadn't broken the anticipated record because the plane had not been able to ride a tailwind.

"You should have called Joe Russell," a sage counseled. "Joe could have gotten you a tailwind."

Joe's personal motivation always was, and still is, suspicion. He is convinced that every stranger in the world is conspiring against him with evil aforethought. Thus, for his apartment, cater-cornered from Jaffe's, he went to no little expense to have the hinges on his door put on the *inside*. To let you through this portal he also had to unlock a series of chains, bolts and double locks that would have frustrated Houdini. Once inside, you stated your purchasing desire—let us say a bottle of imported French perfume. The following routine was then unleashed.

Joe would lead you to a closet that also had locks, stocks and blocks. Getting these items opened, he would turn his attention to an enormous chest of drawers, each drawer of which was sealed with everything except cement. You would get your item. Then Joe would lock away all his goodies and painfully lock you outside in the hall again. He had prison bars embedded inside his single window. We all feared that, one day, he would die of some dread disease in his own handmade prison. Our fears doubtless were groundless, since he spent most of his waking hours in Jaffe's rendezvous. Indeed, when the building's only recorded fire came, Joe and his objets d'art were not even singed.

Now and then all of Russell's fears were realized. There was the time, as an example, when two Jaffe regulars traded cars for the weekend. The trade was necessary because one press agent had a family and needed a bigger car. He took his pal's bigger car and, over the weekend, managed to get it banged up rather badly. This caused an argument between the car owners, an argument that was terminated when one owner (I forget which) belted the other. The slugger left the building in a hurry when the sluggee called for the police. Everybody else also deserted the Jaffe apartment, one of the rare times the place was left unattended.

So, of course, it was then that the worried Russell made his entrance. Nobody was there. As he looked around in dismay, he was joined by two cops from the local squad car. They wanted to know the nature of the crime and who did what to whom.

Mr. Russell testified that he knew nothing about nothing and was simply on the premises because he was minding his own business. "What is your business?" the cops wanted to know. This was a question impossible for anyone, including Russell, to answer. So the annoyed cops left a summons for the owner of the apartment, charging the miscreant with making a false report. However, they misnumbered the apartment on the summons, listing the scene of the crime as Jack Tirman's, the multiple domicile just down the hall. Jack had to go to court and explain things as best he could. The explanation was confusing enough for any case to be dismissed.

The complex event so unnerved Russell that he took to leaving his exact itinerary with the Jaffe Foundation every time he left the building. Please do not ask what benefit such action was meant to ensure. One day he went out "for just one hour" and left this fact with the nonstop card players at Jaffe's. Shortly after his departure, a Western Union messenger knocked on Joe's door and, getting no response, sauntered in through the open Jaffe entrance and asked for Russell. He was told to come back in an hour.

Russell arrived before the messenger's second delivery. He asked if he had received any calls, either in person or by phone. "Yeah," said one of the card players, not pausing in his deal, "there was a Western Union messenger here for you." Russell frowned in worried concentration.

"What did he look like?" he demanded suspiciously.

And now we move down the top floor hallway to the only other apartment there—the one that had Jack Tirman's name on the lease, was used in daylight for Nat Hiken and his staff to write radio and TV epics, and used after dark for any acceptable guest who had run out of places to sleep. A favorite press agent in every newspaper office to this very day, Tirman moved back and forth between his apartment and Jaffe's like the tides. Tirman's speech pattern can best be compared to that of a machine gun, his chatter often outracing his thoughts, but he is a quick man with a funny answer. After marrying a lovely Welsh girl named Myfawnwyn Weixell, he called in a decorator to brighten up the honeymoon pad.

The decorator swished in with his swatches and samples and gushed, "What can I do to brighten up your home?"

Jack stared him in the eye. "Stay out of it," he ordered.

It was not long afterward that the bride moved Jack to more commodious and sensible quarters. But Fawn's problems—we have never known her as anything but Fawn—continued. Married only a few weeks, her husband came home with his usual winter trip to Miami all planned. He had his usual airplane ticket—one. He explained, simply, that all his life he had been going to Miami Beach in February alone. Mrs. Tirman pointed out that men took their wives to the winter resorts.

"Oh, yeah," said Jack, the revelation taking hold. He went out and bought another plane ticket. "He seemed dumfounded by the idea," Fawn recalls.

Working for a film company and mentally involved with a project for publicity he planned to lay on Walter Winchell, Jack once left his office and entered a taxicab. He sat silently in the cab, thinking.

"Where to?" the driver finally asked.

"Murray Hill 2-1000," Jack ordered, giving the phone number of the New York *Mirror*, Winchell's office.

Small tragedies seemed to stalk his career in those early days. For the premiere of a movie based on Cole Porter's life, Jack dreamed up a fine stunt. He rented an English bulldog and had specially knit a blue dog's sweater with a hugh white *Y* on it. He hired a pretty model to complete the deal. Jack figured he was all set. Everybody knew that Porter was a Yale grad and that a bulldog is the Yale mascot. And if anybody missed the point, the big *Y* the dog was wearing should be the convincer.

So he escorted dog, girl and sweater to the box office of the theatre and had the dog photographed with "the first ticket" sold for the Porter epic firmly held in his bulldog mouth. The dog—named Boola Boola, of course—drew no legitimate news cameramen, so Jack had his own hireling take numerous shots, all of which were quickly routed to editors around town.

No newspaper editor paid the slightest bit of attention to these photographic works of art. Now Jack was in a professional pitfall. He had spent the film company's money, promised a big news splash, failed and now had to devise some sort of excuse and deliver it fast. He figured one out.

He entered his film boss's office in simulated fury. "How could anybody," he demanded, "get any newspaper to print the picture of a dog as ugly as that?"

He could be tactful, too. Once having coffee with Otto Preminger in the film producer's hotel suite, the waiter spilled coffee in Preminger's lap. Preminger, never noted for an even temper, went into a Teutonic rage. He seemed about to physically attack the waiter.

"Don't worry, Otto," soothed Jack. "Remember hotel coffee is never hot." Preminger had to giggle.

Jack's frequent unintelligible attacks on his chosen profession often tripped him up. Once he was dialing an editor on the phone and simultaneously sputtering at a compere. After about five digits he suddenly hung up. "Who am I calling?" he asked his fellow laborer.

On another occasion he called columnist Earl Wilson and, as Wilson answered, Jack (talking again) forgot what he was calling about. Without uttering a word he hung up his phone. He then turned nervously to Eddie Jaffe. "Do you think Earl knew it was me?" he asked in mild terror.

Possibly Tirman's most spectacular early campaign, even though it ended in humiliating disaster, was his publicity for the dance team of Gomez and Weinberg. At the time he was handling a restaurant that had no entertainment at all and where the food and liquids hardly called for epicurean attention. Jack needed "a handle." He invented one.

He dreamed up a dance team that he labeled Gomez and Weinberg and sent out press releases that the team had been signed "for a limited engagement" at his café. The announcement routinely made the amusement pages. Jack couldn't let go of the lucky dice without one more pass. He announced the dance team had been held over. That made the papers, too. Success went to Our Hero's head like strong wine. He compounded his mild felony as follows:

He announced the end of Gomez and Weinberg's engagement and their new contract to do a musical film. He brought them back for "a repeat engagement." He announced the pregnancy of Miss Weinberg (thus revealing at last that she had been secretly married to Señor Gomez). He then came forth with the saddening news of Miss Gomez's loss of the baby. The tragedy had an immediate effect on the personal lives of the dancers. They had a marital quarrel and separated.

The nonexistent Gomez and Weinberg were going through more routines than such real-life stars as Tony and Renee DeMarco, Veloz and Yolanda, Paul and Grace Hartman and even Fred Astaire and Ginger Rogers. The "separated" dancers were often noted, singly, in their old café. Gomez "held hands" with various beauties. Miss Weinberg seemed to prefer the company of young male movie stars. After a few weeks of such nonsense, Gomez and Weinberg reunited, forgot the sad past and went back "to work" in Jack's café.

The only tense moments, so far, were suffered by the Mafiosa-type club owner who nightly had to find new excuses as to why the famed dance duo wouldn't perform that night.

But retribution was at hand. The New York *Post* in those days had a bald and cynical fellow named Dick Manson as its amusement editor. An old and firm friend of Jack's, he nonetheless discovered the hoax and determined to teach the press agent a lesson he would understand. Manson "reviewed" the nonexistent dance team in his column and panned the be-Jesus out of Gomez and Weinberg. He reported that they couldn't dance at all, which of course was the literal truth. He told them to go back to the farm. Worse, he identified the club owner and said he was a cretin for hiring the team in the first place. That did it. Mr. Tirman lost the café account and turned his imagination elsewhere.

Lest we put away Jack Tirman as a clown, it must be hurriedly admitted that he has a sharp eye for talent. He "edited" the sleepers allowed in his old apartment and, one day, asked Sid Garfield to meet a couple of them. Mr. Garfield, now a veteran publicist with the CBS-TV family, was then doing the best he could, as all of us were. Tirman took Garfield to his nominal apartment. Sid remembers that there were eight or ten out-of-funds types either already sleeping on beds, chairs and floors or preparing to do so.

Tirman roused a long, lean fellow and asked for a copy of his play. The author didn't have one on his person but promised to deliver it next day. He was as good as his word. And following this prompt delivery came a prompt phone call from Mr. Garfield to Mr. Tirman.

"You think I want to get bedbugs all over me from the script?" Garfield hollered at his pal. "Get it off my hands in an hour. I wouldn't even touch it."

"But what'll I tell the guy?" pleaded Jack.

Garfield softened. "Tell him I said that the script is great. Tell him I said it will make a fortune."

The message was duly delivered. The script turned out to be the tremendously successful play and film, *Stalag 17*. The "sleeper" was Edmund Trzycinski, who had written it with Don Bevan, the caricaturist with whom he had once done other sleeping in the real Stalag 17 when both were prisoners of war.

To this day, when Trzycinski meets Sid Garfield on the street, he is inclined to embrace him. "You are the only one who ever gave us any encouragement," he will assert. "We were willing to give up. We owe it all to your help."

Another "sleeper" on that historic night might also have been awakened and exposed to Sid Garfield's reactions. This chap was Bernie Fine, who later created the TV series *Hogan's Heroes* and is still in the big-time writing field. Mr. Fine was sleeping over that night because a fire had ruined Red Kullers' apartment across the street. Mr. Kullers was an early (and late) Jaffe regular and, in due course, will contribute his own footnotes to this memoir.

Nor was Mr. Garfield, the nondiscoverer of sleeping talents, immune to his own gaffes in his chosen trade. Once he was busy promoting the image of a successful radio producer and things were a little difficult since the successful producer did have a rather bad radio series for which he was taking the blame. But, Sid discovered, his client also did have a mother. That opened up some ideas. Further conference developed that the mother insisted on still living among old friends in the old ghetto, although Sonny was rich and successful. And, further, it developed that the very next week mother would have her sixty-fifth birthday. Mr. Garfield was immediately alert to such publicity factors.

His first story was all about the producer who had taken care of mother's birthday in the Great Big Way. He had hired car and chauffeur. He had booked a big suite at Grossinger's famed resort in the Catskills. He had rented a charming little apartment not too far off Park Avenue for his mother's declining years. He was, indeed, a jewel of sons. The story, of course, got printed.

Thus ends our first act. The second act was also a planted newspaper story. Sonny had later learned, to his dismay, that Mama had not gone to the baronial Borscht Circuit resort, she had not moved into her new apartment. No indeed. She had insisted on staying on the Lower East Side with one of her childhood pals. Better story yet. All the human elements. Everybody looked just great. Sid Garfield sat back happily, dreaming of a fat raise and a long-term contract from his producer client.

The Great Idea continued to build. The Associated Press called Sid, who called his boss, for Mama's downtown address. A national feature was the idea, printed in hundreds of newspapers. Other newspapers called. Where could they get photos? The story was a natural, especially since Mama's birthday was falling on a dull holiday that usually furnishes no pictures except auto wrecks and inert bodies scattered around same. And then the Great Story began to get complicated.

It developed that Mama hadn't lived in the ghetto for years. She wore nice clothes, shopped and argued in the same stores as you and I, had indeed been set up in a small West Side apartment by her son many years ago. So Garfield and Sonny had to go over to her and make their plea. Sonny got her some old clothes. Garfield scuttled around downtown until he found an old neighbor who would go along with the gag at a price. Sid even bought a used mop to accompany Mom in the photographs of her busily scrubbing her old pal's floors. Sonny got Mom down to the ghetto publicity rendezvous.

The Associated Press found Mama hostile. So did the photographers. So did everybody else. No story. No pictures.

"She was most furious at me," Sid Garfield remembers. "She even tried to hit me with the mop I had bought her. She kept screaming that I had ruined her social standing with all her uptown Mah-Jongg cronies. I lost Sonny's account the next week."

On the floor beneath the homesteads of Jaffe, Russell and Tirman-Hiken were only two apartments. One was rented by a song plugger named Johnny Farrow, who kept himself mostly in the world of music and dodged the insanity upstairs. The other apartment was, for years, the pied-à-terre of Irving Hoffman. Irving was one of the most fantastic (in the good sense) men I have known in all my years around the city. In the first place, he had an eye ailment that, I believe, was called cornucopia. His eyes were formed more like footballs than baseballs, and he squinted continuously through heavy glasses. Despite this handicap, he started his life on the Street as a caricaturist and became one of the very best.

Franklin D. Roosevelt always kept Irving's caricature of himself on his desk, a quick likeness Irving had made using only the letters *FDR* and the cigarette in its familiar holder. Nothing else. Many famous folk still have Hoffman's caricatures. But no sooner had Irving established himself in art than he turned his back on the drawing pad to become a press agent for Hollywood studios and a columnist for Hollywood trade papers. It must have been a wise decision. When he suddenly died at too early an age, it was discovered that, of all the flacks we knew, he was the only one to have banked almost a million dollars. He was an intimate friend of Zanuck, the Schencks, the Skourases and all the movie giants of his time. He had great heart, an intense interest in almost anybody and was responsible for at least half a dozen bright Hollywood careers.

Irving "retired" at around fifty years of age and was suddenly struck with one of the most compulsive wanderlusts in anyone's memory. He traveled everywhere. He would just pick up and go. He was, as ever, fascinated by new people, so in no time at all he was the half-owner of a geisha house in Tokyo and half-owner of a famed Italian restaurant in Rome. At home, his only companions were two cats. At home, also, he kept cardboard boxes full of foreign money. This loot was to save him time and inconvenience when he got the urge, possibly in the middle of the night, to get up and go somewhere. Wherever he went, he had the right type of money to at least get him settled.

It was in this apartment that somehow a fire started. Hoffman got second degree burns on his hands trying to put out the early blaze. The fire laddies soon came clanging from Eighth Avenue, a couple of blocks away. Irving left his home for the nearest doctor. The two cats left with him.

"One went down to the sidewalk and sat out the whole affair," Eddie Jaffe remembers, "and the other for some reason went upstairs and tried to get into Joe Russell's apartment. Fat chance!"

Hoffman finally came home to his burned and drenched apartment. The cats came home also, one descending and one ascending. Mr. Russell remained in his fortress, unmoved and unsmothered. Once the fire was out, only the fire department troops seemed upset. One of them came up to Jaffe's apartment with a metal wastepaper basket in his hands. The basket was full of Mr. Hoffman's money—money of various nations.

"This looks like money," said the fireman, holding forth the pail of soggy banknotes, "but I wouldn't even ask you to try and make me out a receipt."

Such was that afternoon. That night continued on its normal way. Another world traveler and later author, Doris Lilly, arrived to explain that she had just had dinner with Victor Mature.

"I'm glad I took along a couple of pieces of rye bread," Miss Lilly said of her recent film star dinner host. She made this remark to Red Kullers and a chap who had been introduced as a potential "rich backer" for Broadway shows. Mr. Kullers had a play for the rich backer to produce. He usually did.

Sometimes one of Red's Broadway projects would be by an

unknown—he was among the first to hawk *Stalag 17*—and sometimes it would be a project of more magnitude. It might, for instance, be a musical version of an Ernest Hemingway novel with music by Cole Porter to be directed by Joshua Logan and starring Ethel Merman, Henry Fonda, Bobby Clark and Ginger Rogers.

The only flaw in such Kullers projects was that Red hadn't gotten around to contacting Hemingway, Porter *et al.* about his plans. But his talk of his newest project, whichever it was, on this night fascinated the rich backer. The latter asked for a script. Red considered the request and told the backer that if he would report to his, Red's, office at noon the next day, a script would be delivered. Red gave his office address.

Little wonder that the big backer was impressed. As Red revealed his great plans, the backer had to notice that Sammy Cahn and Jule Styne were working out the score of their next musical on the Jaffe piano which, at the moment, was being "flotted" by two showgirl beauties. Flotting, we had all been informed, was the pasting of flowers and paper designs on the piano's woodwork. This, please remember, was a generation before the flower children. Doubtless the rich backer was also impressed by the audition of an ambitious young comedian named Wally Cox, who had just finished a routine and was being sternly told by Jaffe to stick to his current trade as a jeweler's helper.

At any rate, the rich backer was driven by his chauffeur to Red Kullers' address the next noon. The address turned out to be a corner orange juice stand. The backer sent his chauffeur to inquire at the open orange juice dispensary where a Mr. Kullers' office was located. Greeted by a fellow in a white uniform as he approached the squeezers, the chauffeur asked for Mr. Kullers.

"I am Mr. Kullers," said the chap beneath a white cap, feeding halved oranges into the squeezing machine. Somewhat staggered, the chauffeur asked if Kullers had a script for his boss. Red said sure, of course. He reached up behind a stack of oranges, pulled out the script and handed it over.

The chauffeur returned to the limousine and, in turn, handed over the dramatic gem to his boss, the big backer. The limousine rolled off. To this day Red Kullers sometimes wonders why he never heard from that big backer again.

Being a Broadway press agent in those Depression days was

always a hard go and most often was disheartening. Let us recall, however, an incurable optimist and regular at Jaffe's compound named Jay Faggen. Jay has since gone on to bigger and more lucrative things in the music world. In the old, hard days he had a two-room office on Broadway, and one employee was the aforementioned Sid Garfield. He had another apprentice to the "big time." Each of these worthies was being paid $15 a week— or, rather, they hadn't been paid for three weeks.

They were about to quit and try, as a last resort, for honest work. But on the day of decision Faggen called them into his "private" office. He told them both, with a big fat grin of sure confidence, that on the following day he would close a deal for the office to publicize the Government of Guatemala. It was all set. Just the finalizing. The next day he left for his big conference, wearing his best suit and an air of superiority.

The staff waited several hours for his return, biting on their knuckles, doing little work. In the late afternoon their leader returned. He went straight to his private lair. His door remained closed. The apprentices gnawed more deeply into their bruised fingers. Ultimately Faggen opened the door of his den and beckoned in his serfs.

"We didn't get Guatemala," he said flatly.

The faces of the coolies fell. Not Faggen's. His face lit up.

"But," he informed his helpers brightly, "We start on Tony Shayne on Monday." Shayne was a radio singer who could, possibly, afford to pay $25 a week. I do not know what the Republic of Guatemala could have paid had it been more Broadway-minded.

There was another very busy press agent around Jaffe's in those days, an explosive little fellow named George Lottman. George's theory was "Get 'em all in and try for twice." Thus, he once sent out the following paragraph that was printed on two amusement pages in two real newspapers:

"Lee Wiley, singing star at the Famous Door, lost her prize spaniel, bought at the Broadway Pet Shop, in front of Ching Chow's restaurant yesterday. Miss Wiley offers a generous reward for the return of the dog to the Famous Door or the Broadway Pet Shop. Dog answers to the name of Ching Chow."

Every name that has capital letters in the above communiqué

was, of course, a Lottman client. He managed, indeed, to get 'em all in twice—although Miss Wiley owned no dog at the time.

The Jaffe enclave was also the scene of a momentous press conference when Chico Marx decided to break away from his brothers, Groucho and Harpo. He hired a publicist named Sam Geisen to explain to an eager press why he would no longer work with his kith and kin. Geisen knew that no newspaper was interested in anything more than the bare fact that Chico was determined to go it alone. But since Chico demanded a big press conference, Geisen stage managed one for him.

All Geisen had to do was assemble the Jaffe regulars and then bring on Chico. Chico was introduced to one regular as "from the Associated Press." Another was "from *The New York Times.*" And so on through a long list of publications. These twenty-odd "newspaper writers" took copious notes of Chico's reasons and complaints. They asked intelligent questions (indeed, who knew better how to do so?) and then they dispersed for "their deadlines."

The next day the newspapers carried the fact that Chico Marx, for years a stalwart member of the famous Marx Brothers, who would always be remembered for his piano-playing antics with the brotherhood, had decided on a new career as a single entertainer. Chico was understandably disappointed.

"I told those guys so much," he sighed to Geisen, "and they printed so little."

The approach of press agents to newspaper editors—and to such exalted heroes as Walter Winchell, Ed Sullivan, Louis Sobol *et al.*—was often a little bit too masochistic. There even was an approach called "the weep." This came hand in hand with the press release and was to the effect that the boss would fire the bearer if the story wasn't printed, that wifey needed another operation, or even that the bearer himself had been told he might have a deadly disease. "The weep" went too far when one expert dressed a small girl in tired old clothes and led her on the rounds.

"My daddy's sick in bed again," this outrageous child tried to tell newspaper writers, "and Mommy said I should stay out of school today and help him get well by bringing you this envelope."

It was considered that this lowered the dignity of the craft. Higher ethics were represented by a more aloof and arrogant type named Art Franklin. When the bandleader Cootie Williams, after sending Art his check every week during a long road tour, came back to the city, he charged into Franklin's office and bitterly complained that he had received little for his money.

"Are you kidding?" demanded Art. "Why, everybody in town is talking about Cootie Williams."

Cootie softened. "What are they saying?" he asked wistfully.

"They're saying, 'Whatever became of Cootie Williams?' " Franklin answered honestly enough.

On another occasion Franklin handled a young musical comedy singer and, to his credit, did a far better job than the singer's talents deserved. Yet the day soon arrived when the singer phoned to say she was breaking her contract with the publicist. Franklin naturally asked for reasonable grounds for such an act.

"Well, for one thing," explained the singer, "my mother doesn't think you are doing a very good job."

Franklin was unimpressed. "I doubt if that will hold up in court," he told the girl coldly. "Because my mother thinks I'm doing a helluva job for you."

Clients in those days were always unpredictable and often unmanageable. A humorless chap named Arthur Murray franchised a nationwide string of dance studios and hired a long, unending stream of press agents. He demanded that the flacks keep incessantly planting "Arthur Murray says" jokes in the newspapers. One day he fired a flack who thought he had been doing fine except for the past two weeks. He asked Murray why his services were being terminated.

"You have lost my sense of humor," said the humorless Murray.

The Jaffe Era ended many years ago (although in retrospect it seems like only yesterday) and possibly many of us should have seen the handwriting on the wall. We heard continuous rumors that the building would be torn down or renovated or just simply made to disappear. Then one day an annoyed Mr. Jaffe demanded the presence of the landlord. The landlord at this time was a Mr. Gumm. Jaffe had a complaint. Rats had invaded the building and, worse, his personal living quarters.

"Feed them up fat and keep them strong," advised Mr. Gumm. "Then when I finally get the chance to throw you out of here, maybe they can help you move that sow's bed you call a couch." The end was obviously near.

The other day, riding through the West 48th Street block, I looked out the taxi window and tried to identify old Number 156. I couldn't. The old inhabitants, the old ambiance, even the street-level restaurant were gone. The building front looked spick-and-span. Today, indeed, even the padrone himself, Mr. Jaffe, looks spick-and-span. He has long since "gone straight" and is interested only in legitimate business.

In the mood of today, with the shrinking of newspapers and the disappearance of columns and Broadway features, with the death of New York night life and, indeed, the night dangers of a Broadway that has slowly decayed, the Jaffe GHQ would be impossible. We no longer live in an atmosphere of the wild, the nonsensical and the studiously insane. Today, with the press and TV full of bad news only, it would no longer be possible to have printed in a daily newspaper such a gem as:

"Celebrities in the Macy's Day Thanksgiving Day Parade can be viewed from the front window of Joe's Broadway Restaurant."

Nor could any loon plant such an item as:

"Helen Craig, star of *Johnny Belinda* at the Cort Theatre, yesterday was elected a member of the Book-of-the-Month Club. She will start receiving books almost immediately."

It must be admitted that in compounding such minor literary felonies, the newspaper editors and columnists were as responsible as the creative culprits.

No, it couldn't happen today. But there are reminiscent moments when I am inclined to close my eyes in memory, giggle in mild senility and sort of wish it all *could* happen again.

Ken Strong, an early stalwart of the New York Football Giants. Football was actually his second sport: The Detroit Tigers were sure they had a second Ty Cobb until Strong broke a wrist against a fence and turned to football—and a 17-year career.

Wilbert Robertson and one of his star "Daffiness Boys" of the
Brooklyn Dodgers, the slugging Babe Herman. It was Herman, who, by
passing two runners on the base paths, managed to turn a triple into
three outs.

Ebbets Field of wondrous memories. The marbled rotunda was under
the sign. At the grand opening (naturally), nobody could find the key to
the front door!

Some bad companions. Jack "Legs" Diamond second from left; Joseph Walsh, who was to die by Diamond's gun in the Hotsy Totsy murders; and (far right) Charles "Lucky" Luciano. At left is Diamond's brother Eddie.

The Depression didn't apply to everybody. Café society's young queen, Brenda Frazier, drives a "team of gallants" at the Velvet Ball. (*Associated Press Photo*)

Brenda Diana Duff Frazier—here supporting the Metropolitan Opera, instead of one of her café haunts.

Will Morrissey and his wife, Midge Miller, after one of the many things which were always happening to them had happened.

The senior statesman of crime in the 1930s—Owney Madden—leaving jail with friend Joe Gould, who later was manager of the heavyweight champ Jim Braddock.

The elegant John Perona, always more worried about the stock market than his elegant El Morocco nightclub.

The bully boy himself, Toots Shor. When two men came to him and said they were Philadelphia newspapermen in town and were broke, Toots lent them ten dollars so they could drink at his bar. They sent back the four dollars' change. "They're no newspapermen," said the sage.

Two of the best friends a hungry actor ever had—Vincent Sardi Jr. and Sr. (*UPI*)

Alas, none of us would have suspected that this home away from home would eventually be a pocket public park.

Eddie Condon—portrait of the artist as a young man, when he strung a banjo like a ukelele instead of stringing a guitar that way, as he did later.

Joe Frisco, doing his famous Frisco Dance. Once, at the height of a casual romance, a starlet broke the tense silence with a question. "Never m-m-m-mind, little girl," Frisco admonished, "we'll dub in the sound later."

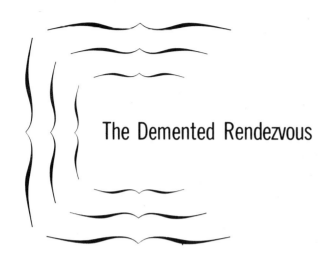

The Demented Rendezvous

AS A GREENWICH VILLAGE LAND-
mark, the saloon named Julius is fairly typical in Village history. It
is only one of several bars where Eugene O'Neill worked on his
plays, where Maxwell Bodenheim wrote poetry on borrowed paper
and where Theodore Dreiser wrote a novel upstairs. It is not the
only rendezvous to draw the uptown celebrity and society trade
over the years, and it may or may not be the oldest Village saloon
operating continuously on the same premises since 1892. The
present management refuses to argue the latter point with much
vigor.

But Julius has always had certain unique qualities. It is, for
instance, doubtless the only groggery in town where the Health
Department makes regular inspections to make sure the dirt is
permanent, probably the only drinkery whose most famous house
cat could work the cash register, and the only place of employment where the bartender once arrived for work through the
overhead ventilating machine. It is also the only oasis in my
memory where it is frequently necessary to go out onto the
sidewalk to find a throughway to the rest rooms.

Julius occupies a triangular patch of land formed by the angled
streets of West 10th and Waverly Place. It has no outside hanging

sign or neon light. The name *Julius* is scrawled in a moldy green paint on the two street windows. There is a door at the apex of the triangular building and another entrance on West 10th Street. Through these portals, at least in days past, staggered some wondrous characters ranging from the fistic to the philosophic. Once inside they were at home. Let us examine the interior of this home.

Back in the bleak days of Prohibition, Julius was raided regularly, and with each raid the saloon was usually described in the press as "the haunt of the literary and artistic set, the best known oasis in the Village." The saloon seemed to infuriate the Prohibition enforcers. "Why," one sleuth aggrievedly told a reporter after a raid, "you can walk in here and get a drink with no talking at all. You don't even have to know somebody. The commissioner is furious."

Although the management (or series of managements) stood up bravely under the legal assaults, the one-room booze mill began to exhibit a sort of punch-drunk appearance. Some unusual decor was obviously needed. There was, it developed, no lack of volunteer decorators.

One such artistic adviser decided the place called for an English atmosphere. Various items of armor were soon hung on the walls. With a new era promising more customers, the saloon added an adjoining 10th Street store to the premises by breaking through the wall.

For this back room, another artistically minded customer pointed out that for years everybody had sat on beer kegs and whisky crates in the main room. There were no chairs. So the backroom tables were constructed on beer keg bases. Another well-wisher had a bright idea for a hatrack. He found (or ripped up) a strip of picket fence and nailed it to the wall, the pointed pickets slightly above head level.

And then it was time for everybody to cast aesthetic eyes at the "armor" that had been obtained as the basic decor for the bar itself. Ah, that armor! It consisted originally of the following: A stiff straw hat supposed to have belonged to the original Julius. A cane carried by Billy Kennedy, a dead but never forgotton bartender. A Kentucky long rifle. A trophy presented by the Greenwich Village Boys Boccie Bowling Club. A railroad switchman's lantern. Four Irish flags rescued from a forgotten Saint

Patrick's Day dinner. A World War I shell case. A decoy wooden duck. Old footballs supposedly used by the Chicago Bears. Linked bronze whippets. An 1810 scatter gun. Gingerbread Russian porcelain Easter eggs. A brown derby allegedly worn by Al Smith. Forearm armor popular with knights of the Middle Ages. A small rosette. A big assegai. There were other items, but memory reels.

But with all this imagination and effort expended, everybody looked around and had a sinking feeling that something, somehow was wrong, "It looks too new," was the spontaneous decision.

The transformation from new to old was not exceedingly difficult. Everybody turned to and simply sprayed everything with linseed oil and added dust grabbed by the handful from everybody's home vacuum cleaner. The linseed oil was new and apparently slippery, so that dust and dirt dropped off ceiling and art objects in a patter of light rain—globules of oil and dirt usually landing in somebody's drink. It was unanimously decided to abandon the "aging look." But time refused to cooperate. Soon the dirt and dust decided to cling to walls, ceiling and decorative objects with the stubbornness of adhesive tape.

The dirt and mold became as permanent as the saloon itself. Once a month or so, the Health Department sent an inspector to make sure it was sufficiently solid. Somebody had to get the electric fan and turn its breeze on directed spots. For years not a dust mote had been dislodged. The muck was as integral as the bricks in the wall.

It was this demented-looking cave that for years sold eight hundred pounds of ground steak a week, did a capacity of six hundred persons daily in a room that has sit-down objects for sixty, and on any busy hour still has two hundred people jammed in. Thus, when Julius is really jumping, a regular at the Waverly Place end of the bar will leave by the main door, walk along 10th Street, reenter the side door and thus be enabled to fight his way to the men's room. Even this inconvenience is an improvement on the system the regulars faced back in the 1930s.

In those noisy days the saloon had only a single toilet and washbowl in what amounted to a closet. Bill Funaro, then managing the place, stole a red flag from a nearby excavation. When a lady went to the rest room she asked the bartender for the flag, took it with her and stuck it on the outside of the hinged but lockless door.

The most wonderfully wacky era of Julius endured through the long ownership of John Boggiano and Pete Pesci, veteran Village natives who not only adjusted to an almost completely oddball clientele but seemed to encourage more of same. Neither Boggiano nor Pesci, for instance, ever chided a series of bartenders for taking time off to act as human alarm clocks for various late risers. These stay-up-late customers would nightly leave wake-up times at the bar. The next afternoon the bartender on hand would call the numbers listed and the routine would go as follows:

"When you hear the gong," the bartender would announce when the sleepy voice came on the other end of the line, "it will be exactly 5 P.M. Rise and shine!"

The bartender would then hold a metal cocktail shaker full of cracked ice near the phone mouthpiece and shake it vigorously. Sometimes, when it was too much trouble to reach for ice, the bartender would just clout the shaker with a knife or spoon.

One of my favorite regulars in the old days was a steeplejack painter named Roy. In the summer Roy specialized in painting bridges; in the winter he painted chimneys. He explained that chimneys were warmer than bridges. Roy got very mad at the U.S. Government for refusing to grant him a $300 deduction for his year's supply of overalls. The tax men cut the figure in half. Since painters' overalls in that era cost about $5 a set, the other Julius regulars used to argue about whether Roy bought a new set of overalls every week or whether he was having his work clothes designed by Dior.

The official Julius historian has long since retired to the suburbs. His name was Jake Qualey, a veteran newspaperman and a master of forensics who would argue, pro or con, the causes of Bunny Berigan's split lip, the imminence of socialism, nuances of Puerto Rican immigrations or how many angels can dance on the head of a pin. If he had nobody to argue with, Jake would argue with himself, or otherwise conversationally amuse himself. Thus, once the afternoon barflies watched Jake silently commune with himself and finally break into gusty laughter.

"Nobody," Jake told himself aloud, "can tell that story as well as I can."

The lunacy quotient at Julius was comparably high. Let us consider the crisis faced by one Ira. He always wore a big hat and was, of course, known only as Ira Under the Hat.

Ira was never without a small dog of doubtful antecedents named Pixie. On the night of this incident, Ira buttonholed Johnny Windhurst, one of the best jazz trumpeters, and told him that Pixie had wandered from Julius and disappeared.

"She must have taken a taxi," said Ira, almost wildly. "She loves to ride in taxicabs. Let's ask all the cab drivers." In those days cab drivers usually worked a set territory, but a poll of familiars revealed that none had seen Pixie, much less collected a fare from her. Windhurst suggested that they repair to Ira's apartment house, to which the dog had probably returned.

"No good," wailed Ira. "We've moved."

Then, suggested Windhurst, they would go to the new home.

"She doesn't know where we've moved to," cried Ira, as though explaining something to a backward child. Then, persisted Windhurst, Pixie would surely have gone back to the old home.

"No," insisted Ira. "She doesn't know where we've moved but she knows we've moved."

Both homes, old and new, were visited. In front of the new home, huddled against an ash can, was a sopping wet but intact Pixie.

The saloon also had a daily girl customer known as the Gourmet. This lassie had a few drinks before dinner, wine with dinner and a couple of brandies with coffee. She did not, however, eat any dinner or drink any coffee.

But let us not overlook a onetime bartender named Bobby Earle. Bobby was a nut on mechanics. He could fix anything, and he claimed he was the original Do-It-Yourself Kid. He fixed the plumbing one day and a water tank fell on Bill Kennedy, possibly the most legendary of all Julius bartenders. Bobby fixed the electric wiring on another day and the place was dark for forty-eight hours, not that anybody cared. Then Bobby came in early one afternoon and decided to repair the ventilator.

Julius in those days eschewed air conditioning as firmly as it ignored television. There was a roof ventilator with a revolving fan. This led through a square outlet in the ceiling to a wide ventilating duct. Bobby, laden with wrenches and pliers, ascended to the roof and went to work on the fan. There was a loud sound, muffled cries of terror and down came Bobby through the ventilating pipe. He landed right in front of the bar, wrench in hand.

"And," the awed Bill Kennedy told all listeners, "he was exactly on time for work, too."

A rendezvous such as this would, of course, develop its own official malaprop. The Julius language scrambler in the old days was Tony de Nisco, who ran a tiny grocery store across the street. Tony once had a pal hospitalized with "ferocious liver" and another with "precious anemia." Between his one enemy and himself, he admitted, the feeling was "neutral." He could handle any assignment if you would just give him "the peculiars."

Cast against such types were almost all the current stars from the uptown theatres, the literary lights, many highly placed city employees and even Mrs. Eleanor Roosevelt. A forgotten bartender once rescued Mrs. Roosevelt and her dog from a snowdrift and she formed a habit of dropping in now and then during the late afternoons.

With its two doors, Julius was always something of a challenge to parched souls looking to beat the place out of a free drink. Only one used much imagination.

This was a girl who came in one slow afternoon, ordered a drink, laid an extra dollar on the bar and asked for change so she could make a phone call. She drank her drink and went to one of the two phone booths. Soon the other phone rang. Pete Pesci, doubling behind the bar, answered it.

"Julius?" a voice asked. Pete said it was.

"Hold the wire." said the voice. "Long distance calling."

Pete held the phone until he tired. When he emerged from his booth, the gal was gone and the phone booth she had been in was empty. The phone in the gal's booth was, of course, dangling.

The saloon took on more musical overtones when Nick Rongetti opened Nick's on the corner of Seventh Avenue, just a pretzel's toss up the street. Nick set down a hard-and-fast rule in his jazz saloon. No musician could drink on the home grounds—Nick's. So, once through with their set, whatever musical stalwarts were featured would simply dash out the front door and across the street to Julius' more friendly bar.

In the 1930s, Dixieland jazz had developed a solid following of college students and Village youngsters. So when their heroes crossed Nick's border, headed for Julius and ten cent beer, the kids would take hold of their own thirty-five-cent Nick's steins and follow their gurus. Once it was time for the oiled-up musicians to be back on Nick's bandstand, the kids would follow the pied pipers back home.

This caused some tension between the two saloons because the devoted followers, having taken their beer glasses with them on the short flight to Julius, would return minus the glassware. Things were smoothed over when the Julius management agreed to collect all Nick's housewares and return them the next morning.

There was always a great esprit de corps among Julius regulars. Once the guitarist, Rod Cless, fell four stories out of a window and was taken to a nearby hospital in critical condition. Blood was needed. Among the first volunteers were Pete Pesci and Eddie Condon. Condon had eaten nothing for breakfast, but Pesci had packed away his usual big meal. Blood was extracted from both and analyzed. It was apparent that Eddie's blood was too thin and Pete's too thick. Mr. Condon was indignant.

"Either mix them together like brandy and soda," he instructed the doctor, "or else put both of them back where you got them from."

And now we sing of Leonee, the house cat. She arrived unsung and unheralded. She remained to become a house legend and as bossy an old broad as one could encounter.

As in most old New York buildings, Julius had a colony of cellar rats who were smarter than the customers and tougher than the Prohibition agents. A retired bartender named Joe Bamberger remembered, some years ago, that he talked the owners into buying two ferrets and setting them loose in the cellar.

"The rats killed the ferrets," Joe recalled with proper awe.

It was soon after this that a magazine owner who had to go off to war left his cat in the saloon for safekeeping. The cat was named Leonee. She was a long-bodied and fearsome beast. In a week she had the premises under control. The rats fell before her hatred like duckpins hit by a bowling ball. She made her own working hours. She demanded, and received, huge quantities of the house hamburger. When bored, or possibly when she thought she should go shopping, she would jump up on the back bar, hit a few keys on the cash register and scratch out some currency, which the bartender had to retrieve from her after a loud argument.

There was an old and fairly large peephole in the West 10th Street door, about five feet above the floor. Virtually every old regular will tell you, with the proper figures, how he measured the circumference of this hole and then the circumference of Leonee's body. The hole was simply too small for her to get through. It wasn't possible.

Yet several times a night Leonee would coil herself together on the floor, sail five feet up through the air and, possible or impossible, somehow sausage her body through the old peephole and out into the street. Home from her wanderings, she might suddenly land in your lap, a rather startling effect since it would appear as though she had come through a solid wall.

Harold Fitzsimmons, one of a long series of Julius bartenders, was Leonee's principal sponsor and tutor. He tried valiantly to teach her to ring up the right amounts on the cash register. A picture of Leonee punching the damper hung behind the bar until very recently. The cat's ultimate death was a bitter blow to Harold. He told Pete Pesci the depressing news and Pete, his mind on bigger matters, merely suggested that Harold get another cat.

"That's just like this joint," said Harold bitterly. "The cat's dead? Get a new cat. The bartender's dead? Get a new bartender."

The history of Julius can be traced fairly accurately even up to the present. Originally it was just one more German saloon in the Village. When bought by a man named George Feste, the new owner was told that it dated back to 1892. John Cummings bought it from Feste and sold it to John Boggiano and Pete Pesci, who operated it for thirty years or more. A few years ago they sold it to Boggiano's son-in-law, Bill Fugazy, of the travel agency and Diners Club, and his partner, George Case. And who was Julius? Why, in Prohibition times all saloons were known under the bartender's name. The Julius was a bartender named Julius Von Posch.

I went back for a visit not long ago. Only a few things have radically changed, but the charisma is somehow different. The old beer keg tables have been replaced by more formal serving surfaces, Scotch whisky now goes for $1.25 a pop and some of the integral dirt has been cleaned away.

Of course, the Village itself has changed. Like so many Village saloons these days, Julius seems to get more than its share of homosexuals. Such a trade would have infuriated old Julius himself. Julius liked very few customers and no off-beat ones.

"The more I see of people," Julius used to tell his drinkers, "the more I like dogs."

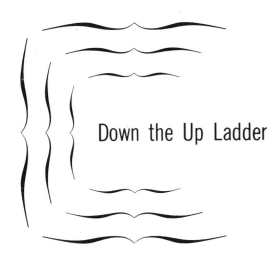

Down the Up Ladder

IN RECENT THEATRICAL SEASONS
we have heard some wild keening indeed when big musical
comedies closed out of town. It is nothing unusual for a musical to
close out of town—indeed, it often seems the norm—but these were
different. One of these musicals admitted to having lost a
production investment of over $500,000. The next big flop
admitted to about the same amount. And then came one that
everybody said, set an all-time record. This one went down at a
loss of $800,000.

Now we hear of a new musical that will be the first to cost
$1,000,000. How the theatre has changed, sigh the old-timers.
Remember when you could do a Broadway play for $25,000?
Nobody can stand off the economics of today's theatre. No? Well,
forty years ago when things were considerably cheaper than they
are now—George Abbot could produce a farce for $8,000—a man
produced a play on Broadway that cost him $1,500,000. And he
lost the money without a whimper.

The man's name was Edgar B. Davis. The play was *The Ladder*
by J. Frank Davis, no relation. The saga went like this:

Edgar B. Davis was a man who had made millions planting
rubber trees in Sumatra and calmly waiting for them to grow and
produce. He took some of these millions and calmly tried new

places in Texas for oil. While the veteran oil hustlers laughed at him, he began to bring in wells. He made friends everywhere. He loved to give away money. When he brought in a well, investors who had long since written off previous stock purchases in dry Davis holes found that all of a sudden they owned shares in a Davis gusher they'd never heard about.

One of Davis' friends was a writer named J. Frank Davis. Together they shared a belief—the belief in reincarnation. J. Frank wrote a play about the subject called *The Ladder*, and Edgar B. brought it to Broadway and had the successful producer, Brock Pemberton, put it on stage in late 1927.

The critics dismissed it. Davis did not. He moved it from theatre to theatre. He spent more and more on advertising and publicity. He hired the famed scenic designer Robert Edmond Jones to furnish new settings and costumes. He brought in a parade of play doctors to rewrite it and punch it up. Still nobody came.

Davis would not give up. He simply announced that he was keeping *The Ladder* running and anybody who would come to the box office and ask for tickets could see the epic for free. For free, the play sometimes did SRO and sometimes played to almost empty houses. After backing it for almost two years, Davis put the play back on a paid ticket basis. Nobody wanted to buy tickets. He reversed his field and offered it for free again.

Meanwhile, he paid the cleaning women bonuses if they kept the theatre nice and neat. Box office staff and maintenance crews and publicists and all connected with the most expensive flop in stage history were all getting more money than they would have gotten from the hit show next door. The actors in the cast changed almost monthly. Any actor in *The Ladder* who could get a role in a more promising show quit *The Ladder* to take the new gamble. Always there was some out-of-work actor only too ready to jump into the vacated role.

Through it all, Davis never complained nor, indeed, made any public statements. Although he became pals with many of the newspapermen, he never permitted an interview and was never quoted until the show was over. He would merely admit to friends that he liked the play, believed in its theme and was happy to support it.

Oddly, there were few funny anecdotes concerning this rather lunatic operation. One that is remembered occurred when the husband of the temporary leading lady walked into the theatre during a matinee. Seeing only four people in the audience, one of them Davis and one of them the director, hubby walked down the aisle and leaned across the footlights, interrupting what he assumed was a rehearsal.

"Honey," he said, "do you want to eat home or eat out tonight?"

No answer. Hubby repeated the question and was ignored by the leading lady again. Behind him, hubby heard one spectator hiss at him to be quiet. Light broke in upon him. He wasn't watching a rehearsal. It was a matinee. For four.

On the other remembered occasion, Davis was in the lobby talking to his friend, the humorist Dorothy Parker. One of his business associates rushed to him through the lobby, all excited.

"Edgar!" he cried. "Two more wells came in!"

"On passes?" queried Miss Parker.

A native of Massachusetts, Davis contributed vast sums for parks, children's projects and community improvements in his former home town. When his first oil wells gushed around Luling, Texas, he was so open-handed with civic projects there that the main street of the town was named for him. Then varied misfortunes struck. Massachusetts claimed he was a resident and demanded $700,00 in back taxes. Davis countersued, claiming "harassment" because he was obviously a Texas resident. He lost this suit in a high court. An Oklahoma oil venture failed, and then another. He closed *The Ladder.*

"It cost around $1,500,000," he admitted in one of his rare statements. It may have cost considerably more.

In his last years he was "broke," although "friends" saw to it that he lived well. He never got lucky with another rubber tree or oil well. Just before he died he was amiable and unperturbed when asked if he didn't resent being broke after all his successes and all his generosity to worthy causes.

"I am perfectly content," was his answer.

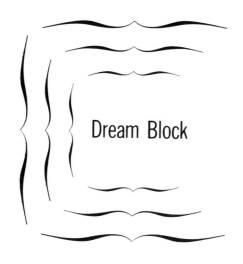

Dream Block

THE CITY BLOCK OF WEST 44TH
Street which starts at Broadway and comes to its end at Eighth
Avenue is still, after perhaps fifty years, the heartthrob of the
legitimate theatre. In all those years it has lost only one historic
marker—the 44th Street Theatre, with its experimental showhouse
in its attic and the nightclub in its basement that became the
fabled Stage Door Canteen during World War II. The 44th fell to
the expansion necessities of the august *New York Times,* and now
delivery trucks pour out of exits that once received and bade
farewell to the glamorous stars and troubadors of a theatre in its
great days. It is still hedged by six theatres, and the only
businesses contained within the strip are Sardi's restaurant,
Mackey's Ticket Agency and Joe Lopomo's barber shop. Thirty
years ago, as now, it may not have been Dream Street, but it was
surely Dream Block.

True to its singular character, Dream Block really starts in the
middle and runs two ways. Its focal point is Shubert Alley,
midway in the block, which connects it to West 45th Street. The
Alley is a narrow strip of iron-fenced, bill-posted, stage-doored
pavement where "No Thoroughfare" signs are blithely disregarded
by the unemployed stage minions on foot and the chauffeurs of
the limousines that eight times a week deliver and remove the

glamorous stars who are exhibiting their talents in the nearby theatres.

Today, with every show an immediate smash or off-to-the-scenery-dumps on Saturday, and with the economic situation such that there is little time for the professional theatre operator to enjoy laughs or gambles, the Dream Block is just another crowded, busy, business thoroughfare. Thirty years ago it was something else again. Thirty years ago it was headquarters for the dreamers; the open-air forum for the exchange of plans and swindles; the marketplace for tip brokers, information traders, small and big promoters and the myriad torch carriers of the art.

The Alley was the bourse for these characters—many of whom went on to solid fame—and the strip of sidewalk across from it their union hall. The stretch of sidewalk ran past Sardi's and Mackey's Ticket Agency, which still stand shoulder to shoulder. Here, any noontime, the multimillionaire Lee Shubert, the practical dictator of the living theatre in those days, would pause briefly to listen to a proposition from some shoestring producer who had lain in ambush for Shubert over, possibly, many days.

Nearby a hungry young actor would be borrowing a dinner jacket or sports coat so he could audition for a role in the play about to be presented by that producer—standing right over there—waiting to collar his newest "angel" and try to hook the money he needed to do the show, for which the young actor was simultaneously trying to borrow the dinner jacket and/or sports coat.

If it were a matinee day, on the typical noon hour we are remembering, the rotund millionaire and aesthete Gilbert Miller would probably roll up in his long limousine just as Lester Sweyd, another producer, arrived on foot from his cubbyhole office. And a glittering Hollywood star, taking an amusing flyer on the straight stage while her agent ironed out an argument with her film bosses, would step from her fancy carrier and possibly bump into the Major, the unpublished poet and lyricist, who had as usual fallen asleep on his feet.

Off one inner wall of Mackey's agency, owner Lou Schonceit would be in his closet office, deciding whether or not to stake a playwright to a rented suit while he read for a producer and, once again, refusing the playwright the privilege of making an outgoing call on the office telephone. It was the Depression. Things were tough. Bills were hard to meet. Any Dream Block hustler could get all the *incoming* calls he wanted on Lou's office phone and do telephone business in privacy. If caught making a phone call that *cost,* he was drummed from the corps.

Next door, just inside the Sardi entrance, the red-haired Renee Carroll would be at her hatcheck post. Since virtually everybody who checked a hat with Renee also checked a playscript, Renee would already be riffling through the first scripts, quickly analyzing the basic casting. She would then be in a position to give early tips to all of her struggling young friends on what upcoming plays had suitable roles they should apply for, before publicity started the inevitable casting stampede.

Renee was one of our foremost oracles and an acknowledged drama critic. Once the Sardi waiters collected a pool for her expenses to a nearby tryout city. Renee went, saw a play on its first out-of-town performance, came back and predicted that it would be a hit. It was booked to play down the block. Vincent Sardi, Sr., listened to her critique and, reversing himself, opened the upstairs room for the expected extra customers who would be flocking to the play.

It was about this time, too, when Lou Schonceit lost his patience with the "option playwright" Irving Kaye Davis. Davis was the most prolific writer of unproduced plays in history. He would write a play and somebody would give him a few hundred dollars for an option on it. Irving could never wait for production (and anyway the play wasn't going to get financed for production), so he would immediately start writing another and seeking another option.

Schonceit was Davis' patron and the Mackey Agency was Irving's headquarters. One day the sidewalk regulars were horrified to see Lou pull a revolver from his cash drawer and chase Davis out onto the street, where he jabbed the gun in the playwright's ribs.

"Get back in there and sign that option or you'll never write another line in your life," the ticket broker ordered.

It developed that Davis did not want to take $300 for a new play because that option wasn't enough. Schonceit was determined that Davis take $300 and pay off his patron, Schonceit.

It was not surprising when, after years of common problems, Renee Carroll married Lou Schonceit. But it was totally startling when, after only a few more years on the block, they betook themselves to live in Majorca, of all places! Or was it?

The outstanding figure on Dream Block, spanning two generations, and the single most important force in the American theatre of our day, stood at the other end of the Dream Block spectrum. This was the legendary Lee S. Shubert. In those days Mr. Lee (he was called Lee only by intimates and Mr. Shubert only by strangers) owned or controlled all but a few New York theatres and virtually every other first-class playhouse across the nation.

A small and rather spidery man, he would and could walk and move faster than his business associates even before his death at age seventy-one. During the deepest financial despair of the Depression, he fought banks and bankruptcies to keep his theatres and theatre business alive. He was an anomaly. He would gamble untold sums, for the times, and lose without blinking an eye. But he could scream like a stuck hog if a bill showed that one of his theatres needed a new mop and pail because the old one had been carelessly lost. He lived in taste and luxury in the best hotels of the world, on the best ocean liners and in the epicurean restaurants.

But he operated his vast empire from a tiny circular room in a turret of the Shubert Theatre in the block with one secretary, Jack Morris. If he would sit outside and wait his turn, anybody could get in to see Mr. Lee. He was the last of the solo entrepreneurs, the kind of one-man operator who has long since gotten lost in the limbo of mergers and fragmented management and decentralization and amalgamations. For twenty-five years he did not speak to his younger brother, Jake, a minor legend in his own right.

Until well into the night Mr. Lee would sit in his tiny roundroom, the only wall decoration a picture of Charles E. Lindbergh, and tell people simply: "All right. You put up half the money and I put up half the money and the show plays a Shubert theatre." It is doubtful that in the long and fabled span of his career he ever read a script, heard a composer sing a show's songs or listened to a comedian tell a joke until the show was actually on the stage and playing in some tryout city.

But there was not a fact or figure, report or audit, that passed through the accounting system of his serpentine and complicated United Booking Office which wasn't first scanned and digested by the lone little man in his small office. His realty holdings alone would, today, probably require a floor full of agents and financial experts. In Mr. Lee's day he was all that was needed.

Memories of his diverse and perverse personality are endless. One night he stood in his Shubert Alley and was approached by a bedraggled old woman who asked him the directions to a stage door. Instead of pointing it out to the old crone, Mr. Lee personally escorted her to the door and mildly inquired what she wanted there. The woman said the stage manager had sold her a pair of fancy shoes that didn't fit and weren't wearing according to the guarantee.

Because he was polite enough to escort an old woman to a stage door, Mr. Lee thus discovered, by following through on the meager information he had been given, that crooked employees in his warehouses were selling thousands of dollars of used Shubert costumes and properties.

Too intense to be clownish, he nevertheless, when relaxed, would tell amusing stories on himself. There was the time, for instance, when he turned up at one of his theatres to find the lobby doors locked. Inside a porter was sweeping up. Mr. Lee rattled the door. The porter looked up and shook his head, Mr. Lee pounded. The porter was unimpressed.

Then, as now, in every lobby of a Shubert theatre there is a photograph of the dead brother, Sam, who died young after launching the empire. Mr. Lee finally got the porter's attention and the employee opened the door.

"I didn't know it was you, Mr. Lee," explained the porter.

"What would you have done if I had broken in the door?" demanded the annoyed Shubert.

"If you had done that, Mr. Lee," the porter told him sadly, "there would have been another picture in the lobby tomorrow."

Embittered competitors and stage folk with whom he quarreled spent many waking hours repeating and sending around anecdotes of Shubert's inherent cheapness and penury. Many of the stories were probably true. It is also true that the last time I saw him, only weeks before his death, I asked him how he had spent the recent Christmas.

"Quietly," he admitted. "My wife and I sat in front of the fireplace and burned up a half million dollars in IOU's."

There were several other authentic theatrical tycoons on the Dream Block, as well as our assortment of hustlers, strugglers and characters. Our two earliest monopolists were Arthur Rosenfeld and Leo Brode. Arthur made the frames and displays that stand in theatre lobbies. Leo painted the marquees and boards. Brode considered himself a recognized critic. So if he believed the show would be a hit, he painted the marquee and wall signs solidly, giving them two or three coats.

A flop was something else again. "I once painted the house for a turkey," he would recall, "with signs that faded out the very day the storehouse trucks drove up to cart the scenery away."

John Golden, who parlayed his song "Poor Butterfly" into an almost endless stream of hits over forty years, had his office in the block. So did Brock Pemberton, a master at producing frothy but highly profitable comedies. Also the sensitive and scholarly Arthur Hopkins. Ditto Eddie Dowling and hundreds of other producers who appeared there briefly. The steady, solid fellows such as Golden and Pemberton and Hopkins had one thing in common— they never gave up their grubby little offices that were usually in a theatre building and ideally in a theatre owned by them.

It was at the St. James Theatre, on the block, that an unknown English actor named Maurice Evans convinced a comic-accented Russian in New York to invest Russian money to finance—of all things!—Shakespeare's *Richard III.* An immediate artistic and financial success, Evans and "Richard" launched the Shakespeare revival that continues to this day, and Evans was the point man for the invasion of English actors which, wave after wave, still inundates Broadway.

"I can never make up my mind," said the critic George Jean Nathan, no fan of the British theatre, "whether all actors talk like Englishmen or all Englishmen talk like actors."

Vincent Sardi, Sr., was another solo entrepreneur who ran his business according to his own lights. The restaurant started the fashion of hanging caricatures of its better known customers on the walls. The waiters and captains would usually be able to seat Helen Hayes, for instance, under her own cartoon. Sardi did this one day for Greta Garbo. The staff studiously paid no attention to the "I-vant-to-be-alone" girl, and Miss Garbo left before finishing her meal. It was later to become known that Garbo was a trial in most restaurants. If the staff fussed over her and customers wanted autographs, she got up and left. If everybody leaned backwards to honor her privacy, she got up and left anyway.

There is many a famous film and TV star today who would have lived a much hungrier life except for the senior Sardi. There were times—and this was in the era of the Great Depression when a buck was a buck—that Sardi's carried $20,000 in unpaid food tabs on his books. He did not worry about them.

"I never worry about real actors," he said. "They're the best risks in the world. I've had them come and pay me fifteen years later. But you've got to be careful about these new movie and radio people. They're not good risks."

Every now and then glamour would brighten up the block. One of these occasions was when Katharine Hepburn was brought back from Hollywood, with all the fanfare any project could ask, to star in a play called *The Lake*. Her producer, Jed Harris, went about things as though he had revived Sarah Bernhardt. One of the more publicized gimmicks was to have a screened alley for Miss Hepburn, leading from her dressing room to the stage, concealed from vulgar stagehands and unimportant supporting actors.

This screened alley annoyed the veteran Blanche Bates, who had an important role. "It isn't catching, you know, my dear," she finally told Miss Hepburn.

What wasn't catching, asked the film star.

"Acting," said Miss Bates, pointing a furious finger at the screens.

But most of the remembered color and characters happened along the sidewalk during the day. We had our own two shoeshine men and were loyal to one or the other. One was Old Joe, who put gloss on the Shubert shoes and many others. Once Jimmy Durante flew out to Hollywood owing Joe for a week's shine. It was merely an oversight, since Jimmy has always been open-handed to the point of slobbishness, but the regulars tried to steam up Old Joe into dashing out to Hollywood and demanding his money from the comedian.

"No," said Joe firmly. "There are enough phonies right here. No Hollywood for me."

Joe's competitor was Jerry Thomas, a colored ex-vaudeville performer. His box had the sign: "Formerly of Vaudeville. Clean

Humor. Philosophy. Music Theatre Prizefights. Entertainment with a Shine."

We also had our two official cab drivers, big Irving Schaeffer and little Irving Domashevsky. And there was the road show press agent Ned Alvord who wore high-buttoned shoes, gates ajar collars and knee-length Prince Albert coats, and looked like a country deacon. His costume was not from eccentricity but for practical purposes. He would go out in advance of a girlie show, plaster a town with seminude posters—his favorite was a semi-nude with her back to you and a plaster over her backside saying "Next Week at the Bijou Theatre She Turns Around"—and then go up and down streets ringing doorbells, introducing himself as the Reverend Alvord, and trying to work up a strong civic protest against the "dirty show" coming to town.

He got a lot of customers that way.

Some of the sidewalk regulars were known to each other, but there were some whom none of us really knew much about. Mike the Playwright was one. Mike was a now-and-then playwright. Other times he was a waiter in any one of several small Greek restaurants. Mike waited on tables and saved his tips. On his off hours he wrote. Once the play was finished, he would canvass all the waiters and cooks in the city's Greek restaurants and get enough money to put his play on somewhere. Each play would quietly open and quietly fold. Mike would quietly go back to waiting on tables.

There was Lester Sweyd, a play agent and frustrated producer, who gave an early lift to Moss Hart and other writers. When not agenting, Lester spent most of his time suing Great Britain for possession of Labrador. It was his claim that the whole of the cold territory had been deeded to an ancestor who saved William III from drowning.

And there were the girls we called Stage Struck and the Girl in the Evening Dress. Stage Struck was a rich youngster who would take walk-on roles for a dollar a night. She would arrive at her theatre in a chauffeur-driven limousine, do her chore, collect her dollar, hand it over to the parking lot attendant and be driven off again. She did not have the success of Betty Perske, part-time usher at the St. James Theatre, who one day changed her name to Lauren Bacall.

The Girl in the Evening Dress was more of a mystery. She would appear once a month, maybe, always in the late afternoon and always in an evening dress. You had to look closely to see that it was always the same evening dress. She would just stand at Sardi's bar, apparently waiting for her date. Somebody would buy her a drink and so would somebody else. She then vanished into the night for another month. She never told anything about herself, nor was she on the make.

Among us, also, was the late, great Jimmy Savo, endorsed by none less than Charles Chaplin as the greatest pantomime talent of all. Jimmy saved money all his life to buy a real ancient castle outside of his native Rome. He finally bought it—a few days before Pearl Harbor. With the advent of warm weather, Jimmy always had his head shaved. He then carried a wig in his pocket that he would slap on his head if he were going somewhere where hair was in order. We knew how despondent he was when, that summer after Pearl Harbor, he didn't even bother to shave his head.

Every now and then a crisis would occur which, because it was free, drew all the regulars in a body. One of these happened when Earl Carroll had a big idea for the first-act finale of his musical *Vanities* and had a staff member go out and rent a whole flock of pigeons, which were to be released to circle over the heads of the audience.

At rehearsal the pigeons were released. They flew, one and all, up into the gridiron that held the scenery, and they found perches elsewhere in the top reaches of the theatre. Nothing would bring them down.

"Go buy me an air rifle," ordered the producer. "I'm a dead shot."

He was. He was blissfully sitting in an orchestra seat potting at the pigeons when an aide rushed up feverishly. Did he know who the pigeons had been rented from? Carroll did not.

"Owney Madden," gasped the aide, naming the top muscleman of the era. Mr. Carroll put down his new air rifle.

And there was the time when a lot of us were invited to consider the dress rehearsal of *Rosalinda,* which a Hungarian lady was launching to revive the glories of Mittel-European light opera. Another Hungarian lady named Marta Eggerth sang the lead, which has an aria that goes, "Velia, oh Velia, the witch of the woods."

The imported soprano sang, "Velia, oh Velia, the vitch of the voods."

An amateur critic sitting behind the lady producer tapped her on the shoulder and pointed out that the soprano was singing "vitch" and "voods." The producer turned in her seat.

"Vell?" she demanded.

In those days on the block, the drama critics were important fellows indeed. They made or broke a show with their criticisms. Most drama critics were scholarly fellows who had impressive backgrounds in theatre knowledge, but there were some who seemed to be in it for sport. One of these was the late Kelcey Allen, of *Women's Wear Daily,* who loved a good cigar even more than he loved an opening night. Consequently he usually appeared at curtain time with a cigar only partially smoked. When it came time to enter the theatre, Kelcey would look around and pick the fender of a nearby parked car, lay his cigar on it, retrieve it at the first intermission and relight the butt.

Kelcey was an incessant anecdotist whose humor eluded another critic of the time, the late Rennold Wolf. "Here comes Kelcey Allen," Wolf would say, "with three million dollars worth of useless information."

We witnessed some spectacular goofs. There was a thieving little promoter who had a foolproof gimmick. He would pay a small advance on any bad play, then finance it three and four times over. Each set of investors thought they were the only ones involved. Thus he would raise, say, $80,000 for what should have been a $25,000 production, produce it with warehouse scenery and rented costumes, have it panned critically and fold up the operation after the first week.

This scheme left him with all the oversubscribed money, and he went along his crooked maze until he made his first mistake, a deadly one. One of his shows was, somehow, a popular hit. When the district attorney finally unraveled the figures for a show that was playing to capacity but paying investors nothing, Our Hero was kicked out of the operation, the mob of investors took over and put in a straight theatrical manager, and everybody came out even. His first success sounded the knell for this little cutpurse.

Once we had what amounted to a funeral at Sardi's. A wonderful guy named Tommy Van Dam, who with his wife Florence did all the theatrical portraits and photos for the best stage productions, spent years and years standing against Sardi's Little Bar when his camera chores were done. Tommy died suddenly and, since he was a British subject and World War II was well on, his widow had to give some thought to his burial. He could not, in those times, be sent home for burial. But Florence remembered that he had once expressed the wish to be buried at sea. And, at the right moment, there arrived home at Sardi's the actor Tom Ewell. Tom was commanding a gun crew on a freighter, and he was just the man to give Tommy's ashes a burial at sea.

So Florence turned over the urn with her husband's ashes to Ewell and that worthy, reporting immediately to Sardi's bar, gave them to the bartender, named Orestes, to hold until Ewell shipped out again and could complete the funeral. For more than a week we all drank "to Tommy," who stood among the back bar bottles. I have always suspected that Van Dam might have wished, if he could have foreseen the situation, that he be sprinkled on the bar floor and swept out at leisure—as he had seen so many other regular customers swept out bodily. Instead, Lieutenant Ewell eventually took the urn to sea and gave his old friend a full military burial.

The Dream Block's contribution to the war effort probably wasn't too heroic. Most of the regulars were found to be too spavined or mentally unstable for military service. The military services generally kept actors and entertainers at acting and entertaining real soldiers and sailors. But the block did produce one of the great morale builders of all time—the Stage Door Canteen in the cellar of the 44th Street Theatre.

This barnlike former nightclub had a kitchen. Opened as a rendezvous for armed service men who were friendless in New York, it was jammed nightly. And the Canteen cast was more glamorous than that of any show in town. Alfred Lunt, possibly America's leading actor of the time, was the cook. His wife, Lynn Fontanne, waited on tables. The greatest bands played for dancing, and the highest priced entertainers furnished the talent. Shirley Booth—the "Hazel" of TV—was a nightly attraction doing wild jitterbug dances with "Killer Joe" Piro, who is still extant as a dance teacher and exhibition dancer.

But World War II took most of the color and many of the

personalities out of the block. After the war it never really came back. It is still one of the two busiest theatre blocks in the world, but things are more frantic, economics are completely different and what was once a way of life is now a more matter-of-fact business. Vincent Sardi, Jr., is probably doing better with the restaurant than his father ever dreamed, and David Merrick probably produces more shows than Lee Shubert did, and is an equally important theatrical tycoon.

It's all changed, all different and most of the laughs are gone. But it sure was fun while it lasted.

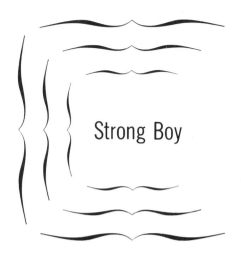

Strong Boy

FAR OUT ON QUEENS BOULEVARD, at the point where weary Long Islanders make the turn to the parkway and the bumper-to-bumper fun trip home to their housing development, there stands a fine broth of a marble man. This statue faces life with sword on shoulder, a modest wreath around his loins his only protection against chill or heat. With one foot on her neck, he holds prone a fallen lady. The other foot has recently felled another lady. He looks serious. His muscles bulge. He's ready for any action.

Not long ago I drove by him and, sure enough, he was having his bath. City employees were washing him down and restoring some of his pristine purity. I was the only motorist who paid him a passing glance. Few motorists even note that he is there. For more than thirty years he has been exiled to the metropolitan sticks, a repository for pigeon droppings and the oily exhausts of passing cars. It wasn't always thus. Once he was a celebrity.

Back in the more amusing 1930s he stood, watchful, in front of New York's City Hall. Officially his name was Civic Virtue. The girls being ground under his big, virtuous feet were, officially, Vice and Corruption. We were never told which was Vi and which was Cora.

What hell he caused among the liberated womanhood of the

1930s! There was scarcely a women's club or organization that didn't hate him. The very idea! That horrible, naked man with one foot on one lady's neck and the other foot kicking another lady! Rise in arms, women of New York! You have nothing to lose but your insults! Tar and feather the sculptor, Frederick William McMonnies! Smash him along with his false idol!

None of us had much to do in the dreary days of the 1930s, but we had plenty of time to do it in. Everybody took sides about the statue, and soon he was known to his defenders as Strong Boy. Irreverent members of the press hailed him. The girls at his feet were intimately referred to as Vi and Cora. From the other side came the strident voices of women critics. Dr. Ella Boole, heroine of Prohibition, viewed Strong Boy with agony. The National Women's Party, the Civic Modern School and other viewers-with-alarm besieged the mayor's office for Strong Boy's deportation. Finally Fiorello LaGuardia took the mayor's chair. Never one to antagonize a minority bloc, the Little Flower cut the pedestal out from under Strong Boy's feet.

"I won't look out of my office window one more day," he told us newsmen, "and have to see that big, bare ass of his."

Nobody wanted him but the Borough of Queens, which must have then been a far more sophisticated and art-minded community than it is now. Out went Strong Boy, Vi and Cora to the darkest stretches of Queens Boulevard. With the new trend toward nudity everywhere, maybe Strong Boy, Vi and Cora will make a comeback.

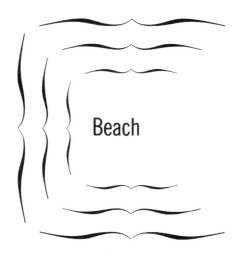

Beach

I STRATEGIZED MYSELF INTO A point of rough return driving the Montauk beach, the other weekend, and actually had to pause long enough to shift gears. I was maneuvered up against a big rock and a bigger chunk of driftwood, and backing out would be a problem. Nothing to it. I shifted the Jeep into low gear, waited for a wave to recede, and the four-wheel drive took me right around everything and into the clear. In the clear, I had to laugh. I had to laugh thinking about what the same situation would have meant when we were surf casting in the old days of the Beach Buggies.

In those long-gone times—yep, at my age twenty-five years is a long-gone time—Beach Buggy was usually an average Model T Ford with what Detroit calls "accessories." A buggy's accessories were a set of the oldest, smoothest, roundest tires that could be found, the fatter the better; two strong jacks; a four-by-four beam long enough to use as a lever; a coil of rope; a hand winch; a shovel; some old pieces of carpeting; and that gimmick that hooked into the number two spark plug hole and ran a tube to the tire valves so that they could be pumped back to normal pressure after having been deflated to ten pounds so they would give that thump-bump climbing traction.

There would be at least two other accessories—surf fishermen. No fool would venture the tides, especially at night, without additional strong backs to help with the inevitable blockades.

Not much more space was required. Just enough for a half dozen surf rods sticking out the back, several tackle boxes, the coffee containers and the water jug, the extra parkas and boots, the woolen shirts, the gaffs, the chains to hang fish to the belt, the Coleman lantern, the can of carbon tet or etheroid to throw on the spark plugs if they got wet, and usually the dog.

Getting a Beach Buggy bogged in the sand or, worse, disabled by a wet motor, resulted in horrible loss of face to any surf fisherman of my day. Other buggies would come by with kindly, straight-faced offers of help. Our society was rigid on this subject. Any damned fool who hung himself up got himself out. The shovel went to work. The carpeting went under the wheels. Didn't work? Deflate the tires. Jack up the embedded wheels. Push the buggy forward off the high jacks. It should land out of its self-made holes. Sometimes. If not, get the winch and find something to tie the rope to.

Meanwhile, down the beach, the miners' headlights strung around other surfers' necks would be flashing. This meant fish were being caught. Dig quicker! Push harder! Embarrassment was bad enough; humiliation was too much to be suffered within the cult.

And a cult we were. We knew each other and fished shoulder to shoulder. Pete the Tramp, a Brooklyn waiter, might fish with Perfume Roger, the rich essential oils man. Garbage Whitey, a Manhattan garbage collector, would exchange information with Gunnar Clive, who owned a wonder drug company. Harry Watkins, now a senior vice-president at Bankers Trust, might be trying to outcast Freddy the Flounder, who repaired refrigerators. Only the Mad Russian–Teddy Gusdanovic, neither Russian nor mad–would be doing the loner bit.

In this day of fiber glass and star drags and monofilaments, our equipment in retrospect seems pretty primitive indeed. The rods were of varnished, pieced bamboo. The slightest knock on the varnish cracked it, the salt water hit the bamboo–throw the rotted rod away and buy another one with your life's savings. Mostly we made our own lures–jigs, to the initiated. These came in various shapes and were of a mixture of lead and tin. We poured the hot metal into brass hand molds. There was always some penitent who worked in a machine shop. We would work out the design and he would make the mold.

The reels would be just too much trouble for the modern fisherman to learn how to handle today, but they were things of beauty. The two models from our personal Tiffany and Cartier were the Vom Hofe and the Perez. They were narrower than the moderns, but they were items of pure, handcrafted genius. You would load up one of these beauties with the old Cuttyhunk linen line, and all you had to do was sort of push it with your thumb and the spindle and line would evenly revolve, literally for minutes.

Of course, your thumb was all you had to hold a hooked fish. You laid that rod back over your shoulder, cast out that lead jig and when it hit the water you started reeling straight in. When a bass hit, you let him run or held him fast by the pressure of your thumb on the reel. After a while you developed an indestructible thumb. Ah, Herr Vom Hofe! Ah, Señor Perez! My nine-year-old kid can now take a spinning outfit and cast just as far. Without even paying any attention.

Our costumes were colorful but inadequate. It was before we could get those belly-high waders and lightweight waterproof parkas, so we wore rubber boots and over these we put yellow sou'wester overalls. And for the torso we used anything semiwaterproof we could find. Down around the ankles we put rubber bands, also around the sleeve cuffs. It was impossible that water could seep in through these tightly applied protections. So how come so many gallons of it always did? In my day no surf fisherman ever came home more than half dry.

Montauk Point was still in its almost natural state, back then, and I have stood under that lighthouse and seen the great V-shaped tail fins of those striped bass sticking right out of the water while the big pigs grubbed around the bottom on mussels and clams. You could throw out your hat and hit one, although that didn't mean they would always take a lure. However, bringing home twenty or even thirty striped bass was no big deal. Sometimes we would stop fishing because we were plumb tired out.

There would be other sorts of days, too. We could see bass breaking too far offshore, and we knew they were feeding out of reach. What to do on days like those? Get the lure out further, that's what. How? Figure out some kind of a casting aid, that's how.

Ah, those casting aids.

Chauncey Poole experimented with a kite. He would attach the jig to the kite with some sort of secret breakaway he devised, run down the beach, get kite in the air and—theoretically— then release the jig right among the feeding fish.

Splendid, imaginative idea. But I never remember the kite ever dropping the jig anywhere near the fish. And that left Chauncey with enough reeling-in to be discouraging. Another hero invented a catapult. This infernal machine worked on a spring, like a clay pigeon projector. The inventor—was it Pie Way?—would release the reel clutch, lay the jig on the infernal machine, hold his rod in the air and release the jig by spring propulsion.

It would rocket off in any direction. He nearly killed us all. He did manage to hook Sam Cox's Chesapeake bitch, Ginger, in the back of the neck.

Another doctor of research built a tiny boat, the propeller operated by crossed and tightly twisted, heavy rubber bands, like the ones kids used to employ to fly model airplanes. The idea was to put the little boat on the end of one reel of line, put the jig in it, send the boat churning out to sea, capsize it with a strong jerk and reel in boat and lure separately, both going through a problematical school of starved striped bass.

This charter member of our lunacy group had suffered the pounding of waves against his chest and belly all his sportsman's life. It just never occurred to him that even a small wave would turn over a toy boat and wash it back on the beach.

For a while I was tempted to try and throw out a jig with my jai alai cesta. I have always been convinced that had I been born a Basque, and thus not discriminated against, I would have been the greatest jai alai player in the world. My plan had only one uncorrective flaw—it called for a round lure without a fishhook.

Being a cult, and largely a moon cult at that, we were all very superstitious. One must never, for instance, curse at the lack of fish. Talk nice about fish—they'll come nearer that way. Speak nice to seagulls, send them on their explorative flights. If they find anything they'll start talking back and pretty loud, too. There were other and less rigid rules in the general classification. But the personal superstitions were perhaps most noteworthy.

One of the brethren would only fish in a floppy white hat. It could be a bitter November dawn and there he was, balanced on a greasy rock, wet and miserable, but wearing the sort of headgear Churchill used to wear when he was painting in Africa's Marakesch.

Another member always had a towel wrapped around his neck. He must have meant it as an emblem, since it was useless as protection. A soaking wet towel around the neck is even less satisfying than getting an occasional dollop of cold water on the thorax.

The late Frank Tuma—with Louis Cihlar the last remnant of surf fishing's days of elegance (more anon)—would wade out a seeming mile into the heavy seas taking with him only one lure. His tackle box he left on the beach. He had to catch his fish with one lure at a time. It would be posturing before fate to flaunt more than a single-o. If he snapped off his jig (a rare occurrence), he had to wade all the way back over the stumble-trap rocks to get another solo.

Teddy Gusdanovic, a Croat who was our smartest and most productive technician—and thus naturally was always known as the Mad Russian—always walked the beach with his lure wrapped in newspaper and carried in the hand not carrying his rod. The rest of us peasants walked with jigs dangling on a length of line hanging from the rod tip.

Another star-crossed practitioner would never so much as step foot in water until he had flashed his neck light on and off three times. No more, no less.

Such antics always amused me. A reasonably sophisticated man is above superstition. I never indulged in such nonsense. But it is a peculiar fact that I never caught a fish in my life unless I was wearing a blue flannel shirt. The fact that I always wore one had nothing at all to do with silly superstitions.

Back we went to the buggies after the night's fun and games. The tires on the buggy, as heretofore stated, had been deflated to give them an uneven traction, which works best in sand. But for the six-mile drive back home the beach pressure was far too weak for old smooth tires on hard concrete highways. Many a gimmick was tried in search of a way to quickly reinflate the tires. Most of us settled for the motor pump, or whatever it was. And whatever it was, it demanded time and patience. It could be purchased in many auto appliance stores and it worked thusly:

You opened the hood and with a wrench removed the number

two spark plug. Into the exposed hole you screwed one end of a tube. This tube ran about six feet to a pressure box, and from the other side of the box ran another tube. This was attached to the valve of the first tire. You then set the pressure box to the eighteen or twenty pounds of pressure you wanted, got back in the car, turned on the motor and let it idle.

By some marvel of dynamics the engine went huff-huff-huff and air came out of the engine block and went puff-puff-puff into the tire. You sat and yawned while the tire slowly—I said slowly— inflated. Then you repeated the process three times with three more tires. You didn't dare go to sleep. At more than twenty pounds any or all of those worn old tires would blow out into small bits. One of them was probably going to blow out on the way home anyway.

The only Beach Buggy I remember that must have been an untroublesome joy was the hot rod of our fleet. It was a real sedan owned by an auto mechanic named George Dietrich. Bigger than any of the others, it cruised with a select party of four or five sportsmen, seemed to have the power of a locomotive and was driven by a veteran who knew how to avoid every rock and trouble spot on both north and south sides of the Point.

It made no noise at all. Further, Dietrich liked to run the beach at night without headlights. To be casting in the dark, to hear that "whooooosh" and look over your shoulder and see a dark mass sliding by was enough to shake a stoic.

As colorful as the old Beach Buggy days look in hindsight, they must have represented a very vulgar change in sporting life to the last of what we used to call the Elegantes. To explain the Elegantes, who were dying out even in my early days, we must take a quick gander at Montauk history.

On Oct. 22, 1879, Arthur Benson (*ref*: Bensonhurst, Brooklyn) bought 13,000 acres of Montauk land from the Montauk Indians. Price: $151,000. It was a gift for his son, Arthur W. Benson, who had always wanted a farm for a toy. Instead, Arthur Benson may have been the first of the surf-fishing aristocrats. He was soon followed to Montauk by a gaggle of social, political and just plain rich folks.

Harrison Tweed, a famed corporation lawyer, socialite and philanthropist, was one of the last living relics of these early days of salt water sport. Another, Knowles Smith, Sr., 77, was boss of the Coast Guard in those times. The millionaires built the big, shingled and porte-cochered homes on Cottage Point. These are among the last of the architectural breed. With the exception of Tweed's big but battered white home on the Point, the "cottages" with their black walnut interior trim and great walnut beams—all tastefully executed by an architect named Stanford White—are now boarding houses and country inns.

But the gentlemen of this small community knew how to fish graciously as well as live easily. There is an old photo in the East Hampton Library files of Arthur Benson busily surf fishing. He is doing it first-cabin style. Hearken:

He is sitting in a beach chair, well up above the water line. An umbrella shades him. His rod is held in the sand by a firmly planted rod holder. There is a basket of goodies at his right hand and a bucket of lobster tails at his left. A *bucket* of lobster tails? Yes, but not to eat. Mr. Benson used a whole lobster tail as striped bass bait. No wonder he caught a few.

As more of the rich and "holding" vacationers discovered the wild point of land, surf casting spread like a low-grade infection. With the primitive equipment of those gothic times, the early Elegantes felt the same frustration the Beach Buggy boys were to feel years later. There were too many days when those striped bass could be plainly seen but just couldn't be touched. Too far out. Something had to be done.

What was done was the construction of some "casting aids," the cost of which would have been far beyond the flat purses of us Beach Buggy maniacs. The sportsmen in the Age of Elegance simply had five "stands" built out into the water at strategic and productive fishing points. These were narrow wooden piers built on pilings sunk into the tidal bottoms. They were like early Erector sets, only of wood. Pilings and cross beams and railings and platforms were simply bolted together. With the first hard blow of fall, the stands were simply unbolted, the pieces packed and numbered, and all stored away for a happier spring to come.

There were two or three stands at the Point itself, one at a cove called Stoneybrook and another at Jones Reef. They rose about twenty feet above the surf. The fishing technique was faultless.

If several fishermen arrived to fish the same stand, the first

116

comer walked out to the end of the pier, cast as far as he could and slowly walked back to the base of the stand, reeling in as he walked. He returned along the *left* railing, because coming up along the right railing would be the next caster. He was to make his throw from the end, and in turn walk and reel back along the left rail to allow *his* follower to walk out along the right and make *his* cast.

Fishing into distant waters probably has never since been made so easy for the surf caster. Even so, the method was too tough for a railroad millionaire who fished the stands regularly. Here was an individual with his own ideas of *joie de sport*.

He fished with his butler. The butler wore his uniform striped pants but was allowed a heavy sweater in dirty weather. Millionaire and butler made their way to the tip of the pier. Butler cast. Butler handed rod to millionarie. Millionaire took rod, walked back and reeled in. They waited their turn and took the casting position again. Butler casts again. Butler hands rod to boss. Boss makes with the easy part.

The only way to surf cast with any less effort would have been for the railroad millionaire to have found a way for his butler to cast from his bedroom window.

The stands existed until the great September hurricane of 1938 which, coming early, caught the wooden Erector sets before they could be dismantled. Now and then at Stony Brook I still trip over a piece of upright piling that is all that's left of the fishing stands.

All other traces of the old stands are gone. So is the casting butler. And so—alas—is the abundance of lobsters that made it a cinch for Mr. Benson to use a whole lobster tail to catch a small or large striped bass Gone also are the Elegantes. Sic transit elegance.

Today no surf fishermen needs to join or disjoint a surf rod. The most practical rods come in twelve-foot lengths of fiber glass and are practically indestructible. No winter varnishing nor rewinding of the pretty designs in silk thread. Jigs come factory made and work beautifully. The wooden plugs that have been favorite lures since my day come machine-made and painted by the most expert machines.

On the subject of the wooden plug as a lure, allow me to digress for a moment. A forgotten man discovered that a painted piece of wood, shaped like a cone or elliptically carved, and set with several hooks, is a fish killer. He has been unfairly ignored in sports history. In Montauk, in the mists of surf-casting time, somebody stumbled upon this fantastic fact. Just take a plug, paint it (in those days) half red and half white, and bingo! Back then, Montauk had two authentic hotels and perhaps half a dozen boarding houses. Within a week there was not a mop or a broom in the entire town that had a handle on it. The handles were sawed off in two-inch pieces to make our primitive fishing plugs.

Now plugs of plastic work even better. Now the spinning reel can be handled by a baby. Monofilament line is not rotted by sea water and neither is the nylon line universally used on standard casting reels. Our waders are lightweight, parkas can be folded and carried in a lady's pocketbook, felt soles attached to waders make it easy to stand on the most slippery rock, and all the surf fisherman really need hope for is some kind of electronic lure that will induce the fish to jump onto his hook while he sips a hot toddy on the beach.

The Beach Buggy—alas again—is another anachronism. Why a buggy when you can take a Jeep or a Volkswagon "bus" on the beach and practically have a nap while it tools you around? The surf casters who use the Volkswagons or Jeeps need never again live off bottled coffee and meat sandwiches. A full meal for four can easily be cooked up on an electric or gas grill in a Volkswagon or a Jeep station wagon. Life on the beach today, indeed, is an unending ball.

So we get where we're going quicker, we fish with equipment beyond our dreams, we are scarcely ever faced with discomfort. It's summertime and the livin' is easy. Fish should be jumpin' and the tide is on high.

So why is it that nobody catches nearly as many fish as we used to in the bad old days?

MOONLIGHT

The late Frank Geraghty was a precise, formal and dignified man with a clipped white mustache. In the great era of New York restaurants, Geraghty was headwaiter at a topflight chophouse run by another fine gentleman, the late Billy La Hiff. The place was called the Tavern after a play by George M. Cohan, a favored customer.

One night Geraghty was called from his post to soothe, calm down and admonish an important man who was dining with friends and also belting the old gutgripper too fast and too hard. With order and good manners restored, Geraghty calmly returned to his headwaiter's post. His face was faintly contemptuous.

"You can always tell a sucker," he said simply.

"How?" I asked.

"Because he's drunk," said Geraghty.

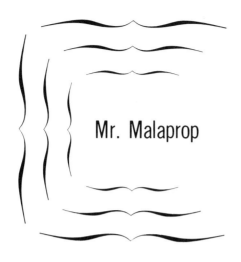

Mr. Malaprop

FROM THE EARLIEST DAYS OF THE movie business until age slowed him down, Samuel Goldwyn was known for two things—he only made high-class films, he was also a champion mangler of the English language. It is hard to reconcile two such attributes, although there were many who were even more amazed by the movies because they could never find an ounce of class in Sam himself. But there is probably a logical explanation. Goldwyn's pictures were made by high-class directors, designers and stars. As the world's champion Mr. Malaprop, it was ultimately generally accepted that the title was a fraud perpetrated by his own associates.

Goldwyn actually belongs to the history of Hollywood, but he and Cecil B. De Mille were the only two movieland colossi who often charged into New York and who became loud if brief factors in the life of New York's show business. This was because both these men, although primarily movie manufacturers, immediately dropped their roles of producers the very moment their newest film was finished and cut to their taste. Then each became his own press agent. Or at least his boss press agent. They would descend on Broadway like the Assyrian on the wolf and start their promotional campaigns. Thus we of the press and the publicity worlds were intermittently brushed by double genius.

It was back in the 1930s when Goldwyn's first malaprop was

printed by almost everybody who wrote about the world of amusements. Ending a conference one day, Sam is supposed to have uttered his famous, "Gentlemen, include me out."

In the years to follow, we "insiders" just didn't believe all the garbled English attributed to Sam. We knew, or figured we knew, that his entire staff was inventing Sam's literary scrambling to get his name in the papers, an accomplishment Goldwyn never derided. The Goldwynisms, as they came to be known, started to pop all over.

"The girl is colossal in a small way," he was quoted as saying of an actress. "A verbal agreement isn't worth the paper it's written on," he told a dismissed actor. "A director is always biting the hand that lays the golden egg," an interviewer quoted him. "You can get all the Indians you want from the reservoir," he advised a casting assistant. "Don't tell me the story is too caustic," he was supposed to tell his advisors, "because I don't care how much it costs."

There were many more. As his perverse prose came to be accepted by Hollywood historians as though it were the hand-writing on the wall, Goldwyn often turned his analytical pronunci-amentos to matters outside his ken. When the Suez debacle occurred he was disconsolate. "If Disraeli were alive," he said, "he would be turning over in his grave."

Communism, he feared, "was spreading like wildflowers." He couldn't see why there was so much tension in so many lives. "Anybody who goes to a psychiatrist," he offered "should have his head examined." He got mad at one of our national leaders because the fellow was "always taking the bull between the teeth." He came East to see the play *Tea and Sympathy* under the impression that it was titled *Tea and Crumpets.*

And then, as he got into his seventies (he turned eighty-eight in 1970) he apparently decided that he needed a new image. He began denying that he ever asked to be included out, and he named the man who originally was supposed to have uttered that. He would tell interviewers that, being a man born in Warsaw as Samuel Goldfisch and a former glove salesman of little education, he doubtless did make mistakes in English and grammar. But the malaprops? Just things other people thought up to make him colorful or, in some cases, to embarrass him.

Of course, we wise guys had known this all along. Sam was not our favorite comedian or our favorite anything else. Possibly because, at one time or another, some of us had gone through the trying experience of trying to write or work for him. Just a fraud, we said. Always had been.

So then Goldwyn made one of his promotional trips East to hawk one of his glorious movies, and I happened to be on hand at a Dutch Treat luncheon where the other speaker was a Washington newspaperman. It was at the time of Dwight Eisenhower's first run for President. A man named Richard Nixon was up for Vice President.

If you will remember, there was a brief but potentially dangerous brouhaha over who from or how much or where Nixon had gotten some of his campaign funds. Eisenhower, as was his wont, was sitting back and letting the affair settle itself. The Washington expert told us what he thought was Eisenhower's attitude, what he predicted about the Nixon embarrassment and then made other predictions which, as so often with Washington seers, later proved groundless.

With the dessert I noted that Sam, on the dais, was in deep whispering conversation with the Washington prophet. That's Sam all over, I thought. He's trying to get a plug for his picture from Eisenhower.

But, getting our coats at the checkroom, I happened to be standing behind Sam as he was telling an aide what the Washington oracle had told him in confidence at the table.

"Eisenhower told him," Sam said with all confidence, "and I quote: 'That boy Nixon has to be as clean as a hen's tooth.'"

DIRTY JOKE

When the producer-composer and very bright fellow, Billy Rose, was married to the great comedienne Fanny Brice, Billy put on his first Aquacade (later to be the smash of the first New York World's Fair) out in Cleveland, Ohio. For a star he hired the legendary backstroke swimmer and true beauty, Eleanor Holm. Soon word drifted back to New York that Mr. Rose had developed a personal interest in Miss Holm outside the water and, while such rumor often fails to stand up to the facts, this whisper had a solid basis as can be recorded by the fact that Mr. Rose later married Miss Holm and the marriage lasted a goodly number of years.

However, with Rose and Miss Holm in Cleveland, Fanny Brice was committed to Hollywood film and radio work. It was inevitable, of course, that good friends would bring her the bad news. So, after having her husband trailed around Cleveland, one night she got the whereabouts of Rose's exact location. She picked up a phone, called a hotel in Cleveland and asked for Miss Holm's apartment.

Like a chump, Billy answered the phone.

"Billy, what on earth are you doing *there?*" demanded Fanny Brice Rose.

"Why . . . uh . . . why nothing, just playing cards with some of the cast," stumbled her husband.

Fanny made no accusations, no more questions, nothing. She just made small talk about the Rose show and her own activities and hung up. But Billy knew *something* was wrong, and he hurried out to Hollywood the next day. He arrived at the connubial home, took Fanny to dinner, and afterward they went home and talked some more. Finally Fanny undressed and got in their bed. Rose, too, undressed. But he sat on the edge of the bed, nervously talking some more, waiting to see if a blow would strike. Nothing.

At last, Fanny Brice used to tell friends delightedly, he got out of his robe and picked up the end of the sheets on his side of the bed, preparatory to crawling in beside his wife. It was then Fanny spoke, clearly and firmly:

"Don't you bring that water snake in here with me!" she ordered. The divorce came in a few weeks.

The Innkeeper

NEW YORK PROBABLY HAD FAR more first-class restaurants back in the 1930s than it has today, although restaurants in the former era had to fight a thing called the Depression. In those days, too, there was night life in the city, and the nightclubs, believe it or not, furnished conversation and newspaper stories, legends and anecdotes. New York, at least the midtown part of it, seemed to live more at night than during working hours. Of all the feeding troughs of the era, there were two nightclubs and three restaurants that probably furnished more newspaper copy and conversational grist than all the others together.

The restaurants were the aforementioned Vincent Sardi's, Toots Shor's and Jim (Dinty) Moore's. The nightclubs were Sherman Billingsley's Stork Club and John Perona's El Morocco. It would be a tough chore indeed to find five more dissimilar men who operated with high success in the same business with such perversely different personalities and approaches. If one could have put them all at one table—which would have been a physical impossibility—and let them talk, one might have thought he was listening in at a subcommittee UN security meeting of the ambassadors of five countries, each virtually at war with all the others.

Vincent Sardi, Sr., who died a few months ago at age 83, was an old-world gentleman who ran his restaurant with quiet and comfort and respect for his customers, who were also his friends. Jim Moore was another old-world gent, but from a different background. He had been a vegetable huckster on the West Side, and even in his advanced age he was almost always belligerent, particularly toward his best customers. Toots Shor is the only restaurateur in my memory who could and would—and occasionally still will—outdrink his customers. This is almost 100 percent fatal in restaurant operation, but Toots's following not only includes the sports mob but also highly placed pals in areas you would not expect to find them.

Billingsley and Perona shared only one motivation—their jealousy and mistrust of each other. Perona's place was the rallying point for the then international set and the more exotic flowers of society. If Billingsley's oasis could have found the ideal patron, it would have been Frank Merriwell or the chairman of the board of the All-American National Bank. Perona's favored guests sat in banquettes against the wall, where they could be amused by the antics of the lower echelon at the crowded ringside tables. Billingsley put his stars in a special small room, the Cub Room, where they could admire each other.

But the most complete anachronism, in a business depending on the goodwill of the public, was old Jim Moore. He, his wife and his brother-in-law opened the restaurant on West 46th Street the year Montgomery and Stone opened *The Wizard of Oz* across the street at the Globe Theatre. All you youngsters must remember that night, 1903, only sixty-seven years ago. The three originals of the Moore clan are dead several years now, but the white-tiled restaurant, which still snubs neon lighting for bright, old-fashioned white bulbs, is still in very active performance under a surviving daughter, Anna.

In Old Jim's day, directly in front of the entrance to the restaurant, blocking arriving cabs, limousines and private cars, stood his black Packard touring car. Remember the touring cars? They had side curtains and running boards. Moore's was elegant enough for a bank president or a Chicago mob chieftain. It was used mostly to take him back and forth to the Polo Grounds, where his pal John McGraw ran the baseball Giants.

It was used for one more bit of travel—Moore would get up at dawn, stick a roll of money in his pocket, and his chauffeur would tool him down to the market district. There he would inspect, and finally buy for cash, the biggest baking potatoes available, or the best onions or something else particularly good. He paid cash on purchase, not weeks or months later, so whenever a marketman had some particularly oversize item, he would get on the phone and call Jim. Moore would be there in the morning.

Trucking was no problem. Moore would have the potatoes or onions or carrots or cabbages loaded into the back end of the Packard, and the chauffeur would tool the vegetables and their owner back to the parking space at the restaurant front door. Often the long black car would stand there for hours, spilling an occasional Idaho or Bermuda onto the sidewalk.

Inside, things weren't so easy. Moore died in 1952 at the age of eighty-four. For possibly forty of the last of these years he did not speak to his wife, his son Willie Moore, and one or more of his three daughters. It was a house divided, although at one time all the Moores lived in separate apartments in the building that houses the restaurant, which they owned. All used the private elevator from their apartments down to the restaurant on a careful schedule.

Old Jim's territory was the restaurant proper. Willie commanded the bar. Out in the bright, immaculate tile kitchen, Mrs. Moore sat in her wheelchair and her dark glasses. The obergruppenfuehrer of Moore waiters was a flat-footed veteran named Moran. Every once in a while Moore would order Moran to stop serving customers and join him in a far corner of the kitchen for a game of pinochle.

Moore would argue with anybody, including his dearest customer. He worshiped Al Smith, at the time of the following pastiche a recent governor of New York, and Smith was a steady customer whenever in town. This time Moore kept haranguing Smith on how to run the state until Smith threw down his napkin in disgust.

"Moore," he said firmly, "I've known you for forty years and in all that time you haven't been right once."

Moore turned to the hushed, crowded restaurant.

"Al should never be in politics," he told the room. Smith nearly laughed himself off the chair.

Moore was also devoted, for some reason, to the two Chinese

who ran his downstairs men's room. Once he received the news that one had been arrested for smoking opium. He got right on one of the phones—both phones in Moore's were and are right out in the open—and called New York's mayor, Bill O'Dwyer. O'Dwyer checked into the arrest and reported he could do nothing because it was a Federal narcotics squad pinch and thus beyond his control.

"You round-headed chump," Moore hollered at the mayor over the phone. "You want to be governor of New York and you can't even get a Chinaman out of jail."

Old Jim was an enthusiastic analyst of all athletes and was somewhat critical of the talents of former heavyweight champ Gene Tunney. "All you ever had was good health," he told Tunney one night.

Tunney's good health probably came from a different source than Old Jim got his, which was out of a bottle of castor oil kept at the bar. He was convinced it was the complete panacea. When he went to the bar and reached for his castor oil, veteran barflies would clear away from the area. Jim was more than apt to make them take some oil with their brandy.

Toward the very end he began to feel more and more poorly and, for the first time, his doctor made him stay in bed for a couple of days. He reappeared in the restaurant with a wondering, betrayed look.

"The oil failed me," he complained.

Almost up to the end, he was convinced that he could have been a baseball star for McGraw if life had taken a different turn or two. He would get up from the table, bend double and make a sweep along the floor with both hands. "That's the way to field a ground ball," he would explain.

He would not only insult and argue with his best customers but would frequently drive them into the street. He abused the Hollywood agent Billy Grady into leaving in a huff because Billy wanted the liver without the bacon. You could get thrown out, conversationally, for ordering rare hamburger or fried or sautéed fish. Once a misguided epicure tried to tell Moore how to prepare striped bass. He didn't even get to the sauce.

"That's for dagos," Old Jim told him.

One summer night a Supreme Court justice and his family, old friends of Moore's, or at least so they thought, sat at the big table at the head of the bar. The table is against the big French windows of the 46th Street front. The justice leaned over and opened the window for some fresh air. Sitting back in the room, Moore watched this and sent Moran to close the window. Moran did. When he left, the justice opened it again. Moore sent Moran back. There was some dialogue. The judge scowled back at Moore, rose with his family and left the restaurant. Moran came back to the boss's table.

"The party left," he said accusingly.

"Good," said Moore. "He's been coming in here for twenty-five years and I never did like him."

One must wonder why such old and solid customers would ever come back for more abuse and insult. The answer, probably, was that Moore's was and is one of the best restaurants for solid, good food throughout this land. Lou Holtz, the comedian, once swore he would never pass through its doors again. He was back in a week.

"I won't let that old bastard spoil my eating," he told everybody in hearing.

The family fights were sometimes equally funny on the surface, but a cause for sadness to any eavesdropper. Looking back, one wonders if there mustn't have been a deep sadness in all the participants. There was an unbending verboten against anybody giving Willie Moore, then in his full middle age, a drop of anything with alcohol in it. Nonetheless, Willie managed to get quite a bit of the stuff down his capable throat.

One night Old Jim faced Willie down and an argument ensued. Old Jim ended it by slugging his son with a roll of nickels he had hidden in his hand. Willie went down. He got up and seemed more amazed than hurt.

"To think," he told the shocked room, "that a man his age would use a cheap hoodlum trick like that. Who do you suppose taught him?"

On another night his mother sat in her wheelchair back in the kitchen and steadily watched her favorite child sneak drinks here and there. Around eleven o'clock she was wheeled to the elevator to be lifted up to bed. Her pride and joy came over to dutifully say goodnight. She listened, smiled and nodded. Then Willie leaned down to kiss mater goodnight.

She gave him a belt in the nose with all she could put behind her right fist.

Priests, judges, counselors, doctors, famous folk all tried to heal the family wounds over many a year. Never to any avail. There were observers who believed that quarelling kept the two old folks alive. If they ever let down, was the theory, they would simply wither away. There was the night when an argument involving almost the entire family threatened to erupt into real violence. A famed theatrical producer got into the act, soothing everybody down, and for his pains got a bottle of ketchup and a bottle of mustard all over his nice sharkskin suit.

"Well," Mom giggled when the producer complained to her, "why didn't you mind your own business."

Willie Moore did have one fine triumph over the entire family, and it had to do, of all things, with World War II rationing. The government upon our entrance into war decreed that all spare automobile tires must be turned in for rubber reclamation. This of course split the Moore family on the destiny of the spare on the big black Packard. Three of them were for being patriotic, but Old Jim's side sneered. "I wouldn't give a perfectly good tire to that bockety-legged son of a bitch Roosevelt," he said firmly.

The argument waxed. One day it was noted that the spare was out of its well on the Packard's side. Willie appeared. He seemed satisfied with himself.

"I just threw the goddam tire in the Hudson River," he advised. The solution seemed to satisfy both sides. "People wonder why I drink," Willie said to the room at large.

The Moore attitude toward the war was almost as divided as the main combatants themselves. One night the whistles blew and we knew it was another blackout practice. All over Broadway lights darkened. Moran turned out the lights in Moore's, which are not only bright but bounce added light off the tiled ceiling and walls. Moore got up and flipped a switch that put the lights on in his section of the room. Soon a very serious air raid warden in white helmet was at the table.

"Get the hell out of here before I break your head," stormed Old Jim. The air raid warden said he would have to call a cop.

"I'll have him sent to Staten Island," promised Moore. Soon, sure enough, a young cop appeared with the warden. "Mr. Moore," he said respectfully, "it's a blackout. You must put out these lights."

"It's cowardice, that's what it is," Moore told him. "When Hitler starts coming up Eighth Avenue, that's when I'll worry."

"I'll have to take you in," said the young cop.

"Try it," suggested Moore. "I'll have your job and the job of that clown Valentine, your boss, too. Outside, son."

The cop and the air warden stood uncertainly, apparently torn between duty and the consequences of an old man's potential charges of harassment or even mishandling if he were to be forcibly moved. It was a bad situation. And then, from the darkened kitchen, came Mom's clear voice.

"Officer," she called clearly, "strike the lights out with your club."

Without a word, Old Jim got up, went to the switch and turned off the lights.

Old Jim Moore is long gone now, dead in 1952 at 84 years, right up to the end refusing to be called Dinty. That was what the town knew him as ever since George McManus brought fame to the place with every sequence in which Jiggs, of Jiggs and Maggie, left the cartoon strip "to go down to Dinty Moore's for corned beef and cabbage." The corned beef and cabbage to this day is enough to make anybody leave home.

Mrs. Moore departed this vale before her husband. To the amazement of us all, Willie Moore went on the wagon, became a successful restaurant operator on his own for many years, and died sober. One theory is that he stopped drinking when it no longer caused arguments with his father.

Anna Moore, an amiable and competent woman, ran the restaurant quietly for years. Neither its decor nor its kitchen, its bar nor its food, seemed to change an iota.

A lot of us miss the mad atmosphere of the old Moore's. But, of course, if a Jim Moore came along today, they'd computerize him.

The Clubkeepers

BACK IN THE YEARS WHEN THE doings, scamperings and flutterings of something called café society—and *that* is surely a self-contradictory description—caused the general reading, radio-listening and conversing general public to utter many "oohs" and "aahs," there were only two—count 'em, two—nightclubs that steadfastly over the years could point to a socially restricted trade and uninterrupted financial success. These two boîtes were John Perona's El Morocco and Sherman Billingsley's Stork Club. Within these unhallowed walls was café society born and nourished. Here social and professional reputations were made and broken. Here came the debutantes who would be tomorrow's social leaders. Here came princes and aristocracy from far-off lands. Here came the post-college young men who would soon take over Dad's big business.

And here, to sort them out, were two men without education or social background of any kind—except, perhaps, of the suspicious kind—each of whom sat near a guarded door at the entrance of his establishment and decided, on reason or whim, which applicant was "fit" to enter. The applicant admitted on any given night might be a no-account loafer who just happened to have the right friends, and the applicant denied might just as easily be a pillar of his community and the trustee of ancient wealth.

If the Stork Club had succeeded in knocking out El Morocco, or vice versa, we could look back and analyze how and why the great café of the era was designed and carried to its natural success. We could trace the methods, rules and modus operandi of the successful joint and set down a diagram for other operators to follow. The confusing truth, however, is that there could not have been two nightclubs more dissimilar than the Stork and Morocco.

There was one valid comparison. Each was not only owned and operated by a single personality but, in all truth, was fiercely *dominated* by a personality. Yet the very characteristic differences and viewpoints of Perona and Billingsley were so opposed that it is impossible to draw from them any common formula for success.

John Perona was a self-made millionaire of Italian birth. He wore soft, striped flannels of European cut, and his jewelry was delicate and expensive. He was reasonably handsome, talked fast and volubly, had mannerisms that were inclined to be nervous and somewhat jerky, displayed great physical energy, was gregarious, loved night life and was not averse to tipping the bottle with his cronies. He owned foreign cars and in the past tried to drive them before hiring top racing drivers. He was a gentleman farmer who took an atavistic joy out of growing things from the soil.

Sherman Billingsley was a self-made millionaire from Enid, Okla. He wore solid color suits of conservative, almost shapeless cut. He was nearly bald but almost handsome in a business-executive way. His talk was slow and controlled, his mannerisms deliberate. He managed to give the impression that he was either tired or aggrieved. Although possibly the most famous host in restaurant history, he was apt to be socially remote even with old customers. His close friends were few, his hobbies nonexistent. He had the veteran saloonkeeper's wariness toward alcohol and he seldom drank. He was a thoroughly unsuccessful gentleman farmer who ultimately had to abandon the fields.

Each ran his individual oasis on equally contradictory lines. El Morocco never opened until six in the afternoon because the boss was busy daytimes trying to outsmart the stock market or having his portrait painted by Salvador Dali or buying a new racing car. Or he might even stay at home all day and listen to the dozens of radios that were perched on almost every flat surface in his New Jersey home or his apartment across the street from his club.

There were no telephones in either of his habitats. A caller would be told by the club operator to "try again after nine o'clock."

Billingsley might arise much later in the day than his competitor. But from the moment he opened his eyes, every waking thought and act concerned the Stork Club. He would most likely appear at his place for the luncheon crowd, lunch being an important part of the Stork operation. Inevitably he could be found talking on one or another of the dozens of telephones he had cached around and about his creation. Although, somewhere in his past, he had acquired several pieces of midtown real estate, he seemed to look upon these holdings with a bilious eye. They were digressions from the main job. He always seemed vaguely annoyed when somebody phoned to buy or rent or lease one of his properties.

As children, the two entrepreneurs did have one thing in common. Billingsley would cheerfully admit to exactly four years of formal schooling. Perona would vaguely refer to his "elemental" education. Perona's professional education, however, included apprenticeships in some of the great eating places of Europe, which put him in the lifetime restaurateur class. Not so Billingsley. The latter was fond of remembering his first "job." His older brothers in Enid gave him a toy red wagon. He could keep it only if, once a week, he let them load it with "soda pop" and then he took it down and sold the bottles to the Indians. Since selling firewater to Indians was, and is, against the law, Billingsley could truthfully boast that at seven years of age he was the nation's youngest bootlegger.

Perona was somewhat evasive about his American career, but speakeasy contemporaries remember him as a leading light in the old Club Sportiva, which was a sort of recreational annex to the Unione Siciliano, now always referred to as the Mafia or Cosa Nostra. At one period he ran a West Side speak when Luis Angel Firpo was in New York to fight Jack Dempsey. Perona met Firpo and his friends. As a consequence, to the end of his career Perona held the rich and open-handed South American visiting trade.

Billingsley's career took an entirely different tangent. He ran drug stores. He operated garages. He sold and bought real estate. In 1928 two visiting Oklahoma friends decided to go into the booze and food business. Billingsley found them a spot on West 58th Street. The friends grew more and more nervous. They were country boys in the big city. They asked Billingsley to come in as a one-third partner.

"I told them," he would recall, "that the commission I would make on the lease would have to be bigger than what I would pay for a partnership. They agreed."

Perona's debut on the big time was, as might be surmised, somewhat different. In 1931 Federal agents were not only aggressively raiding speakeasies and locking up the owners, but they had also adopted the nasty habit of using axes to break up anything they could find in a joint. Perona, after a smashing raid, decided to make a bold move to the unexplored reaches of the East Side. He rented a ground floor at 154 East 54th Street. He hired Vernon MacFarlane to decorate it. He decided upon a "desert decor" because the more barren a speakeasy could be, the less expensive furniture would be obliterated by the heavy axes of the Federal snoops.

Meanwhile, Billingsley also had made the trek east. He abandoned one location because "it was too much up and down stairs" and settled in at 3 East 53rd Street. Hark now, to a series of small accidents and offhand, careless decisions that were to have future import, although they hardly contribute to the formal success story.

Let us consider, for instance, the origin of the names these men chose for their clubs. Perona pondered over such titles as the Desert, the Sahara and the Sands. His decorator, meanwhile, had worked out a pattern of blue and white zigzag stripes for banquettes and background. These reminded Perona of zebras and, for some mysterious reason, Morocco. There was another club in town named Morocco. "He once told me," says a veteran customer whose liver stood off nightly attendance at the place, "that he put the *El* in front of Morocco because the Third Avenue Elevated was just a few steps down the street."

The Stork Club label had been pinned on Billingsley's watering place before it took residence in its third and final location. Veteran waiters there contend that a forgotten customer once left a toy bird on the bar. It was placed behind the bar in case the drunk should return for it. It looked a little like a stork and customers began referring to the place as the Stork Club.

"I realize," Billingsley used to say, "that I should have dreamed up some colorful and romantic legend about the choice of the name. Actually, I can't remember how it got named. I forget why I picked it."

For more than twenty-five years, El Morocco and the Stork ran one-two, taken in either order. They shared a hard core of celebrity customers, but the overall clientele was as different as the two iron-fisted and hardheaded owners.

"We never give anything away," Perona would say, a note of contempt for such lunacy in his voice. "We feel that gifts would embarrass our customers."

"If I'm having a slow night," Billingsley once related, "I start bringing out the gifts with both hands. I send bottles of perfume after bottles of perfume, and instead of a bottle of champagne to good customers I send a magnum. That way when those people go out they are not saying the next day, 'Geez, it was slow in the Stork last night.' They're saying, 'How does he do it?' I know what I'm doing with gifts."

Of the two men, Perona, despite his rigid customer control and his adoration of the rich and social, was the antic member of the pair. It is possible that he thought of himself as something of an amateur comedian. He guffawed louder than anybody when Woolworth Donahue, a playboy whose manic didoes bored an entire generation of saloongoers, crawled into the hooded roast beef wagon and had himself trundled about the nightclub one late evening. He was hilarious when Michael Famer, onetime husband of Hollywood queens, had the men's room attendant bring articles to his prominent table so he could shave before dinner. He was even amused by the sight of heavyweight champion Max Baer crawling under tables with lighted matches to give friends a hot foot.

Such impolite gaucheries would have given Billingsley an immediate triple coronary attack. About the time Perona would be calling for another bottle of wine, Billingsley would be ordering more hot tea.

Of the two, also, Perona was indeed the most complex. One day he might be in a legal battle with the New York Health Department over—and this is a historical fact—the age of some prunes he was serving. That night he would be at the Metropolitan Opera with a millionaire customer-friend. Twice he was brought before magistrates for walloping, with his fist, unruly customers. A day or so later he would be named Knight Commander of the Order of Saints Victor and George by no less than the Pope for his "work in aiding the poor of Italy."

He was unpredictable in business. He originally rented the rooms that housed El Morocco for $350 a month. Twenty years later he would cringe with guilt when admitting that the rent had gone up to $2,500 a month. It apparently never occurred to him that, with all his success, he should have bought the building early in the club's history. Instead, he *did* buy the building across the street. The ground floor of that one almost immediately started to shelter a series of nightclubs, all of which did their damndest to steal away Perona customers.

Yet often what seemed his perversities had a way of returning unexpected dividends. For most of the club's bright history, a headwaiter named Carino stood at the entrance rope, with the assurance of a Marine sergeant and the analytical ability of a high-priced psychiatrist. He was gifted with a camera eye, an iron memory and a genius for "dressing" the room—which means spotting famous customers to the best possible advantage.

Why and how Perona and Carino worked out their master plan remains unfathomable. As much so as why Carino called himself Carino, which was his middle monicker, instead of Frank or Beccaris, which were his Christian and surnames. Everywhere else in the nightclub world, the classiest customers get the front tables. Perona and Carino somehow became convinced that the best tables in their club were not those crowding the small dance floor. Out there service was impeded and some overactive samba dancer might knock a glass of wine down milady's girdle.

So the curved banquettes became celebrity land, and you had to dance around the floor maybe twice before you realized that the girl half hidden by the curve of a wall seat backrest was Rita Hayworth and the thin woman a few places down was the Duchess of Windsor. "We have no show to watch and our best customers should be comfortable," was Perona's theory. "Of course, if they want a ringside table they can have it." Hardly any of them did.

Nor did the club have any identifying ashtrays on its tables. The background of those zigzag zebra stripes was more than enough to identify where the news photo was taken. You remember those stripes.

Very few truly funny anecdotes—as opposed to the many laughs launched in the Stork—came out of El Morocco, but one is remembered. A sailor from a Spanish ship in town, a seaman who must have been dressed in his churchgoing suit, was allowed in early one night.

He had himself a chicken dinner and two bottles of red wine. When a sixty dollar cheque was presented, the sailor copped a pauper's plea and was hauled off to night court. The sailor said that he thought he had gone to a Spanish restaurant because of its name. The magistrate wearily dismissed the charge.

"For sixty dollars at El Morocco," opined the learned judge, who indeed may have been there himself on occasion, "this defendant probably didn't cheat the place out of much more than a club sandwich."

Contrast this story with one involving the often dour but also very complex Sherman Billingsley. One day Billingsley got a letter from a sailor on an aircraft carrier. The sailor admitted that he had bragged to his pals that he hung out at the Stork all the time and "the boss" was a great pal of his. Please, wrote the sailor, when the carrier docked at New York shortly could he come over and just get through the door? All his pals would follow him, ready to laugh and humiliate him if he was turned away.

Billingsley promptly wrote back inviting his "pal" to be sure and come in and have dinner as soon as he made port. Bring some friends, too. The sailor arrived, bringing fourteen shipmates. Billingsley served them dinner and booze. There was no check, he explained, for his old pal.

Unlike Perona, who did not even own his own store, Billingsley owned every inch of the eight-story building that housed his club. Before the bitter labor strike that ended the Stork's history and ultimately brought Billingsley's fatal heart attack, it was a fabulously valuable property.

"I don't know exactly what it's worth," Billingsley would contend, "but I know I've refused $850,000 for it."

It was the seventh floor of the building, to most old-timers who knew the clubrooms as familiarly as their own homes, that was the most colorful of all. This was the private lair of "the Boss" himself. After you were admitted by the club guardian—the Stork had nothing so common as a velvet rope, it had a gold chain—you reached the residence by elevator, rising past the twelve accountants, the banquet rooms, the radio and TV studio, the carpentry shop and the rooms for private parties. There was also a floor devoted to the perfume business which, for years, entranced Arthur Godfrey, Morton Downey, Steve Hannagan and a rather reluctant Billingsley as fourth partner with his pals.

You could find almost any facility in the Boss's lair. There was a phone in every corner. There was a closet with twenty freshly pressed suits and dozens of neckties, all kept in Beau Brummel perfection by a tailor who worked in a tiny room with his spotting, cleaning and pressing tools. There was a machine that whirled coins around and separated them into compartments. There was an old-fashioned bathtub with reading board and lamp. There were bureaus of haberdashery. There was a monastic single bed. There were more unusual articles.

A rather esoteric gadget was his special chair. He would insist, with the eagerness of a child, that his visitor sit in it. Then he twisted dials and flipped switches and the chair would vibrate, rock, roll, tilt and bounce like an old trolley at high speed. He would thrust another gimmick in your hand, turn another dial and the gimmick would get warm.

"See how good it makes your hand feel?" he would cry, his face alight. "Wait till you get out of the chair and see how rested you are. It's better than a night's sleep."

During the last years of the Stork, Billingsley brought a small dog in from the country, meaning to give it to a customer. He instead fell in love with the puppy himself. One day he reached to pet it and the puppy cowered. This convinced Billingsley that somebody had abused it. Up in front of the elevator went one of the typical handprinted "S. B." signs. It read: "God damn it! Anybody who hits or kicks this dog I will hit or kick back. S. B."

The "S. B." signs could be found almost any place out of sight of the paying customers. The kitchen had a full collection. A typical one might be: "God damn it! Son of a bitch! How many times have I said if a customer wants a baked apple and we don't have it go the the restaurant down the street and buy one. God damn it! Son of a bitch! S. B." Underneath it would be another: "God damn it! Son of a bitch! I said when a customer, etc. . . . ."

On the reverse side of his personality coin, he had many shrewd and perceptive ideas about the running of a saloon.

"You take when a place is filled," he explained once. "Three or four people get up and leave. Then another party leaves. It's catching. Soon half the people in the place have decided to leave. The idea is to stop the exodus. That's when I start buying drinks and sending bottles of champagne to the tables."

There were other reasons for his openhandedness.

"How much does Dorothy Lamour get for a guest appearance?" he once asked a newspaperman.

"Oh," said the writer, "probably about $5,000."

"Well," said the delighted Billingsley, "tonight she's making a guest appearance here free. And she's not going to end her guest appearance as long as I keep sending perfume and wine to her table."

His eye for detail approached the fantastic. One night he sat at Table 50, the home base for Walter Winchell and always reserved for the biggest name in the place, speared a shrimp with his fork, got it halfway to his mouth, stared at the plate, put the shrimp back and commanded the presence of his chef. On the double. To Table 50.

Gabriel Beaumont, the Parisian kitchen aristocrat with his profession's blue ribbon, came up from below decks ready to answer thrust with riposte. Billingsley fairly snarled at him.

"What's wrong with this shrimp cocktail?" he demanded.

"There's nothing wrong with it," Beaumont gritted back.

Billingsley repeated the question. Same answer. It began to sound like an old Dutch comedy act. Billingsley scowled at the cocktail and then his face slowly softened. There ensued a long technical discussion on the merits of the lettuce, the shaved ice, shape of receptacle, color of doily and napkin and God knows what all. Billingsley's basic theme was that the cocktail just didn't *look* right.

"I know what it is," Billingsley said finally, his face lighting up. "There isn't *enough* of it!"

The crisis was resolved. Henceforth the Stork Club shrimp cocktails had six shrimps instead of five.

His distrust of anybody else being in charge of any feature of his club was such that he took over the hatcheck, rest room and cigarette concessions himself and shared the profits with a club employee he installed to run same. Nellie Fitzgerald, the ladies' room attendant, was considered the ideal choice because she had been nurse to one of the Billingsley daughters until daughter no longer needed a nurse.

And then there was the three-act drama over how much whiskey should go in a bar glass. First, the bar had been serving drinks in glasses that had a line almost at the rim. As these nearly full glasses were pushed at customers, Billingsley noticed that some of the whiskey would slop over on the bar. So the padrone threw out all the bar glasses and bought bigger ones that had a line well below the rim. He instructed the barmen to fill the glasses to the line only. It was not that he worried about giving a customer an excessive portion. He didn't want that whiskey slopped.

The barmen, out of long habit, kept forgetting. Billingsley raved and ranted. The bartenders denied all guilt. They had many and varied answers and excuses. Billingsley instituted a series of fines, but since he couldn't watch the bar all the time, he had to have a monitor.

Thus it was that one morning after everybody had left, a crew of workmen arrived and replaced the mirror behind the bar. They replaced it with one of those one-way see-through mirrors. Behind it they set up a movie camera. Beside this camera, for several weeks, sat a Billingsley employee with notebook and pad. At the end of a convincing period, Billingsley assembled his barmen, showed them the film and the spy's notes as to time and occasion and levied his fines.

The whole thing must have cost him hundreds of dollars and probably didn't save him a dime. But it helped convince the barmen that when the boss wanted something done his way it was going to be done that way.

He seemed to have a special antenna for anything relating to his nightclub. "Tell the orchestra leader," he instructed captain Gregory Pavlives, whose only duty was to follow the boss around and transmit messages, "not to play sad music on a sad night." Another time, without apparently looking, he observed that the hatcheck girl near the entrance door was jigging up and down because of the chill coming through the open door. "Tell that girl to stop dancing," he ordered Gregory. "This is not the Harvest Moon Ball."

As Billingsley moved about his club, Gregory would follow at a discreet distance, never taking his eyes from the boss. Often no words were exchanged. Commands were given by an intricate code of hand signals. If Billingsley pulled one ear, for instance, Gregory would materialize at the table and rescue the boss from a bore with the message that the boss had a phone call.

There is one funny story that inclines a historian to the conviction that Billingsley somehow thought he owned and ran the entire block of East 53rd Street. When two former lieutenants opened the Harwyn Club, Billingsley was furious. He got himself into an even worse pet when a captain, remembered only as Red, left the Stork for the new competitor. Red took the subway downtown every afternoon, got off at 53rd Street and walked west to his new employment. This route brought him past the Stork Club.

One afternoon Leo Spitzel, Billingsley's day adjutant, came running down the street after Red. Catching up with the deserter, Spitzel told him firmly, "The boss doesn't want you to walk on 53d Street."

For a man who was running a social establishment, he had definite and prejudicial ideas. He despised the exotic, the erotic and the noticeably foreign. The gigolo type raised his hackles, and he was deeply allergic to Latin specimens. He liked true-blue, All-American types. He would prefer a Hollywood starlet eating and drinking free to an overage Aly Khan spending money but wearing hair too long and striped suits in extreme cuts.

Once an old customer called him for a reservation for a party that would include the Maharajah of Jaipur, one of the richest princes in the world.

"I don't want none of those colored men in here," said Billingsley flatly.

The customer, aghast, pointed out that the maharajah was not only one of the world's richest men but one of the most important royalties in the East.

"He's still colored," Billingsley insisted, ending the conversation.

Of course, the maharajah was taken to El Morocco where Perona practically tore the place apart to impress and entertain him. But then, of course, Perona was also "a foreigner" in Billingsley's eyes. And the maharajah was just another Indian. Billingsley remembered Indians from his boyhood. To him the only good Indian was a dead Indian.

In all the great years of the Stork Club, Billingsley never took a single advertisement in any publication. He would give a donation to a charity affair rather than take an ad in the program. The vast publicity he received over the years was all free. In the earliest days, he remembered, he did take some ads in college magazines, which he paid for not with money but with food and soft drinks when the college editors came to the club.

Many of these kids were rich and social. They talked about the place and their parents came. As the years passed, "the kids" grew up to be executives on their own. They kept coming. All clean-cut American types, Billingsley would proudly point out.

Some of these clean-cut youngsters could, however, get a little exuberant. Bing Crosby, who eschewed neckties for the inevitable sports shirts, would be admitted to the Stork, but a necktie would be ostentatiously brought to Bing at his table. So one night when one of the clean-cut kids arrived without a necktie, he was sternly informed that he wouldn't get through the door until he had properly knotted the house necktie that was produced.

This seemed to annoy the young man but he complied. He joined his party at the table and immediately became one of the most enthusiastic dancers on the floor.

It was a half hour or more before a captain wildly reported to Billingsley that the clean-cut young man was dancing *in his stocking feet!*

The demise of both the El Morocco and the Stork Club was predictable. Perona lived to see his landlord take over the East 54th Street building that he had negligently failed to buy at rock-bottom Depression prices. He moved to a new and bigger location on Second Avenue and died in 1961, shortly after the new place was launched. He was sixty-four years old. The "new" El Morocco has been operated by one or more or a "syndicate" of owners, but the sheen and the glamour are different, if not, indeed, gone.

Perona died before realizing his greatest dream, which had nothing to do with his or anybody else's nightclub. His dream was to stage the biggest international automobile race in history. Where? Why, in New York's Central Park. Where else?

The death rattle of the Stork Club was more prolonged and even more painful. In 1956 the waiter's union tried to organize the club. This was akin to Chiang Kai-shek telling Mao that Chiang's army would henceforth police China. For ten years Billingsley bitterly fought the union, one man against the trend of the times. His customers and his help slowly drifted away. He became more and more embittered. He kept up his stubborn, fatally expensive solo war for a whole decade. Then one night he told his secretary not to bother coming in next day. He closed the door for the last time.

He died in his sleep in 1966. He was sixty-six years old. Once a millionaire, he had previously provided for his family. Friends, enemies and just plain snoops wondered how much money he had left. It appeared that there was no will. It further appeared that he had nothing to leave.

After his death the club premises were bought by William Paley, head of the Columbia Broadcasting System. Paley razed the building and installed a charming and restful little "vest pocket park" dedicated to his father. It is, in a sense, still an oasis in the crash and clatter of midtown New York.

Perona and Billingsley, nearly of an age, grew and flourished in the same era. It was an era the like of which we will not know again.

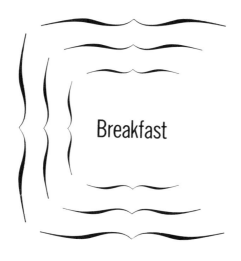

Breakfast

WALTER CATLETT IS A COMEDIAN
who is long gone and scarce remembered, but he was funny
enough to star in *The Ziegfeld Follies* and later to be a stalwart in
the early talking movies. On stage or on screen, on East Coast or
West, Walter was a man never exactly frightened by the sight of a
bottle of whisky. Back in the early and mid-1930s when they were
making films in the makeshift studios out in Astoria, Long Island,
Catlett was signed to play a lead role in one. The night before he
was to report, he hung over the bar of an actors' club and got
himself thoroughly stoned. Friends tried to warn him and slow him
down because, then as now, movie making starts early in the
morning.

When it became evident that Walter was smashed, two friends got
him home to his small apartment, put him to bed, went home and
went to bed themselves, and set their own alarm clocks. With cock
crow the two pals got up and rushed to Catlett's pied-à-terre to
make sure the comedian answered the studio roll call. Getting him
awake and on his feet was a Gargantuan chore in itself.

And then everybody was faced with a more acute crisis. Nobody
could find Walter's false teeth, neither upper plate nor lower. The
small apartment was combed as thoroughly as a police shakedown
could have done. It was only two rooms with bath and

kitchenette. No teeth. Even Walter, having had a nip for breakfast, couldn't understand where the choppers were hiding. Everybody agreed that he had all his teeth in his mouth the night before.

Walter's only roommate was a big tom cat named, of course, Harrigan and Hart (great comic names of an even earlier era), and as the search continued and the clock ran on inexorably, Harrigan and Hart kept rubbing up against everybody's legs and meowing loudly.

"What's the matter with the damn cat?" one pal finally asked.

"Oh," said Walter, "he hasn't been fed. There's a piece of liver for him in the refrigerator."

So a friend went to the refrigerator, opened same, and sure enough, the sole content was a fairly big piece of beef liver and clamped into it, like a vise, were Walter Catlett's false teeth.

Sometime during the night Walter had decided to have a bite of breakfast.

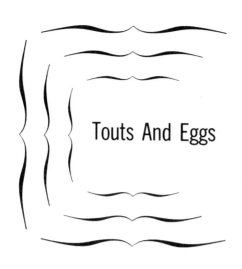

Touts And Eggs

THE CLASSIC DAMON RUNYON adage that "all hoss players must die broke" has been accepted as gospel over the years. Among racetrack touts, a dying breed born to live on its wits, there was also a descriptive proverb, "You can't educate a sucker." Translated, as applicable to their own field, it means that a true horse player will keep falling for myths and fairy tales no matter how many times he get financially burned, ruined or crippled. To the tout of the "great" era—a time when street and telephone bookmakers were always near enough to take an immediate bet—a confirmed horse player was "an egg." When a tout said he "layed an egg," he didn't mean he came a cropper. He meant that he had found a "sucker" who was hooked on horse betting.

There is still a truism often heard around the racetrack. Asked how some stubborn horse player—known to the trade as a "degenerate"—can be out there betting when it is well known that recent gambling has cost him his wife, car, home and business, the veteran horse player merely shrugs and points out that "a real horse player can always find money."

The Kefauver hearings, in the early 1950s, brought new laws and police activity that broke up bookmaking as it had existed for generations. In the old days there was not only a bookmaker in every corner candy store (and another on the corner sidewalk), but there were large and well-organized credit operations. These latter bookmakers had offices across the Hudson River in New Jersey, but they had somehow prevailed upon the New York Telephone Company to give them midtown Manhattan phone numbers.

You called your contact, who had been recommended by a horse-playing friend, and made your bets over the phone. Mondays the bookmaker's man called on you—just like the elegant and gentlemanly Tattersall Clubs in England—and either handed you some money or took some from you. The Jersey bookie ring was, in fact, a much safer operation for the horse player. Whenever a Jersey bookie got overloaded with bets on one horse—giving them what is for some reason known to their trade as "a Dutch book"—a stooge got on the long distance phone and "laid off" the appropriate percentage of the overbet in Boston or Cincinnati or Chicago or even with the bookmaker down the street who didn't have so much action on the overbet horse.

This was called "laying off." It protected the book and the player. Today horse betting is more dangerous and confused. If you find a furtive bookmaker and manage to beat him out of, say, $2,000, you will hurry around to collect.

He won't be there. You are unlikely to ever see him again.

Horse racing, both flat and harness, has made such strides in recent years—indeed, flat racing is now virtually a state project in New York—and television, publicity, advertising, *et al.* have so broadened and extended horse race fans and track attendance, that the harried street bookmaker and, of course, the Jersey operators are mostly memory. This condition has, of course, more or less knocked the old-fashioned tout out of action.

Once it was different. Touts were all over, and it must be admitted that most of them had vivid imaginations. Here are two tout routines I remember that worked very well indeed for many a year:

A known horse player, always a rather heavy bettor, would be in his office when a visitor would be announced. The visitor was calling at the request of "a famous jockey." The horse player could hardly wait to have him ushered in. The visitor would glance over his shoulder, ask if the room was bugged, get assurances that the horse player was truly interested in winning a nice bet. He would then open his briefcase or small suitcase and bring forth a jockey's whip.

But not just an ordinary whip. The tout would take it apart, revealing wires and a battery all well hidden but guaranteed capable of giving a running horse an electric shock that would make him run even faster. This was known as "a buzzer."

"This is the whip Eddie Arcaro [or Eric Guerin or Ted Atkinson or whichever jock] is going to use on his horse in a race tomorrow," the tout would whisper.

It was amazing how many times in a single day this ploy would work. The price for this inside info? The bettor would buy a specified number of winning tickets for the tout.

There were more sophisticated approaches that took more time and study and were never wasted on any "egg," but only on one known to be a very high player indeed. The touts—they almost always worked in pairs and called themselves "partners"—would study the daily routine of the high player. If, for instance, he was in the habit of having a couple of drinks at a railroad station bar prior to boarding his commuter train, the touts would wait for the right day and time when they could range next to him at the bar.

They would never speak to him or, apparently, even see him. Their conversation would go thisaway:

"I got a letter from Eddie Arcaro today" (or George Woolf or Bill Boland or even a leading trainer), the first would tell his partner. "Here, want to read it?" He would hand it over. His partner would look at it and laugh.

"Why does he always write in that green ink?" he would say rather loudly. "He always uses that green ink. Well, he's a great little guy. He's made me a lot of money over the years."

The two pals would finish their drinks and immediately depart. Not until a few days later, when the egg at the bar had almost forgotten the conversation, would he get a letter. A letter written in green ink.

"Knowing that you are a fan of racing," it would start, "and having been given your name by one of your friends who is a friend of mine but whom I had better not identify, you may be interested in seeing an associate of mine who will call and make a date with you in a day or so." The letter would be signed, in green ink of course, Eddie Arcaro or whoever. The "associate" of the green-ink correspondent would indeed call in a few days. He would bear tidings of a race that was a sure win at good odds and, of course, nobody else knew about it. They were letting the egg in on the coup because he was a friend of the unidentified friend, etc., ad infinitum.

If the horse won, everybody made a bundle. And if the gag could be—and often was—worked on eight different eggs for eight different races on the same day, at least one egg did make a score. And so did the touts. For the others, there was always "the story."

Ah, the story. How often has it been used in its untold mutations. "The horse stepped on its stifle coming round the turn." "He got caught in an air pocket." "Didn't you see it? Didn't you see that clown assistant starter hang onto his tail in the gate too long?" "You mean you didn't see him claim foul after the winning jockey hit our horse in the eye with his whip?" There were countless variations.

The degenerate horseplayer, being the egg that he is (and was), would surprisingly accept "the story" and listen to the tout's next caper. It was amazing how often a good tout, having his egg firmly layed with the foundation of the green-ink operation, could keep a sucker going with the losing "story."

The standard form of the tout game, however, was at the track itself, and since it was first devised it has also been the basic caper racetrack cops are seeking. Again, it needs two men, this time called the "Inside Man" and the "Outside Man." Amusingly, their roles are reversed as the swindle goes along. Also, the game is never worked on the veteran bettor, who has been bitten by it long years ago, but on anybody who looks confused and/or yokelish enough to be a beginner at the race game.

This bemused stranger to the exciting world of betting money is approached by the Outside Man. The latter sidles up with an almost whispered: "Say, mister, pardon me. You didn't see who that big guy over there bet on, did you?"

He points to a fellow nearby, an angry looking specimen who is carefully counting a huge stack of tickets in his hands. He is the Inside Man. Our bumpkin says no, he didn't see what horse that man over there bet on. He never even saw him before.

"You know who that is?" demands the Outside Man. "That's Big

Jack Banner. He bets all the money for the syndicate. Yesterday they won more than a hundred thousand."

Our innocent looks again at the big gambling man just out of earshot. The inside man sighs a little. "He won't tell us nothing, I guess," he says plaintively. "But, what the hell, let's ask him. Come on." He takes our victim over to Big Jack, nudges Mr. Innocent in the ribs and whispers, "Ask! You ask."

"M-M-Mister Banner," says our yokel, "could you give me some advice on how to bet?"

Mr. Banner swings on the intruders. He glares at the Inside Man and then snarls at him. "I told you to stay away from me," he almost hollers. "We don't want you hanging around and using our information. You did it before and it knocked the payoff odds way down. Get away from me! Both of you!"

Then he turns to our lambkin.

"Are you with this man?" he demands.

"I never saw him," says our hero, atremble but his own anger rising. "I've only been to a racetrack a couple of times."

Big Jack looks toward the Outside Man. Our victim looks toward the Outside Man. Or, rather, where he had been standing. The Outside Man has disappeared. Big Jack's voice and face soften a little.

"Well," he says, somewhat conciliatory, "you seem like an honest man. I'm sorry I was rude," He pauses, thinking. "Maybe I can help you," he decides. "Come with me."

He walks our innocent to the $10 window and says sharply, "How much money have you got?" The bumpkin pulls out his wallet. This is his big mistake. Big Jack just takes it out of his hand. Maybe our innocent planned to plunge five dollars instead of his usual two on this wondrous, inside information, but instead he finds himself betting all or most of what he's got. If he insists on keeping some of his own money he will be worked on again.

"See me before the next race," Big Jack growls and disappears.

Now the Inside Man becomes the Outside Man, and soon the Outside Man will become the Inside Man. From now until the race is over, the new chore of the new Outside man is to shadow the egg and, if he should win the race, be right there at his shoulder to make sure he goes back to Big Jack and hands over the rather stiff cut that will be demanded. If the horse loses, Big Jack disappears and so does his confederate.

It is merely necessary for them to note where the innocent has taken position. Then the two touts move their operation to another part of the track. A racetrack is of necessity a big place. With a crowd.

In the half hour between races, a good original Outside Man may steer three or even four yokels to Big Jack, who will tout four different horses. In such a case, when the Outside Man changes assignment he needn't shadow four different bettors. He just stands at the cashiers' windows until he sees the one winner—if there is one winner. Then he steers the euphoric winner back to Big Jack for the next inside info. Rather, he steers him to where Big Jack can pick him up. After all, the steerer is in Big Jack's doghouse.

Often this hoary ploy is dressed up with all sorts of trim. The Outside Man may be wearing jodhpurs or even riding boots and may be small enough to be a jockey or exercise boy. Big Jack may be sportily or at least handsomely dressed, and he has that big stack of tickets in his hand, the numbers carefully covered. A big stack of mutual tickets can be had by anybody who wants to bend over and pick them off the floor or lawn of a track. Big Jack even may be seen talking—and this is always a lucky turn—with a well-known trainer or somebody with an official button in his lapel.

The trainer will be real and the man with the button is official, but what Jack is talking to them about is what time it is or how is the best way to get to the first-aid room or the secretary's office.

This "double touting" has infuriated the Pinkertons and racetrack police for years. The villains caught at it are photographed and identified and fingerprinted and barred from the track. With racing drawing more and more sophisticated crowds and track police more numerous and efficient, the Inside and Outside Men are seldom encountered on a major race course these days. But veterans who travel the racing circuit say they are still in action at small meets, hunt courses and bush tracks.

The racetrack tout could never operate, of course, without a supply of material at hand, any more than an artist can paint without pigments or a carpenter work without wood. The material of the tout is the seemingly inexhaustible supply of inveterate horse players.

The inveterate horse player lives up to the adage about a sucker being uneducatable but, as a variance, it is truly said that "a sucker don't want to be told." This means he doesn't want his hopes shattered, his belief in his own shrewdness shaken, his ego deflated. Tricked by one gimmick today, the egg will eagerly fall for just as phony a gimmick tomorrow. This is illustrated by the fact that in the great age of the touts, every tout had a book listing his current suckers all over the country. If the tout had a string of bad guesses and "tapped out" the names on his list, they would inevitably stop their "action" with him.

The tout would then merely sell his list for cash to another tout with another approach, and the latter would start working a new story on his newly bought list after a decent interval. The first tout would buy some other tout's list of eggs.

"You just have to give a busted horseplayer time enough to heal up," one tout explained years ago.

The mental processes of the confirmed horseplayer remain, often, beyond normal comprehension. There is one who to this day works in my newspaper shop, and his attitude toward his life calling—horse playing—is always fascinating. Once, after a week of losses and shylocks, his wife phoned him at his desk. She reported that they had been served with an eviction notice, there was no food in the house, the lights were about to be shut off, the children were crying. She had all the usual horseplayer's wife's complaints. Would hubby please send his paycheck home quick. He got it that very morning, she knew.

Hubby didn't have any paycheck to send because the shylocks had taken it under threat of busting his skull. He argued and evaded on the phone. Finally he hung up in disgust.

"I don't understand what she's beefing about," he said in tired wonder. "After all, I'm just doing it for her and the kids. It's not like I'm spending the money on myself."

Money at hand is the horseplayer's religion. One I know borrowed $200 from a friend after the fourth race, which the pal had won nicely. Three races later the friend was tapped out and Our Hero had won two races. His friend asked for his $200 back.

"This is no place to talk business," said Our Hero in annoyance, looking up from his scratch sheet. "If you want to talk business, come to my office."

It was this same chap who had a big day and brought his winnings into the office where he gave the money to a co-worker to hold for him. The news got around the editorial room, and a chap who had been owed $100 for months by the temporary big winner, a chap who was a middling important boss, just ordered the money holder to give him his hundred out of the winnings. When Our Hero came to collect his loot and go out to break the trotters that night, he was furious that he was $100 short. No matter the reason or who it went to.

"I can pay my own debts," he said steaming. "I don't need you to make a gentleman out of me."

But this champion's greatest moment of glory came at a New York racetrack after the second race. It was his second losing adventure of the day and he was inclined to be glum. And then, under a nearby table at the old Aqueduct restaurant, he spotted nine winning tickets on the floor. Each was a $5 ticket on a horse that had paid $18 and change. He dove out of his chair onto his knees and scooped up the discarded tickets. But he didn't get back on his feet. He still groveled around under the empty table.

"Hurry up!" his friends advised in loud whispers. "That guy will be back. He'll know by now he threw away the winning tickets."

Our Hero kept at his search.

"Nobody buys *nine* tickets," he said over his shoulder. "There's a tenth one under here somewhere."

Almost every big newspaper shop has a house bookmaker, even today, and almost always there is a house shylock who hands out the money that is handed back to the bookmaker. Years ago I asked our resident shylock why he had refused a new loan to one of our desperate punters.

"There isn't enough money in the world," said the shylock, "to keep a horseplayer going every day."

Even the experts in the press box at tracks are susceptible to "information," and they bet mildly but stubbornly on same. There is a classic "expert" story:

The tracks put in a $2 window at the press boxes, which are perched on the roof and thus inconvient to the downstairs window, for the experts who must stick fairly close to their typewriters. On a legendary day at the old Belmont track, the $2 window in the press box handled more than $4,800 in "expert" bets. The same window had paid out $18 at the end of the day.

DIRTY JOKE

It is a musician who claims it happened to him, and the very word "musician" immediately makes the whole thing suspect. But if it didn't happen it *should* have happened, as is so frequently the case with such tales. So from the opening downbeat:

Our Hero awakes with what must surely be a lethal hangover. In the bathroom he tries for the toothbrush and knocks it on the floor, gets the toothpaste on his fingers but not the brush, gulps some cold water and is sick. He looks at the safety razor and the blades and knows that even to make the try would be suicidal. The thought of cold milk makes his stomach jump over twice, but he fights his way to the refrigerator and gets part of a cold beer down his throat. He doesn't finish the beer because he remembers, too late, that a cold glass of beer always sounds so much better than it tastes.

In the living room his clothes are everywhere. All his clothes but his overcoat. He seeks the time. Nowhere is his watch, either. He sits down and trembles for a while. Where was he? What did he do? What happened?

He sits shuddering, memory mostly a blank. But not completely a blank. Here and there a chink stands out, like the ragged standing parts of a broken brick wall. Another brick comes to join the structure. He thinks he remembers being in a big apartment that had, of all things, a gold commode. Slowly and painfully he fights his way into some of his clothes and then sits down to think some more.

Yes, he was at Charlie's bar with that Gino, who plays oboe in the big TV studio orchestra. And yes, it was Gino who took him to the party. Since he doesn't know Gino's last name, no use trying to find and ask that character. But he does know where Charlie's tavern is. He gets into the rest of his clothes and finishes his beer.

On the street the cold perspiration breaks out on face and brow, although the temperature is almost at freezing. A taxi mercifully

154

accepts him and takes him to the closed and darkened Charlie's. A window clock tells him the time. It is noon.

Memory is slowly struggling back. He will fight to help it, he will try to retrace his steps. Something tells him he and Gino walked east about five blocks. He walks east about five blocks. Did they turn uptown? He thinks so. He turns uptown. The territory seems vaguely familiar. He walks further east. There, right down there, that big apartment. It has sort of a familiar look.

There is a doorman in front of the big apartment and Our Hero approaches and asks, "Did you have a big party here last night?"

"Did we," sighs the doorman. "Those drunks were all over the lobby and in the gutter at six o'clock this morning."

"What apartment," asks Our Boy, his voice cracking.

"Fifteen A," says the doorman in disgust.

Well, please God, he tells the empty elevator, please make it the right apartment, the one with the gold commode.

He rings the bell to 15A. A woman comes to the door. She has an icebag on her head. She looks like an escapee from the drunk tank. Behind her, he can see that the apartment is a shambles.

"Did you have a big party here last night?" Our Hero asks timorously.

"Maybe you'd call it that," croaks the woman. "I remember it more as a horror play."

"Tell me," says our overcoatless and watchless principal figure, "was I here?"

"I wouldn't know," says the gal. "God knows, everybody was here."

So far not so good. Only one trump card left.

"May I ask you a question?" says Our Hero in his last, desperate gambit. "Do you have a gold commode?"

The woman turns her head and calls back over her shoulder. "Harry!" she calls. "Here's the guy who pissed in your French horn."

The Early Magic Box

FROM WHAT I READ IN THE SHOW business trade papers, there will be little live TV produced and broadcast in New York for some time to come. TV has followed the movie trail to California. Ed Sullivan, a local veteran, may be the last of the eastern primitives. To me, who might be described as an overage senior performer on the Magic Box, it seems only yesterday that *all* live TV came from New York. And I must, in all fairness, make another point:

Nobody saw it, either!

The first TV shows on which I was a co-star originated from a smallish, square room in NBC's Radio City complex. Up in the corner of the room, high above our heads, was a small box on which we could watch ourselves in grayish image. I have no idea where the programs went, otherwise, except possibly into the offices of disinterested NBC high brass. There were said to be a few boxes in chosen saloons, but I never saw one. The living rooms of our great nation until 1948 were bare of the magic eyes. To this day I am convinced that Frank Farrell, myself and any free guest who could talk, sing, play piano or guitar—there was no money for *any* talent—are possibly the only "TV stars" who did shows principally for our own amusement. Plus an even more entertaining $50 a shot.

This was back in the late 1930s and earliest 1940s before we got those Greetings, put on blue or brownish uniforms, and had to go back to reading USO comic books for our entertainment. In those great years, $50 looked like half the money in the world to a downtrodden newspaperman.

The producer–director–paymaster–casting–agent–makeup–man–coffee-go-for was Martin Jones. Martin had produced Broadway plays and was possibly the first producer for TV. He saw so little future in his closet TV productions that he took an executive job with the Red Cross for the duration of the war, and I have not laid a busy TV eye on him since.

Farrell and I, and other eminent comperes, would once a week (usually at the last desperate minute) start calling our actor and entertainment world friends. We would explain how this was their big chance at future fame. They would be pioneers in the new medium. They would be in at the accouchement. Think what it would mean, someday, to have all that experience. Remember Cecil B. De Mille? Remember Mary Pickford? Remember Eddie Polo? Remember all those hallowed pioneers who had seen the value of the primitive movies?

How much? Well—uh—no money, but think of the publicity! Come to reflect, Ed Sullivan started about the same way on a slightly higher financial scale.

Was it ever fun. Our "nationwide" audience consisted of friends of the guests stars, friends of ours and friends of Jones. They all stood off to one side, under the wall TV box, where the single camera wouldn't pick them up and put them in the picture with the real stars. They applauded everything wildly. Our friends did. Others did not.

Wandering around the radio halls of our floor, we would bump into singers and musicians and actors we knew from Sardi's or Louie's or the stage and nightclubs. They were all pals. Former pals, rather.

"Whadda you finks trying to do?" these radio stalwarts would demand. "Take the bread out of our mouths?" They were afraid of the new medium. If this attitude seems fictional, it was encountered by the first men who went to Hollywood to introduce sound and who were feared and scorned by the silent veterans. The great scenic designer Robert Edmund Jones told me that when he went to Hollywood to pioneer color films he got the same treatment from former Broadway stage pals who had long established themselves out there in black-and-white films.

It seems a pity the epics that came out of that closet studio could not have been preserved on film or tape. They would show the current critics how *good* modern TV is.

We now dissolve to 1948 and what was, considered in its time slot, the dawn of big-time TV. I am a graduate *sin laude* of that era, too. I was called to have lunch with a reformed Hollywood producer and manager named Martin Gosch. Martin had a stupendous idea. We would televise Broadway hits directly from their stages. We would even be allowed two or three TV cameras. I would condense and rewrite the stage hits into half-hour block-busters. Gosch would produce and direct. A man named Bill Gillette would handle the camera shots, switches and angles. We were all set. Away we went.

To launch this brave new project we somehow secured the television rights to *Mister Roberts,* then the number one Broadway smash. The news of this was so important to the trade that I believe we were the first—and *last*—production ever revealed to a waiting public by none other than William S. Paley, then the very definite top man at CBS and now chairman of the board. Mr. Paley, in person, described the new show on March 11, 1948, and said, rather proudly: "The program 'Tonight on Broadway' will have the first truly national exposure. It will be carried on TV stations ranging 500 miles from Boston to Washington. Its potential audience is estimated at over 500,000 viewers."

Imagine *that!* All the way from Boston to Washington and all around the cities in between! And how about a whole half million viewers? Man, we were BIG TIME!

We had already been at work for some time. We even had a production studio. It was Gosch's one-room studio bedroom in the Savoy Plaza Hotel. We sank our teeth into *Mister Roberts* and started artistic surgery on it. I would bring the scripts and Gosch would edit, sitting on his couch-bed. We had no secretary. Gosch also typed sitting on his bed, a portable typewriter on his lap. Of such efforts comes great literature.

The telecast was set for a Sunday night in April. We were so important to the industry that we even had a single sponsor instead of a lot of small, dubious ones paying small, dubious fees.

We had none less than Lucky Strike, over the years one of the most persistent and successful sponsors in radio. We worked feverishly on our script and had it done just two days before deadline. Then things began to happen.

Henry Fonda, a powerhouse star in those days, took one look at the script and balked. He had agreed to do TV for peanuts under the assumption that it was some sort of interview or promotion. He was not—repeat, not—going to *act* on any TV for a measly $125 for a half hour—and much longer rehearsal. That was our price for one of the biggest stars on Broadway. A hundred and a quarter. Other acts got union scale. I forget what scale was in those days, but it wouldn't keep an actor out of the Actors' Home.

David Wayne, a featured player, followed Fonda's lead. Not him, not for a hundred and a quarter. The formula for the future history of the show was set at the kickoff. The formula was rewriting scripts each week, usually a few minutes before we were to go on the air. The only part of the original script retained was a monologue I wrote for Bill Harrigan. He did it wonderfully on the telecast, and a few days later I had the usual author's ague when reading in *Variety* that the show's only highlight was Harrigan's "obviously ad-lib monologue."

Between interviews and monologues and pictures of the set, Gosch put himself on camera and did a fairly long, rambling exposition of the show's accomplishments and aims. Next day the screams hit the fan. Gillette and I reported to our "studio." Gosch was on the phone with the Lucky Strike ad agency. We sat there silently. We sat there long. Gosch was on the phone for eight straight hours, probably a record even for a producer.

Soon the witty and informative John Mason Brown, critic and lecturer, was filling the role of narrator. He had to attend script conferences. That made four of us in the studio-bedroom-TV enclave. It was a bit close.

There were a lot of other excitements. The electricians had a nice little internecine war over whether radio or stage electricians should handle wires and lights. The movies were convinced that any actor on Broadway still under film contract was violating that contract by appearing on a TV "screen." It took Hollywood a long time to stumble into TV's gold mine.

I, too, had some personal minor crises. In my newspaper column

I had been ribbing the stage producer and director, the elder wunderkind Jed Harris. This was safe enough as far as it went, but now I found I had to write the script for Harris' production of *The Heiress.* Harris quickly sent word that the first time he met me he would break my nose.

"We'll get the work done first," Harris said when we were introduced on the stage. "And then I'm taking you out in the alley and knocking your silly head off." This was not a particularly lethal threat since I was convinced that my younger daughter could lick Jed Harris at catch weights. But after the rehearsal we did go out into the alley. We walked through the alley and across the street to a saloon. Harris started on brandy. I forget what I started on, but it was something.

About four hours later we came within an ace of taking the next plane to Paris. It developed that Jed wanted to go there and buy a racehorse stud. The only money to be made in racing was from stud fees, he explained. We would fly over, spend a day or so, and bring back something on the order of Bull Lea, Calumet Farms', immortal stallion. Somebody had convinced Jed that such horses ran free in the Bois de Boulogne. We never did get to make the trip, but Jed and I have been friends, if horseless, ever since.

Another chore I remember was a play called *Monserrat*, which had been a hit all over the world. The American version was doing just fair. The play was a series of episodes involving the fates of several dissimiliar persons.

We read the script and reread it and couldn't find a way to tell its story or make its point in half an hour. Finally I gave up and took several scenes and put them out of context, and we telecast them that way. It was one of our best shows. The critics lauded it. The adapter and director, Lillian Hellman, complimented us. So did the producer.

Nobody seemed to notice or care that our TV version of *Monserrat* ran backwards!

By the time we got to doing shows from nightclubs—where the waiters union and the stagehands couldn't agree on who had the privilege of moving tables, chairs and silverware—Lucky Strike was understandably tired. Our sponsor canceled at the end of 1948.

Were we dead, we early pioneers? Not so, friend. Lucky Strike had scarcely dropped the ball than it was picked up, this time by the equally prestigious Esso gasoline. Esso lacked Lucky's experience and know-how in show biz and was probably a little apprehensive since the new contract called for, I remember, only four 1949 telecasts with an option for the rest of the season. We were understandably jittery. We didn't even know the president of Esso, a conservative type, we heard. His name was M. J. Rathbone. We were to get to know him much better.

I forget the disasters of 1949, but they were even more crashing than 1948. Then Mr. Rathbone called us for a conference. This, we felt, was the deathblow. Mr. Rathbone talked to us at length. He explained that his company had once hired a radio newscaster whom neither critics nor public praised.

Nobody liked the newscaster except Mr. Rathbone and his associates, he related. So, naturally, they had kept the newscaster on the air for twelve years and, sure enough, he had been an ultimate success. We sat listening, our hearts hanging out.

Mr. Rathbone told us he liked us, too. So he would keep our show on for all of that season. He did. And for part of the next season, too.

Well, television today is bigger and better than in those bad old days. But you have to admit one thing: *They don't make sponsors like M. J. Rathbone anymore.*

MOONLIGHT

Miss Lenore Lemmon was a beauty at fifteen and today retains much of what the graces gave her free. Earlier in her life she was a prominent member of what was known as café society. She is an acknowledged humorist and, further, she apparently is on friendly terms with just about everybody in the whole wide world, loaded or bankrupt, on the upbeat or on the hustle. Miss Lemmon is on Old Pal terms with many of our city's upper echelon policemen, and on the same terms with many upper echelon wrongos whom the upper echelon cops would just love to collar.

One of Miss Lemmon's favorite friends is a hero detective whom we will call Jim Stanton, and it is his story, not hers, that is herewith recounted:

We had a big extortion case recently (relates Jim Stanton) and that kind of case is always kept as quiet as possible to protect the victims and also to try and flush out the muscle behind the shake. We pretty well had the shake artists made, and then we got a real steer over a tapped wire and we set our trap. We set out lines around a block in the East 50s, where the rich victim lives.

We went all out, the boss determined to catch the bad guys and show them the light. We had cops disguised as mailmen studying mailboxes, and we had cops looking like delivery men trying to find an address to deliver a package, and we had cops dressed as doormen in front of three or four buildings. We had a cop newsdealer and a cop elevator operator, a cop butler—the works.

Me, I am playing a bum down on one corner, lounging around like a drunk in an old pair of pants and a dirty sweater. We wait and we wait some more. Into the block, at last, comes a car. It stops a ways from the apartment house and only one guy gets out. He starts toward our target. I can almost feel every cop on that block stiffen. We all get busier at our phony jobs.

The guy keeps walking nearer me, which means nothing since he is probably casing the scene, and I lean up against a lamppost like a lazy bum. He's coming nearer.

162

Suddenly who comes along but the Lemm, who also lives nearby. She's walking fast. She gives me a big slap on the back.

"Hello, Dick Tracy!" she fairly hollers. "Who you trying to grab?"

I could have crawled right through a nearby sewer grate. After all, my boss is sitting in a car about ten feet away. The Lemm just keeps right on walking. So does the guy.

Lucky he wasn't our guy. Our guy came later. The boss asked me, "Who was that crazy dame?"

"How would I ever know?" I said, straight-faced.

The Top Cop

SURELY THERE HAS NEVER BEEN a more determined crime fighter over anywhere near such a long period of years as Mr. J. Edgar Hoover of the Federal Bureau of Investigation. His attainments and victories in his chosen field of sheltering his country from assorted villains make too long a list for any monument that inevitably will reward him. Perhaps it is the very nature of his job—remote from control or influence, suspicious of politicians and do-gooders—that over three generations has placed Hoover in an exalted niche from which he is sometimes inclined to gaze down on ordinary mortals and to run the FBI with rather a godlike hand.

He has everybody's respect, including the intense respect of his underlings, but his Zeusian stance in all inevitably has given rise, now and then, to some tittering and snickering when the hard Hooverian outer shell was purposely or even accidentally cracked.

Hoover belongs in any memoirs of New York of the 1930s and 1940s because of his perfect attendance at the Stork Club, one of the towns most glamorous oases, whenever he granted us his presence. He was the constant table companion of the famed columnist Walter Winchell and a fast friend of the club's owner, Sherman Billingsley. It was his predilection for the company of these two celebs that gave some of us one of our biggest (if well-muted) howls.

On this occasion Billingsley and/or Winchell had introduced Hoover to another Stork Club regular who may, some old customers contend, have been a partner in the place at the time. The time was when Hoover and his men were cracking down on crime of any kind or sort. Hoover, discussing something with Winchell, obviously did not catch the name of the gent to whom he had just been introduced. Billingsley's back was turned when the Stork Club official photographer took a flashlight photo of the celebrities at the table.

The celebrity who had just joined the group headed by America's number one cop, and who was deep in conversation with same, was none other than a man named Frank Costello. Mr. Costello at that moment was the acknowledged maximum leader of the Mafia, Syndicate, Organization, Cosa Nostra or you name it.

Billingsley, alarmed by the flash of the camera bulb, ran his own photographer into the kitchen, grabbed the camera, ripped out the negative and personally burned it in a kitchen stove. It wasn't the kind of picture that would have enhanced Hoover's image in the nation's press.

So many years have passed in FBI history that veteran and retired G-men are now willing to open up and pass on a few reminiscences of life under the Boss Cop. Once, one remembers, an agent was called in from the field to write a special report for the director's desk. Director Hoover read the report and wrote across the first page: "This man bears watching."

"But he didn't say plainly," recalls the veteran G-man, "whether he meant we should watch him for possible promotion to bigger and better jobs or whether we should watch him because he was a suspiciously inept or bad performer."

At this point our historian sighs and laughs a little.

"It is twenty years later," he claims, "and that agent is still being closely watched. Nobody knows what for. He's just being watched."

Another old soldier in the G-man ranks recalls a time when he was invited to lunch with the director and the few close associates Hoover has in his Bureau. As they descended in an elevator, an agent whom we shall call Davis also got on the elevator. The man who tells this story knew this agent and knew that he had been brought back to the Bureau for some retraining in a specialized field. Our historian said good morning and Hoover nodded at the strange agent and also said good morning. The agent made a somewhat flippant reply. As our source remembers, it was something like "What's good about it."

At lunch Hoover asked our historian what the fellow's name was and was told Davis.

Now, going back from lunch in the same elevator, Director Hoover said simply "I don't like that fellow Davis."

"None of the group but me knew who or what he was talking about," relates our chronicler, "and I wasn't about to fink on the chap. So what do you suppose happened?"

We had no idea.

"They transferred twenty-four Davises," was the answer.

But the G-man who must have been the soundest thinker and surely the most imaginative agent of all was the one in a Midwestern city. This hero went into a bar one night and, several drinks later, got into a wild fist fight with another bar customer. Glass, mirror, chairs and other articles were damaged beyond repair. Both the G-man and his opponent were soon in the city jail. Once the G-man had identified himself, his superior was sent for immediately.

The agent in charge arrived and naturally demanded: "What happened?"

"What happened?" said Our Hero, who had time to do some quick thinking. "I don't know what happened! Well, I know what happened up to a point. I was in this bar having my usual two drinks before dinner when this stranger started a conversation. Pretty soon he made a disparaging remark about our director. After that I don't *know* what happened!"

The net result?

The agent who couldn't remember exactly what happened got a letter of commendation. Signed by the director.

Old Homestead

WHEN A YOUNGSTER LEFT HOME
in the late 1920s or early 1930s and arrived in the big city to
become a millionaire or even a man about town, he almost always
had his initial step prepared. He knew exactly where he was going
to live. He knew that because other youngsters who had preceded
him had all written home to friends and revealed where they had
located. This soon meant concentrations of emigres from the same
towns and even states. The original kid who came to New York
from Mooseleg, Mont., found a room or small apartment and his
first letter home told where he was holed up. The second kid from
Moosejaw advised the earlier arrival of his arrival in advance and
was invariably booked into the same rooming or apartment house.

Most of these homes-away-from-home were the old brownstones
or small apartment hotels, or even big apartments, which then
crowded the streets off Broadway from the West 60s up to the
West 90s. The East Side in those days was remote and square. So
after a while there would be an apartment house or small hotel
almost entirely inhabited by drop-aways from, say, North Carolina.
Another would have a predominantly Ohio trade. Still another
would be full of ex-Wisconsinites. "It's a Maine place," somebody
would often describe a certain building.

Since all of us were young and salaries were adequate but

scarcely profligate, there were always from two to four—and in times of crisis even six or eight—old hometowners in a single two-room apartment commune.

The one I came to, all fresh and scrubbed up from New Haven, was a Connecticut kibbutz, a small apartment hotel in the early West 70s. As did most of these places, aside from the new innocents, this hostelry also housed its share of petty thieves, hustlers, card sharps, racetrack touts and gals on the make. We will call it the Rugelton, for it still stands in its original location, shape and identity.

The other day some business took me back to the old neighborhood, and afterward I walked a couple of blocks to see what time hath wrought with the old homestead. It had been over thirty years since I had last been in the Rugelton and, walking toward it, I looked carefully at the first-floor windows of the brownstone and graystone houses, or at least those that are left. I suppose I was subconsciously looking for the old, hand-printed, cardboard window signs that would say, merely, "Senorita Carita" or "Pearl and Nanette" or "Mlle. Felice." Under such names would be, simply, "Dance Instruction."

Ah, you Pearls and Nanettes and Felices and Caritas! Your dancing shoes must long be worn to shreds, those satin evening gowns tattered and torn, the dyed blond or black or red hair long since taken over by natural gray. Ah, you itinerant teachers of Terpsichore, where are you now? You used to be everywhere.

The way these girls made their living was simple enough. They would hire the front room of a brownstone, write their sign and put it in the window, take all furniture out of the room but a couple of upright chairs, install an old record player and a few records, and then put a small ad in the tabloids offering the aforementioned dance instruction. "Individual Dance Instruction," the ad would always emphasize.

Unbelievably, these ads would bring immediate results. And the results were unbelievable in themselves. The results would be the appearance of limousines and town cars and expensive autos, each of which would disgorge an elderly gentleman, or sometimes not so elderly, all eager to become the new Fred Astaire. All looking rather like Daddy Browning, a celebrated beau of the day.

Inside, as per appointment made over the hall telephone, Pearl and Nanette would dance them around for the contracted hour. Pearl and Nanette danced real close, to give more intimate instruction. The future Fred Astaires would start to breathe a little heavily. Pearl and Nanette would back off a little, then come back to closed ranks, the while whispering soft instruction in the student's ear. If they whispered anything else they whispered it softly, because in those days there were heavy-handed police-women who made it their duty to drop in every once in a while—without telephoned appointment.

Any other talking, or any other contact, had to be made on two stiff, straight-backed chairs. Police regulations for individual dance instructresses forebade even an over-stuffed easy chair in the studios of Terpsichore.

After two or three weeks, the elderly Ray Bolgers would begin to tire of the lessons and charms of Pearl and Nanette. The early infatuation would cool. Pearl's and Nanette's bodies, sheathed in their satin evening dresses backed by neither brassiere nor panties, would become a little too familiar. Old stuff. The appointments would fall off. The hallway phone would cease to ring. The shiny cars would not be parked in the street. The dance studio was on its last phonograph chorus.

Was this the end of Pearl and Nanette, professionally speaking? Far from it. Each girl would dye her hair a different color, each would go out and buy a couple of different evening gowns. One, or both, would adopt a different and equally phony accent. They would move around the block, hire another parlor room, move in the record player, print up a new sign, put another ad in the *Graphic* or the *Mirror* and bingo!—back in business again.

The only change would be in the window sign. Pearl and Nanette would now be Fifi and Sonia. The hall phone would ring, the big cars would arrive—well, history would repeat itself again.

After a while the landlords of the neighborhood began to tire of the dancing girls. It wasn't that they moved so often. It was that just before they moved they would restore the studio into living quarters and then, when they did move, which was usually at night, would take everything with them except the fireplace.

We had a dance studio on the ground floor of the Rugelton, but upstairs the girl tenants I found most fascinating were known to us other tenants as the Double Dressers. These dolls never went out of an evening without wearing, say, a dark blue dress over a light green one. And they always carried an enormous handbag.

They would sit around the speakeasies of Broadway or Greenwich Village—the latter was particularly good hunting ground—and work their charms until some drunk became definitely interested. They would then promise their all for a certain sum and insist on payment in advance. If this were paid, the Double Dresser would want just one more drink before they left. After that she would need to go to the ladies' room before they took off for a night of love. "Just a teeny minute," she would promise, and head for the john.

Even if suspicious, the drunk would raise no objection. All he had to do was watch both the ladies' room and exit doors. But time would drag and he would usually have himself a nightcap.

Meanwhile, in the privacy of the john, the Double Dresser would have slipped off her dark blue dress and stuffed it into the big handbag. She would rearrange her hair and take a hat from the handbag. Then, looking quite casual in her light green dress, she would stroll through the saloon and out the door, keeping as far as possible from Casanova at the bar.

The doorman and waiters, when later queried by an enraged drunk, would and could honestly testify that no girl in a dark blue dress and long hair had left the place. It was infuriating for the drunk, but it paid the Double Dressers a pretty good living. Every now and then, it must be admitted, something would go wrong. Then one of our Double Dressers would be confined to quarters for several days while a large black eye or painful split lip underwent healing potions.

I lived with three roommates, all from near my hometown. We formed the permanent but by no means total habitation. There were often floaters left over from some party, and of course any hometown boy—or girl—was welcome to the floor or a couple of chairs until he could get straightened away on his bright new city career.

In a way it was a fact that one tenant of the Rugelton had an automatic introduction to every other tenant. Most doors were almost always open, and it was not hard to track down the nightly Rugelton party merely by following one's ear, so to speak.

The Rugelton party, as I remember it, was itself a permanent affair, although it shifted about from apartment to apartment. You entered almost any door that was open for ventilation and joined the gaiety. After a reasonable period you were expected to send out for a bottle of gin and pay two dollars for same. There were empty gin bottles in the hall and empty gin bottles in the corners and just about everywhere else. Rugelton tenants removed their own garbage. Or didn't.

There were casual liaisons and desperate romances going on everywhere, and there were also intermittent fights. Often you went to bed in a room of screaming celebrants, somehow slept and somehow got up in time for work. A constant din hung like a cloud.

Once a week the management collected eleven dollars from every living, breathing body under the roof. It doesn't take advanced arithmetic to figure that our tiny apartment, with its four householders, brought $176 per month. In those dear, dead days, a management would put up with a lot of noise for such rentals.

My neighbors to the left were four sharp youths of mysterious origin and motivation. The only one I ever knew real well was Joey. Physiognomists (and the cops, too) tell us that there is no such thing as an honest face but, nevertheless, Joey had one. He also had a pleasant, effervescent personality and—where did he learn?—spoke no less than nine different languages.

With such attributes Joey could certainly have found himself a respectful and even envied job with a fine future. But no, he was a Rugelton tenant and as such had nothing but contempt for anything legitimate. Instead, he rushed around all day long selling phony insurance policies to newly arrived foreigners who, in these days before the Great Depression, had no trouble finding boom-time jobs and were beginning to buy homes, cars and even jewelry. Joey could sell them these items also. One hopes that the rise of the labor unions and their protective services forced Joey into honest work. I wouldn't be surprised if he was something big at the UN right now.

On the floor above us were four other wise guys of more criminal stripe. They were busily engaged in what is still, I suppose, referred to as Pushing the Queer. This is the professional term for passing counterfeit money. They didn't manufacture counterfeit. They bought it in packages and stored it away from their domicile, paying a fraction of the face value.

Almost anybody caught passing a single queer bill, if his pockets contain only honest money otherwise, has a pretty good chance of convincing a judge that somebody else must have passed the queer bill to him in all his trust and innocence. But caught passing a phony bill, and with a pocketful of others, almost always means residence in a jail. The U.S. Treasury Department takes a very dim view indeed of counterfeit money.

So my upstairs neighbors ran around all day, one bad bill nestled in with their other good ones, and bought something in a dark candy store here or quickly passed one and got change from a harried bookmaker there. Once the bad item was out of their hands, they had to rush back to the cache and get another one—just one, always. Repeat the process. And repeat again.

Considering the legwork and anxiety involved, it might seem to the normal mind that they would have been better off working at day labor. But not these boys. They were wise guys. In the rackets. Wise guys don't work hard. That's for boobs. Although their job had other drawbacks, they kept their hands on the plough. Since the items they bought with their funny money came from candy stores, drug stores and small haberdasheries, their rooms at the Rugelton were always overstocked with unwanted candy bars, collar buttons, chewing gum and old magazines.

The Ryan brothers, who lived on our floor for a while, looked a great deal like Jimmy Cagney and Pat O'Brien. They were partners in an old-fashioned switch game which, it grieves me to say, is apparently still flourishing at the old stands even though the Ryans first demonstrated it for me over thirty years ago.

The Ryans had an ordinary light delivery truck. There was no firm name painted on it but it looked legitimate, and so did the Ryans in their uniform tunics and chauffeur's caps as they set out for work each day. They would cruise about until they spotted a likely prospect, edge over to the curb and beckon to him mysteriously. When the customer approached, one of the Ryans would furtively show him, in a box with a fancy furrier's name on it, an expensive and handsome silver fox stole. Silver fox stoles in those innocent days rated with pink mink full-lengths today. The other Ryan would go into his spiel.

The fur, he would whisper hoarsely, had just been delivered to a store where the receiving clerk had signed acceptance for it and then forgot to take it with other furs and now it belonged to nobody and couldn't be traced and the boys didn't want to take it back to their heel of a boss who underpaid everybody and the customer looked like a good guy who wouldn't tell the cops so didn't the customer want this wonderful $500 fur for only $50?

While the talkative Ryan was going through his spiel, his pearl of a brother would be blowing on the fur, admiring it, and finally replacing it in its box and stowing it carefully under the driver's seat. If the customer went for the offer, even after financial haggling, he was violently warned not to open the box until he was safely far away. You never knew when somebody might recognize them, the Ryans, selling fur on the street.

Then the box was delivered. Or rather, an identical box was handed over. And the Ryans were off with a grinding of gears. When the customer opened his prize he found a fur in it. But not quite the fur he had been shown. More like cat's fur.

I said earlier that this ancient dodge is evidently still being worked because not more than six or seven years ago, on Sixth Avenue almost at 42d Street, two swifties actually launched it on me. I laughed and gave them a hopeful double take, but they were not my old pals the Ryans.

Two more miscreants are memorable from those dear days. I will call them Mutt and Jeff because they were that dissimiliar in appearance. They were card sharks, graduates of the three-card monte games with carnivals, and they were now working the trains. Their action took fantastic timing, highly specialized card handling and almost man-and-wife extrasensory perception.

I never saw them work because they had to get up before dawn to begin their day. They would ride a milk train out to one of the rich Westchester or Long Island suburbs, hang around a station platform and then board a returning commuter train to New York. On the train, in an hour or less, they would join or promote a bridge or poker game. The money would flow back and forth, the stakes being subtly raised by Mutt or Jeff. Just as the train was slowing down for Grand Central, Mutt or Jeff would deal for the final, biggest pot and Mutt or Jeff would win it, whichever was not the dealer and could not be accused of fast or tricky dealing.

It was almost a vaudevilly act and even with all the effort and skill involved it frequently didn't work for one reason or another—the train came in too fast, the honest players weren't adventurous gamblers or something else would foul up the final deal.

With all these characters, little important violence ever took place in the Rugelton. There were knifings and head bustings and even shootings in some of the crummier hotels nearby, but the Rugelton remained almost pure on the local police blotter. This was probably accountable to a big, tough policeman I will call Big George Wandling. Big George knew almost all of us and probably knew everything that was happening on his beat, but he was interested solely in keeping things calm, cool and in order.

Nobody wanted to argue with Wandling, and when bad trouble threatened, the cry of "Call Big George!" was always enough to quiet the hottest tempers.

Years ago I read that Big George had married an heiress, retired from the force and gone off somewhere to run a resort hotel. I wish I knew where it was, because any hotel George runs should be a good place for a real rest.

So the other day I stood looking at the facade of the Rugelton. There is a new canopy. The front has been sandblasted. There are Venetian blinds in the windows and most have air-conditioning machines. I went in and found the lobby clean. The old bilious green walls had been done over in a soft gray. The registration desk was gone, but an alert middle-age man said he was the superintendent. I asked if there were any vacancies. He said no, not now, and he didn't know of any coming up in the near future. I said I had lived there once and what kind of tenants does he have now?

"The best," he said rather smugly. "Doctors and lawyers, travel agency, people like that."

I asked if he had any plain tenants, just people who lived there. He said no. All professional suites. "It's the only way the owner can get around that goddamn rent control," he explained.

The Rugelton had its own rent controls when I lived there.

The Street Fair

MANY YEARS BACK, A CHAP NAMED Boggio Peppitone had a brief fling at being an owner of race horses. Mr. Peppitone designed his own colors, and they were best described with the racetrack critic Tony Betts' great line: "When that guy sends out a horse, I never know whether the jockey is going to ride a race or lead the San Gennaro Festival parade." To an old-time patron of Italian street fairs in New York, this said enough for multicolor.

As we bring along new generations, the customs and legends of the Old Country do not have the same emotional pull as they had on Grandma and Grandpa, huddled ethnically with their own kind in their own neighborhoods. But the annual San Gennaro Festival, in the still intensely Italian Mulberry Street area is still traditional and colorful and often unpredictable. Over the years it has always drawn more than a million people during its nine-day stand. It needs thirty thousand light bulbs strung over the street so you can see what you're eating. It offers—for free—everything from top-flight opera singers to local street bands, some playing the old music, some playing rock 'n' roll. There are the fresh-fried crullers, the pizza and, back from the street, some of the great Italian restaurants of the world. In brief, it's a blast.

The patron saint of the San Gennaro Society is Saint Januarious, martyred in the third century in Benvenuto, Italy. His statue—the host that is carried through the streets—was scuplted in Italy many years ago specifically for the New York celebration. The host has lived a dangerous life, at times, even though his permanent home is in the Church of the Most Precious Blood. The other sacred relics are three sealed containers that, legend has it, contain the head of the saint and two vials of his blood.

The major sport is traditional enough. A greased pole is set up and from it, on strung wires, are all sorts of goodies. Neighborhood youngsters try to shinny up it for prizes and family prestige. Everywhere there is the frying dough, the peppers, spices, meats and cheeses. There is never a smell in New York to compare with the aroma of the San Gennaro.

There are also games of chance, and since these contribute their winnings to the sponsoring charity, in years past the police were inclined to turn a blind eye at the dice games, wheel games and other hazards. But Mulberry Street has furnished some of our most dedicated gangsters, as well as some of our most prominent citizens, so the Mulberry Street Mob many years ago turned a speculative eye, not a blind one, on the gambling games. After all, gambling was their racket.

The Mulberry Mob called on the Society and demanded its usual cut of the gambling profits. The Society indignantly refused.

Then on the night before the opening of the big festival, those chosen to bring the host to his position of eminence were horrified to discover that he was not in his church quarters. He could not be found anywhere. Hysteria reigned. And then came a phone call.

The Mob would ransom the host for a specified sum instead of cutting in on the gambling. The money was paid and the statue retrieved from a very dirty Mulberry Street cellar.

One must assume that a more pleasant business arrangement has been worked out in the years since. Or maybe all the old, irreligious mobsters have been cut down or tucked away in jail.

The Shoestring King

IN THESE FINANCIALLY BULBOUS times, how would the King of the Shoestringers* have done? Would he have been a nonentity or would he as casually and easily have raised the $100,000 or $500,000 needed for a show today with the same techniques and approaches with which he scratched up hundreds—and even fifties and tens—back in the days when raising the loot for a theatrical production was just about as easy as getting a bank loan on a handshake?

How would he have done as a comedian or an actor? Probably just fine. He was very possibly the very first of what we now immediately recognize as the master of ceremonies. As a comedian, he came along too early. This would have been his time, this time of the offbeat approach, the languid air, the throwaway line and the ambiance. Like so many comedians of his day, he affected a battered top hat. Unlike other comedians of his day, he would not stay on the stage. He was as likely to do his monologue and his ad lib remarks in the aisle, or in an empty seat, as anywhere else.

And on those occasions when he kept to the stage, he liked to lie down in the footlights for an informal discussion of things with his hearers. His name was Will Morrissey.

*"On a shoestring." Theatre jargon for promoting something on little or less money.

Never a stranger to the bottle, he was completely unpredictable, a quirk that frequently interrupted his professional earnings for longish periods. There was the time, for instance, when he was master of ceremonies for the weekly Sunday night vaudeville shows at Broadway's Winter Garden, then probably one of the most famous theatres in the world. All great stars worked these Sunday night varieties: Al Jolson, Caruso, Ethel Barrymore, everybody. On the night in question, an imperious and aloof soprano from the Metropolitan Opera came on stage to add her cultural bit to the proceedings.

The orchestra played its first chord, the great soprano opened her aristocratic mouth—and all the lights in the theatre went out. Silence on stage and in orchestra pit. Mr. Morrissey, introducing the stars while roaming the aisles, rushed into the breach.

"Come on, honey," he shouted encouragingly. "It's not the first time you've worked in the dark."

Next day he was back at his favorite trade—producing a show of his own without any money of his own. Ill fortune never daunted him, his bland Irish face never showed a line of worry.

"I have stranded more stars," he would say firmly, "than Ziegfeld ever made."

His record bore him out.

"I stranded Bing Crosby in Honolulu," he would remember. "I stranded Mickey Rooney in darkest California, Martha Raye in Atlantic City, Hugh Herbert in Peoria, Willie Howard in Boston and Bert Lahr in Milwaukee. Also I forget how many youngsters who went on to fame. When my shows strand nobody has a dime, not even me. But look at the experience my actors get."

Somehow, the Shoestring King could strand actors without even hurting their feelings. Bing Crosby went right back to work for him, singing at $40 a week when it was there. Paul Whiteman came in, listened, and put Crosby to work with the Whiteman band. A skyrocket was fused.

But every now and scarce then, an unbelievable bolt of lucky lightning would strike. Consider:

A writer named Ralph Spence gave Morrissey a script called *The Apes*. Morrissey let it lie around for months and then gave it to Donald Gallagher, who said he would play it if Morrissey would pay his back room rent of $250. Morrissey found the money. Gallagher then disappeared, room rent in pocket, and somewhere, somehow, patched up the script, or at least changed it. The next thing Morrissey knew, Gallagher had actually produced the play for exactly $250. One of the major changes had been changing the title from *The Ape* to *The Gorilla*.

Legend is that on opening night, Morrissey stood in the audience loudly screaming "Author! Author!" Finally Spence, considerably confused from several desperate trips to the nearest speakeasy, was pushed on stage. He gazed at what was left of the audience.

"I. . .I'm sorry," was this author's curtain speech.

You don't remember *The Gorilla*? Nobody does. But in the late 1920s it ran for a year on Broadway, costing nothing and raking in box-office money with Mr. Morrissey long since having declared himself a partner. It went on the road for what seemed like years and was—believe it or not—sold to the movies and made into another profitable production.

Now the Shoestringer had a pocketful of money, a condition that always seemed to have an adverse effect on his judgment and fortunes. With the last of his new loot he did a revue with the then unknown Four Marx Brothers.

"All four of them were never on the stage together for a single show," Morrissey testified. "One of them was always in the box office watching me."

Finances got desperate, but the Shoestringer's confidence remained serene. He loudly announced production of another musical revue and booked it for a break-in in New Haven. On the day the show was to entrain, Morrissey called on Sam H. Harris, former partner of George M. Cohan and in those years the "class" producer on Broadway. Mr. Morrissey explained that Mr. Harris would have to give him the money for the train fares for his new show.

"Who's producing it?" asked Harris, reasonably.

"You are," explained the Shoestring King. So Harris did.

Still later, Morrissey put a musical comedy in rehearsal, his stars rehearsing bits of this and that, learning one song and another, timing a sketch or inventing one, while the Boss went out on the town to raise the money with which to open his epic. He couldn't raise a dime, strangely. On the morrow, Mr. Ziegfeld's *Follies* was coming into the rehearsal theatre and Mr. Morrissey's epic entertainers would be thrown right out into the alley.

Some twenty hours before that happened, Morrissey collared Lee

Shubert, who owned or controlled most of the theatres in the nation, and brought him to rehearsal. Mr. Shubert was too old a hand to back a Morrissey musical.

But he bought most of the songs and comedy material for $10,000, an authentic fortune of money in those days.

Overseas Revue toured for six or eight weeks without anybody getting paid anything. Morrissey stranded it somewhere beyond memory's reach. Yet for this show Richard Whiting and Ray Egan wrote *Japanese Sandman* and *Till We Meet Again*. You're still hearing them. Something—enough—always came out of a Morrissey fiasco to keep alive and kicking the legend of the Shoestring King.

Once George M. Cohan wouldn't give Morrissey any money because Will, as was his custom, was drinking. But Cohan gave him credit with the Cohan printers and sign posters. Morrissey plastered the town with cards and handbills and shoveled up enough cash to debut his newest extravaganza.

While he usually carried his liquor with humor and aplomb, there were times when he lost personality decisions to it. Entertaining Tom Mix at his Hollywood home, somebody-struck-somebody and Morrissey's wife, little Midge Miller, wound up with a black eye. Everybody made court next day, with charges hurled and met by countercharges. Mr. Morrissey had not shaken off all the grape.

"You're drunk," the judge told him.

"You're not so dumb after all," Morrissey replied approvingly.

Five days in durance vile.

But it was during the Depression of the 1930s that Will Morrissey's finest talents flowered. He simply produced shows. More often than not he couldn't pay for a theatre. So he would produce his shows in saloons and pass the hat. He would do them in parks or—no theatre available—on the sidewalk *in front of a theatre*. He once opened a show—and drew newspaper critics—in an alley. It happened thus:

When he didn't come up with the advance rent, the theatre was locked against his troupe. An alley ran alongside the theatre, as such alleys often do. At night there was a grilled iron gate closing the alley. Night before the "premiere," Morrissey climbed on the gate and began barking to the passing crowds about the great show "opening at this theatre tomorrow night."

News somehow got to the nearest police precinct that a madman or a drunk was trying to kill himself by jumping off a gate. Mr. Morrissey was collared and taken in. Somebody phoned the newspapers. It was such a good story that the theatre owner relented—partly. He wouldn't let Morrissey use his theatre, but he *could* use the alley, which would more or less make it a show *at* the theatre if not in it.

The Shoestringer presented his wunderkinder on the opening night as vocally advertised. A crowd gathered. Contributions were made. Most newspaper critics found that "there were some good things in it."

Occasionally, he would actually get one of his turkeys inside a real theatre. But a major problem would invariably raise its ugly head. Once, playing to mild audiences but getting by, Morrissey demanded of the theatre owner why neither the marquee nor the lobby lights were ever turned on. The owner looked fearfully over both shoulders.

"Sh-h-h-h," he warned in a shaky voice. "The bank mustn't know there's anything going on in here."

There was always a crisis, the usual crisis being with one or the other of the theatrical labor unions. Having announced that he would do a variety show in a Broadway theatre and would do it in two acts, he was informed by Actors Equity that if the show was in two acts it was a musical and must abide by Equity rules, one of which stated firmly that bonds for actors' salaries must be posted. A variety show, interpreted Equity, starts with the first turn and goes right through to the last turn.

Okay, said the Shoestring King, he would play his variety show straight through, according to the book. So on opening night he played it halfway through. Then the house lights went up. A girl came out onstage and began to harangue the audience with the story of her life and all its vicissitudes. Morrissey came out and stood in front of her.

"Pretty soon," he announced, "she will start her lousy dance number. It lasts about fifteen minutes." He looked over his audience with understanding and sympathy. "So," he advised, "why don't you all go out on the sidewalk and have a smoke?"

The audience went outside. The girl danced to an empty house for the intermission period.

If he were alive and as honest as usual—however honest that

can be interpreted—he would admit that his grand production in the city of Philadelphia was his greatest triumph as a shoestringer. It was, indeed, quite a feat.

Morrissey and his minions were thrown out of the Philadelphia theatre in proper course. Going back for some reason next day, Morrissey studied the darkened theatre and, by chance, tried the stage door. Eureka! Unlocked. He went in and pulled some levers. Eureka in no trump! Some goof had forgotten to have the interior lights turned off by the electric company. Will Morrissey, King of the Shoestringers, was back in business again.

All that day all members of his cast and four-piece pit orchestra toured the Philadelphia saloons. They sold "passes" to the show for whatever they could get. They planted cut-rate tickets on store counters everywhere, advising that seats were to be had at the theatre at "lowest possible prices." That night a man stood before the dark theatre selling tickets on the sidewalk. He sold them to passersby for the highest price he could get, and if he couldn't get that, any price would do.

All patrons, of course, had the added excitement of entering the theatre through the stage door and seeing a lot of real, live, glamorous entertainers more or less in costume.

Morrissey's mob canvassed the town. Each night the show went on, before a small audience or a goodly one. He kept this operation going, as I recall, for more than a month. Finally, somebody at the electric company remembered to cut off the lighting current. Mr. Morrissey and his stars beat their way back to Broadway, where other opportunities anxiously awaited them.

By this time he was getting old. His wife of better days, Midge Miller, had left him with tears but with reason. She had caught him in a rooming house bed with a strange lady. Morrissey told the press, when questioned about Midge's planned divorce, that the gal had been his landlady. This gave him an opening for one of his last quoted remarks:

"Many a marriage has been broken up by an idle roomer," he pointed out.

It is nice to report that his end was not the expected, or possibly earned, stereotype. He did not die alone or forgotten or in the gutter or in some actors' poorhouse. He died among friends and in comfort. This final act was his luckiest, and possibly his finest, production.

He somehow found himself in the city of Santa Barbara, Calif., a place of trim houses and trimmer flower gardens not noteworthy as a gang-up ground for overage and somewhat moldy stage hams. But, however he got there, he was the first to offer his professional services and long experience in aid of some charity production the city was staging. I believe he starred in it, too.

Well! The citizens of that city embraced him as if he were their own little lost lamb. He was given some sort of a title—Minister of Culture, perhaps. He was never again in want. No more did he ramble. He was home at last. Possibly because he didn't want any of his raffish old playmates to cut in on his act, he would never give an address on the occasional rambling and amusing letters he sent. The top of each letterhead was printed modestly with: "A Recognized Hotel."

He died out there some twenty years ago. I tried to look up the exact date the other day but couldn't find it or, indeed, any obituary. Possibly he wasn't important enough. Maybe not. He sure was resourceful enough.

And so ended the saga of a wandering player in the classic mold, a true trouper who was born either fifty years too early or fifty years too late.

DIRTY JOKE

If you remember the old W. C. Fields radio shows, which have recently been revived on an LP record, you may remember the Stroud Twins, Clarence and Claude. I could never tell them apart, and even now I am not quite sure which one had the leading role in two different military incidents. They were dead ringers, and their humor was very personal.

In the first incident, the Air Force wartime show *Winged Victory* was in San Francisco and found itself needing a new comedian. The IBM files were consulted, and it was discovered that Claude (was it Clarence?) Stroud was in an artillery unit in Kansas or somewhere. Muscle was used, and Stroud was transferred in a hurry to San Francisco where, on one of those steep hills, the *Winged Victory* cast and crew were being housed. In front of these "barracks" were parked the Air Force trucks used to transport the entertainers back and forth from their theatre. The trucks, being on steep hills, were supposed not only to be put in gear and braked, but also have their wheels cramped into the curb lest they break loose and roll madly downhill into the center of the city.

Claude/Clarence arrived at dawn this day and went to bed. Not for long. He had to get up and stand inspection with the rest of the "troops." He was not, as was often the case, in the best of physical condition.

He dutifully lined up in the gutter with the other heroes as an officer walked along the street looking over his artistic heroes. Before he got to Stroud, a truck up the street that had not been properly braked and cramped broke loose and rolled downhill. It hit the bemused Claude (Clarence?) and knocked him flat. It then proceeded to roll right over him. However, the center of the truck passed above his stricken eyes. Not a wheel touched him. They hauled him back to his feet as good as new.

"Send me back to the artillery," said this temporary fighting man. "This duty is too rugged for me."

But it was the other Stroud, Clarence (or was it Claude?), who found a way to spend less time in the military. Clarence/Claude was determined to prove to the Army that he was a mental case, and he found many methods to call himself to the attention of the medical authorities. Ultimately, he was ordered to appear before the company's pyschiatrist. The psychiatrist asked Stroud a long list of questions, to which he answered as he saw fit, and then the headshrinker made his big mistake.

"When did you last masturbate?" he asked.

Stroud looked at his watch. "What time is it now?" he demanded. He was excused from military service soon thereafter.

The Work Of Breeding

NO MATTER WHETHER THE OBJECT is to produce a family heir, a racehorse to outrun all others, or a mink with the blondest coat in the world, the act of breeding should by nature's own rules furnish an initial bonus of pleasure and even ecstasy. Often the heir turns out to be a boob, the racehorse can't beat a trained pig and the mink arrives with a mouse-colored overcoat. Nonetheless, in all such cases there should have been one wonderful memory to fall back on—the original act of the breeding. When this act becomes a chore or a bore there is usually a story involved.

Back during the Depression when we (to us) more sophisticated types had as little money as anybody else, we were forced to study the press to find free—or almost free—entertainment. We were very big for museums and parks, and thus combined healthy long walks with at least some art education by osmosis. But there were other things, particularly on the weekend list. Top-class Army polo was available for a free, pleasant, short ferry ride to Governor's Island plus a fifty-cent ticket. There were poetry readings—with something or other to drink and even nibble on—in Greenwich Village and elsewhere.

Even in those faraway days the literary cocktail party to introduce the new book by the new author was an almost continuous social function. And when you wangled an invite—or crashed—a party given by a film company to hooraw its new epic, and possibly meet the star, you came away full of hors d'oeuvres and usually very, very drunk. It should be also remembered that even the WPA Theatre produced not only some interesting and experimental plays but also gave us Orson Wells, to-be-famous scenic designers and many a now-established actor and director.

But it was when we were holding enough chips to make Long Island, Westchester or New Jersey for the horse and dog shows that we felt most like repressed millionaires. There we mingled with the aristocracy and the sporting. And, personally, I got hooked on the field trials, the ones for working spaniels and pointers and setters who actually had to contest with speed and accuracy in the retrieval of shot-down birds over some Jersey or Long Island marsh.

It was in Westhampton, Long Island, that I first saw and fell in love with a coffee-au-lait Chesapeake Bay retriever with yellow eyes. This gal's name was Westhampton Pink Lady. She was owned by a local hotel man named George Carmody. Was she pretty! Was she fast! Was she smart! A woman with her basic qualities would have indeed been THE woman behind a successful man.

She was the outstanding competitor of her time. On the bookshelves of her owner there were no books. No room for books. The shelves were loaded with blue ribbons and trophies earned by Pink Lady over the years. Six years. She was at middle age. She was the queen. But there was a king.

The king was named Firpo. He lived across Long Island Sound near New London. In his line of work, Firpo never met a Dempsey. He was nine years old.

And then it occurred, simultaneously, to the owners of both Firpo and Lady that their champs had been so busy working that neither owner had ever thought of a natural projection into the future. They had never thought of breeding Pink Lady and Firpo and, possibly, nurturing a litter of all-time champs for tomorrow. A breeding of two such standouts in their art should produce offspring comparable to what might have come, talentwise, from the offspring of an Eleonora Duse and George Bernard Shaw. Or, more accurately, Jean-Claude Killy and Peggy Fleming.

Both Carmody and Firpo's owner decided to sponsor the great

187

event the very next time Pink Lady came in heat. But then Carmody remembered that the national trials and championship were coming up about that time, so he postponed the wedding and started worrying about the nationals. This main event would, he realized, occur just about at the time of Lady's next heat.

So he sought out a veterinarian and asked that he give Lady some shots that would bring on her heat early and, timewise, have her normal and ready for the big show. No indeed, counseled the vet. If he did such a thing, Lady might have a recurrence of her feminine frailty. He had a better medical idea.

What he would do was give Lady *male* hormones and thus postpone her moony attitude until *after* the big tests. Further, the medicine would have to be given to her regularly. He gave Carmody some lessons in injections.

Almost with her first hormones, Lady's personality changed somewhat. As she kept getting her shots, she changed more definitely. She developed a low, masculine growl. She took to looking for insults and answering same physically with the opposite sex. She brooked no nonsense at all and very little attention. Transporting her by train to the nationals, Carmody kept up the regular shots of hormones.

The nationals that year were held in some Ohio swamp, and Lady went into them like a tiger and placed third against the best males in the country. It was, her sex considered, possibly her greatest triumph. She was in due course brought home and Firpo was delivered to stud. He approached Pink Lady with all the confidence of a powerful and experienced lover.

Lady bit him in the neck. She chased him and bossed him. She practically sent this bewildered canine Don Juan to the psychiatrist's couch. His owner had to come and take him, shaken, back to the more sympathetic home kennels and more susceptible bitches.

At this point Lady was now past her seventh birthday. Firpo was soon coming up ten. There was still time, or so everybody thought.

It took eighteen months before Lady's basso growl returned to its normal happy bark and she began to act like the lady of old. The happy owners conferred and studied the calendar. It did them little good. Nobody knew when Lady would become *all* female again.

It took another six months. Lady was now nine. It takes little arithmetic to conclude that Firpo was past eleven. He was carted again to his royal bride. They were put together in the breeding lot.

The poor old guy couldn't make it.

So the veterinarian was called again and this time it was Firpo who had to tender his broad backside for the male hormone shots. After several weeks a wolfish gleam was noted in his elderly eye. He was carted back again to perform his paternal duty.

Witnesses said that he performed in a rather disinterested way. After all, he was about twelve years old. Everybody congratulated one another, however, and sat back to wait for the most famous puppies in Chesapeake history.

No puppies appeared. Nobody tried again. Breeding is no fun that way.

The Wild Guy

HE CALLED HIMSELF TED HEALY. He had a face like the map of Ireland, he wore a jaunty felt fedora on stage and off and, possibly, you have laughed at him on the Late Late Show. His stage name was Ted Healy, although he was born Lee Nash. He was part Indian, part gypsy and part Irish, featuring the wilder strains of all three. It was probably inevitable that he should die following a saloon brawl, but at the peak of his career he set a vaudeville record salary of $6,000 a week in the depressed years, starred in many Broadway musicals and is generally credited with inventing the "stooge" style of low comedy.

The Three Stooges, who had a big revival on afternoon TV kiddie shows a few years back and whose old film shorts are still being televised, were either the second or third set of stooges used by Healy. The two Howard brothers, Shemp and Moe, were originals.

"How much gas have we got?" Healy would demand of Shemp.

"It says half," Shemp would report. Long pause. "But I dunno," Shemp would continue, "whether it's half full or half empty."

Not very funny? You should have heard the audience reaction when Healy & Co. did such bits.

Another faithful stooge was a flat-footed character known only as Swick, who doubled as Healy's valet. He would come on stage at Healy's request and sing "Old Black Joe." After a croak or two Healy would move him to stage center. Just as they took their first step, a sandbag would come crashing down from the gridiron overhead, missing both Healy and Swick by a hair. Swick would croak another couple of notes and Healy would urge him to move upstage where he would sound louder.

Bam! Down came another sandbag and another miss. It went on until an entire audience was waiting breathlessly for a sandbag to hit its target. Then Healy would urge Swick to do his impersonation of Katharine Hepburn in *The Little Spitfire*. Swick would dutifully spit in the footlights and simultaneously light a big sulphur match. Such was the Healy brand of comedy.

He was as wild in his personal life, although generous and loyal to old friends on their way up or down. Once he contended that he had purchased Joe Mendi, a wonderful chimp he used in his act, but the owner contended differently. So Ted simply kidnaped Joe Mendi, possibly the only case of chimpnaping in the annals of crime. If Joe got out of line Healy would box his ears. He would never have believed that the chimp could have torn him apart anytime it took a notion to do so.

But my clearest memory of the Wild Guy has to do with the old Half Moon Hotel in Coney Island and an heiress named Mary Brown Warburton.

Coney Island in the 1930s still had some pretensions as a topflight amusement park, its boardwalk was a nice place for nice people to take the sun and the sea air, and the Half Moon Hotel still had a regular summer vacation clientele. In fact, the ocean breezes at Coney were so accessible to New York that the hotel during the winter had become something of a haven for convalescents and New Yorkers who just wanted to hole in at some quiet place and rest or dry out for a few days.

The romantic interest between the Wild Guy and the heiress, Miss Warburton, was hardly a secret, since Healy's then wife and Miss Warburton had engaged in legal charges and counter-charges. The course of love is never smooth, the poets tell us, and one night Mr. Healy and Miss Warburton had a more than usually rousing quarrel. The result was that Dick Hakins, a Healy employee at the time, and yours truly, who was attempting to build the proper publicity "image" for the Wild Guy, were called on the phone at 6 A.M. and told to report to Healy's GHQ.

Once there, and still half asleep, we were told by the boss that all was ended between Miss Warburton and himself. But, he explained, he had awaked to find that somehow and somewhere during the long argumentative night he had come home with a great deal of the heiress' personal jewelry in his pockets.

"She'll say I stole it," the Wild Guy was convinced. "I know where she is. She goes and hides out at the Half Moon Hotel. I'm going over there and throw this ice right at her, and you two are going along as witnesses."

So we got in the car and went. Without the modern beltways and parkways it was a longer trip to Coney in those days, and it must have been around 8 A.M. when we arrived at the hotel. We entered the lobby and Healy, still steaming over last night's lovers' quarrel, stabbed at the elevator call button. Then we all stepped back.

It must be pointed out here that Healy had spent his youth around the horse trading camps of Texas, and from those early days on it is doubtful if he even visited close members of his family without a pistol in his pocket. It was as natural for him to carry a rod as it was to tote his roll of money.

So as we stood there waiting for the rather slow elevator, Healy looked up and noted an oil painting above the elevators. It was a portrait of a rather stern looking old boy who stared back at the Wild Guy in obvious disapproval. Healy's brow washboarded in a frown. Any new disapproval was more than he meant to bear.

"I don't like you either!" he hollered at the portrait. And with a real fast draw he brought out his pistol and shot the portrait neatly in the right eye!

It was at that exact moment that the elevator doors slid open. Staring out, at a man who was apparently shooting straight at them, was an old couple en route to a bracing boardwalk stroll and some invigorating sea air.

The tableau was frozen for the time of a long breath. Then the elevator doors slid closed again and the indicator showed the car was rising, rising, up and away from the dangerous boardwalk and the cordite-laden lobby air. We hustled the Wild Guy back to the car as fast as we could and lost no time returning to the quiet environs of Broadway.

I do not know how or when Miss Warburton ever got her jewelry back.

Only a few years later, in December 1937, after a series of escapades in Hollywood, Healy engaged in a pair of fistic duels in and outside a nightclub. He was patched up by a nearby doctor, but a few days later was dead of "natural causes."

Anything related to violence was probably a "natural cause" for the Wild Guy.

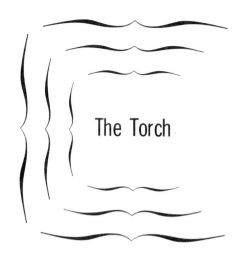

The Torch

YOU DON'T HEAR THE PHRASE much more—what with the new language of "making it" and "the scene" and "hangup" and all the personal youth slang of today—but if once you said somebody was "carrying the torch," everybody knew what you meant. He or she was the victim of a broken romance. I don't know where the description came from, but I once heard a very exact description of the torch.

I couldn't help listening to them. They sat there at a bar, this girl and this fellow, and the chap kept trying to open a conversation but the girl just kept twisting her martini glass and staring into the untouched drink. So finally the fellow stopped talking and, sure enough, the girl took a big breath and began to speak. The funny part was that she spoke in a monotone, but there was so much emotion in her voice that the words carried clearly to me.

"You want to know what it's like?" she asked, asking it as if she were talking to herself. "I'll tell you what the torch is like. It's like this. You sit here and listen to some nice guy, some nice guy like yourself, and you don't even hear what he is saying. All you can think of is, will this chatter never cease? Will I go on forever listening to the wrong voice? Will I never hear the right voice again? So you order another drink and it doesn't taste any better than the first one. And you try to think of someplace to go where it's fun. But you know that nowhere you go will be any fun. I'm sorry, friend. Am I being insulting?"

The guy smiled and told her: "Go ahead. Maybe talking about it will help you."

She took another breath. "And then," she said, "there are the places you can't go to any more. Because if you go there all you'll do is think about the times you were there with him. And there are the dresses you won't buy because they're too much like the dress he liked. And there's that damned song. That damned Our Song. If only they wouldn't play it every time you just begin to think that maybe you're really starting to forget."

She took another breath.

"Sometimes you walk down a familiar street and you think you are bleeding inside your chest. That's what it's like, that's the torch. You carry it with you wherever you go and you're a bore to everybody. And then all the questions about him, and answering them is enough to put you into the psycho ward. It's always some fool who asks about him, of course, but fools can't help being fools.

"And then there is that staring at the wall. You stare at the wall and, staring, you go through all the painful scenes again. Where did it go wrong? That's the unanswered question. And then you go through the old scenes, the great scenes, and you rephrase all the old arguments and tell yourself what you should have said and what you should have answered to what he said. You even remember the words you said for the Great Goodbye, and you know what you should have said instead and then suddenly you have to fight yourself to keep from calling him up and saying those things even at this late, dead date.

"And if you get a little drunk you're sure to get into an argument because you say nasty things to people at the party before you even know who they are—no matter, they've got to be the wrong people. And you don't like new friends any better. You get to the point where you are telling the head shrinker all these things in a dead, dull voice and he is answering in another dead, dull voice.

"Another thing. You get to hate the telephone. Your heart jumps every time it rings. This could be it. This could be him. This could be him saying he's sorry, he was wrong. But it never is. Not ever. It's always a voice you don't want to hear. But still you jump every time that damned phone rings. That's what it's like, the torch."

The man laughed quietly. "There's only one medicine that can cure a bad case like yours," he told this girl.

"You must mean poison," she said.

"No," the young guy said, "it's a medicine spelled *t-i-m-e*. You take enough of that medicine and one morning you wake up all cured. Even the scars have disappeared."

"How would you know?" the girl demanded.

"I know," the fellow said gently enough, "because it takes a torcher to know a torcher."

Broadway as it was during the era of the great moviehouse and the Hollywood extravaganza. Filmgoers then could hardly have foreseen art films and skin flicks. (*Culver*)

Swing Street in the days of its loud glory. The block of 52nd Street between Fifth and Sixth avenues where more star jazz musicians clustered and were born than anywhere else since the days of New Orleans. (*Culver*)

The basic Condon Mob. Cutty Cutshall on trombone, the Master with guitar, Wild Bill Davison on cornet, Peanuts Hucko on clarinet, Gene Schroeder at the piano keys, Jack Lesberg with bass and Davey Tough on the drums. A radio session in the early 1930s.

The man in the center is Benny Goodman, the King of Swing. Lionel Hampton on vibraphone and a younger Gene Krupa on the drums. (*Culver*)

The Palace Theatre, mecca of two-a-day big-time vaudeville. Virtually every famous name in show business—from Sarah Bernhardt to Bob Hope—played here, with the sole exception of Al Jolson. In those days our entertainers protested less: The marquee flag shows that song-and-dance men endorsed the National Recovery Act. (*Culver*)

Texas Guinan on her way out of town—a wise move, since Owney Madden and Big Frenchy DeMange had banished her from Broadway. Once, when she opened in nearby Long Island, still out of favor, a bomb exploded in the place on Saturday night. Texas got the message, but never made peace with her former allies. Her most famous club is now Al and Dick's restaurant, on West 54th Street. (*UPI*)

The home of corned beef and comedy—the original Lindy's delicatessen and restaurant. It was here that the fabled gambler and Black Sox fixer, Arnold Rothstein, was lured from his table to his death—by the pistol of a loser who considered himself cheated. (*Culver*)

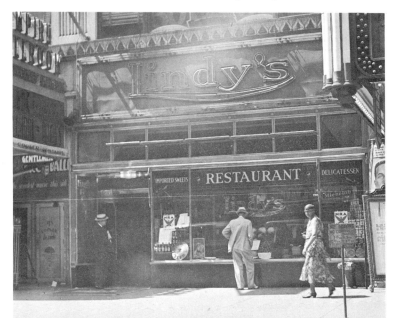

Mister Lee, as he was always called. Lee Shubert virtually saved the living theatre in the dark Depression days by stubbornly hanging on and risking his huge fortune. Never known to whimper or complain after an investment loss, he would moan and groan over the cost of coal or ice for this chain of theatres. (*Acme Photo*)

Who can forget the old international set? Here the portal to their New York playpen. (*Culver*)

Mr. Malaprop himself. Sam Goldwyn, with hand to chin, and producer Arthur Hornblow (seated right) on the set of an Eddie Cantor film. In dark glasses is Florenz Ziegfeld. (*Culver*)

The Great Schnozzola in his early days. Jimmy Durante (center) with Eddie Jackson (left) and Lou Clayton, at Clayton, Jackson and Durante's Club Rendezvous. "We are opening the joint," was Jimmy's announcement, "as soon as I learn how to say it." (*Culver*)

The wistful and wonderful Jimmy Savo. He was called the greatest pantomimist in the world by another pretty fair pantomime artist named Charles Chaplin. (*Culver*)

Firm friends and fast enemies. Walter Winchell and Sherman Billingsley at their regular table 50 in the Stork Club. It was as much Winchell's place of business as Billingsley's. They were always virtually in each other's laps—or at each other's throats. (*Culver*)

An Irish Indian named Lee Nash. As Ted Healy, he was to become one of the funniest, and also wildest, comics in Broadway and Hollywood annals. (*Culver*)

MOONLIGHT

When Mae West was the siren of the screen and her "Come up and see me sometime" was a national catchword, her ample bosom was her basic trademark. At the height of her film fame, Miss West bestowed her presence on New York for a brief visit. Reporters and photographers clustered around. Questions and flashbulbs popped.

"Give us a smile, Miss West," called a photographer. "Show your teeth."

Miss West declined. "It makes my mouth look too big," she explained.

"All right," called the photog, "so will you open your coat and throw out your chest?"

"Gladly," agreed Miss West.

The Last Barrelhouse

ONE NIGHT SHORTLY BEFORE AN unpleasantness known as World War II, and when a restaurant called Toots Shor's was receiving daily, nightly and often twice-nightly attendance from its favored famed folk and also from any transit celebrity who happened to be in town, I asked the obergruppenfuehrer who had generously bestowed his own name on his own place to give me, in his infinite wisdom, the real kernel of truth, the innermost secret, of what made a restaurant successful and, even, legendary.

Mr. Shor thought for a moment. His gourmet's eyes looked into the mystique of the matter. But when he spoke, it was without evasion or uncertainty. "Keep plenty of good peanuts on the bar," the Great Man pronounced. "If you give the bums enough peanuts to eat, you don't have to waste time serving them food. With a lot of peanuts they drink more."

Further proof that Shor, gourmetwise, is a meat-and-potatoes man rather than a disciple of Escoffier was introduced some years later when he returned from his only (and truncated rather quickly) tour of Europe and its epicurean lures. On this late afternoon I sat at a table alone, over a drink, when all of a sudden Joe Rivera, a veteran captain of waiters, approached me with a large tray. I gazed at the tray in some wonder. On it were nothing but small pieces of crisp toast covered by melted mozzarella cheese. You know mozzarella. It's the stuff the pizza joints use.

Even for free, this hors d'oeuvre did not appeal to me. Joe looked pained. "Aw, take a couple," he pleaded. "The boss is watching."

What the hell did I care who the boss watched, I demurred?

"Go on," Joe practically ordered. He turned his back on Shor's house table near the door to hide an amused giggle. "He loves to see people eat these things. He tells everybody that this stuff is the only thing fit to eat he could find anywhere in Rome."

I started to join Joe in his compulsion to giggle. And then I stopped cold as I remembered the other side of this attitudinal coin. Only a month or so before, the wife of a film executive had returned to New York from a place called Paris, France, where she had dutifully journeyed with her husband to be at his side while he spent several months on foreign film matters. Wifey lasted in Paris exactly two weeks. Barely packing, she rushed to the airport and grabbed the quickest available flight home. We were all amazed to see her. Naturally, suspiciously, we asked what was wrong.

"There isn't a restaurant in all of Paris like Toots Shor's," she explained. Soon thereafter she lost her husband. But Shor's has never lost her.

Food in Shor's goes up and down, even though it is in the basic chophouse pattern. One night you may get the best Caesar salad in town, and the next night a piece of good-looking roast beef may turn out to be dull. First-class, second-class is about all that need be said for the Shor menu.

It is the ambiance of the Man himself, and the reactions of those who know him, plus his rather remarkable personal history and foibles, that could fascinate any psychiatrist. There is no pianissimo to Shor's personality. He is at full holler at all times. Nor is there ambivalence in the reactions of those who now, or formerly, studied the man at close range. These are also in full cry on the subject of Shor. He is either idolized or despised. There is no in between.

Physically, he is more than a heavyweight. Harassed by his doctors, he will get his weight down to 210, or when just living a normal drinking life he will balloon up to 275. In recent years we have had a plethora of "insult comics," but Shor was surely the first insult restaurateur. To your face you are called a "crum bum" (his favorite and most monotonous term of endearment) or you are a "meat head" or "creepy" or worse. All too often he further indicates your social acceptance with a muscle-tearing slap on your shoulder or a bone-bruising jab in your ribs.

Such behavior, by a restaurant man who lives on the money you spend in his place, quite naturally produces opposite poles of reaction.

"It's just his way of showing you he's your true pal," says his long-time true pal Frank Sinatra. "He's got a heart bigger than his big rear end."

"I have just found the formula for what will be the most famous restaurant in the world," contrarily says a manager of glittering show biz folk. "I will only let in people who refuse to go to Toots's place."

Such latter opinions bother Shor not a whit. Deep in his big heart he knows that if you don't appreciate and even admire him, then it is obvious to all right guys that you are a wrongo. He is the first to admit that he was a school dropout back in the days when dropouts were still called truants, yet he delights in the company of deep thinkers. A deep thinker, to Toots, "has a lot of class." Totally uninterested in the arts, possibly because he is almost hypnotized by sports and athletes, he nonetheless dutifully attends erudite musical and dramatic events if they concern a friend, patron or hero. These rare occasions have furnished some of the finest Shorisms.

Having lost a football bet to his pal Paul Draper, he could not welsh. He had to get into white tie and tails and attend Draper's dance concert at Carnegie Hall. He suffered through the entire ghastly experience and fairly bulldozed his way through the exiting crowd to the first empty taxi. "I said, 'Take me to Toots Shor's,'" he remembers. "The driver looked at me and said, 'This is the first time in twenty years of hacking that anybody ever left here and told me to take them there.'"

Because Maurice Evans is a pal, Shor faithfully attended the premiere of Evans's *GI Hamlet*. At intermission he loyally praised Shakespeare and Evans, and even GI's, but he also admitted, "I'm probably the only bum here who doesn't know how it all comes out."

He has even been to Carnegie Hall twice. For some forgotten reason he was dragooned into going to hear a symphony concert maestro-ed by Leopold Stokowski. Shor took a backup man this time—the burlesque comic Rags Ragland. He was bored and fidgety through the first part of the program.

"There ain't even any dancing," he beefed to Ragland. "Let's leave at the half." They did.

His attitude toward the arts has not changed over the almost thirty years he has rubbed shoulders with the effete as well as the muscular. Not long before this was written, a dinner guest at Shor's was Wellington Mara, the president of the football Giants, and his wife. Shor sat down to regale Mara with his own football lore. Mara asked to be excused and, with his wife, rose from the table. Mara apologized for his hurry, explaining that he was taking his wife to see the play *Hadrian VII*. Toots was unimpressed.

"I ain't even seen the Sixth," he admitted.

But with an athletic celebrity it is, as the saying has it, a whole new ball game. One night years ago he conferred his favor on Sir Alexander Fleming, the discoverer of penicillin, by sitting at Sir Alexander's table and being pleasant, even polite. That night Mel Ott, a favorite immortal with all baseball Giants fans, had done something spectacular at the Polo Grounds and the news had been quickly flashed to Shor's.

As Shor sat with Fleming, a waiter came with the glorious news that the mighty Mel Ott had just come through the door.

"Excuse me, Sir Fleming," said Toots hurriedly, "but I gotta go see a celebrity that just walked in."

His fascination with sports goes back to his childhood, which was in Philadelphia. He is the product of a comfortable, middle-class home, and as a boy was friendly and popular. There are various theories as to why he quit school to become a poolroom hustler—a chapter in his history of which he is still childishly proud—and to develop a fascination for the glamorous hard guys and night-life folk of the day. There is nothing sleazy or illegal in his adolescent record and, indeed, he soon went square and became a very able salesman for various items of men's clothing. He was a traveling salesman, and his travels took him to New York.

He was immediately hooked.

He did not rest until he wangled a job at the long-forgotten Five O'Clock Club. Today he describes his nightly duty as "inside bouncer." People who remember him in those dim days, and your literary servant is one, recall that he was perhaps the handsomest bouncer that New York's speaks and cabarets ever boasted. Tall, and in his youth built like a telegraph pole, he was sufficiently physically powerful to handle almost any kind of trouble and, more important, had the rare talent of transforming strange combatants into new friends. He was as quick with a gag—or a free drink—as he could be with his hands.

The Five O'Clock Club, like most illicit activities in the big city back then, was owned by Owney Madden and George "Big Frenchy" La Mange, overlords of our early local Syndicate. This was the heyday of Jimmy Walker and Tammany Hall, and all large-scale operations, including those outside the law, had Irish overtones. Madden was boss. He took a liking to Shor, for one reason or another. Possibly, it was because Madden, always a negotiator and mediator rather than a shoot-firster, saw in Shor a promising talent for café work.

Shor dealt more directly, however, with Sherman Billingsley, who hadn't at that point even thought of a Stork Club. Billingsley was a sort of general manager for the mob's speaks and nightclubs. Billingsley's reaction to Toots was immediate. He despised Shor on sight and never stopped. Billingsley and Shor for almost forty years butted heads in an ideological vendetta and personality clash that ended only with Billingsley's death and that at one time—to the shocked disbelief of the entire underworld—was even carried to (of all places!) a real, honest-to-goodness court of law. There Toots beat Sherm out of a big sum for libel.

Nicky Blair, one of the few nightclub operators who was already established in those days (and he is still active with the new Bahamas gambling casinos), sighs as he remembers the Hatfield-McCoy blood feud between Sherman and Toots. "Owney would give Toots a job in a joint," Nicky remembers, "and three weeks later Sherman would arrive to examine the books and the management. The first economic move he would make was to fire Toots. Toots would go to Owney and Owney would grin and, maybe just to needle Sherman, would hide Toots away in another joint. A month later Sherman would arrive and fire him again. Owney would put him somewhere else. Sherm would fire him all over again." Here Blair sighs. "It got monotonous," is his criticism of the whole remembered disrapport.

In 1934 Shor married Marian Volk, a tiny Irish doll who can dominate her lumbering bear husband to this very day. In 1936 Shor left his job at Leon and Eddie's nightclub to become a manager at Billy La Hiff's aforementioned Tavern—the sportsmen's hangout, remember? La Hiff died the same year. His son was disinterested in the booze and food business, and Shor persuaded a Philadelphia businessman friend to buy the storied place and make Toots full partner and manager.

Here, we might comfortably predict, was the turning point in Our Hero's young life, the first stage in his professional rocketry. Alas, we would be fooled. Shor seemed to go slightly lunatic. He became a big-time gambler, winning and losing in those depressed times as much as $10,000 at a clip. It was about here, also, that he really began his running competition with the nation's distillers. He set out to prove that he could drink all they could make. The Tavern was still frequented by Shor's idea of the only true aristocracy—prizefight champs, famous jockeys, popular sports-writers, baseball stars, great comedians and tragedians.

"The place was an established gold mine," a Shor detractor remembers, "and the big boob literally drank and bet it away. You remember Frank Ericson, who was then the top gambling commissioner in New York and maybe in the country. There wasn't a wise guy in town who didn't say, as he passed Shor's Tavern, 'Tomorrow that name comes down and Ericson's goes up.' "

For the next two or three years our Boy Wonder, as usual, was studied from two disparate poles. The pals stood by steadfastly with the courage of their faith in him. They needed both courage and faith, since a financial crisis was an almost daily event in Toots' addled life. The knockers sneered and repeated that anybody could have foreseen Shor's toboggan. He had never been anything but a loudmouth and a no-talent and now, having finally faced this fact himself, all he had left was to drink himself to death.

Through it all, his wife, so lengthily and normally known to us all as Baby that some of us have to call a friend to remember her real Christian name, stuck to Toots, who is known to nobody as Bernard. Taking into account the amount of influence she exerts on him, it is possible that it was she who stopped the aimless slide. At any rate, sometime in 1939 Toots took dead aim on a restaurant of his own, one that would have his own name above the door. First, of course, came the financing.

Ah, that financing. Even what is known of it is a saga, and we may safely assume that we don't know all of it.

One item is perhaps indicative of the overall promotion. With construction under way, Toots found himself one day in a money bind more serious than all previous crises. He thumbed through the list of friends in his memory book. He chose Eddie Duchin, the pianist, man of wealth and inheritor of greater wealth.

"I need money," he told Duchin bluntly.

"How much?" asked the orchestra leader.

"A lot," said Toots just as bluntly.

"How much is a lot?" was the next question.

"Just give me a blank check with your name signed to it," was Toots's suggestion.

Without further quibble, Duchin wrote a check with only the date and his signature. With this blank check on established wealth, Shor was able to browbeat and cajole his creditors until he got his hands on extra cash. At last the restaurant stood completed at 51 West 51st Street, the exact site of the old Leon and Eddie's. At six o'clock on the night of April 30, 1940, Toots arrived at his own door accompanied by Baby and the sportswriter Jimmy Cannon.

Shor paused in the doorway. He dug into his pants pocket and came up with his total wordly cash. It came to forty cents. Lifting his arm, he flung the coins across the street.

"I might as well go in empty," he said simply.

He had the first drink at his own bar. It was not to be his last. Success was almost immediate and, of course, to this day you can listen to a wide variety of analyses from various historians, any single analysis reflecting either admiration and approval or bitterness and ridicule.

There are probably several reasons for the Shor success. The wartime economy had taken hold and, although the hard core of Toots's customers were the same worthies who had contributed to the Tavern debacle, they now had money with which to pay their bills. Shor himself had doubtless seen the light. He transformed himself into a hard-working proprietor and an equally hard-working businessman. And he did something even more important—he stopped gambling. For years he has had a front box at all the racetracks (in addition to his boxes at the stadiums and arenas), but I can't remember ever seeing him in it. The racetrack is for his friends only.

Otherwise he was unchanged and remains so today. Once, after an extended session with the brandy bottles, he and Eddie Arcaro and some kindred souls took themselves off to Saratoga for the health-giving baths. They stayed for a week or ten days, and Shor came back to his bistro looking like a new man. At noon when his place opened and he appeared as usual, he was the picture of heavyweight health.

"Mr. Shor!" said a surprised bartender. "It's really good to have you back!"

"If it's so good to have me here," said the maestro strongly, "why don't you mix me a Bloody Mary?" He was up, up and away for three days. Saratoga had lost another convert.

Yet he made it to his business desk bright and early every morning.

Sometimes one must suspect that deep in his heart Shor is convinced that everybody lives and drinks like he does; it's just that the rest of us try and hide it. A few years ago he fell in a Washington hotel room and broke a leg, which has never properly healed. He was with two old pals, Bob Considine and Frank Coniff, who both suggested he sue the hotel because a rug had slipped beneath him. They would and could both be witnesses. Shor sneered.

"You been drunk for thirty years," he told Coniff. "What'll you answer on the witness stand when they ask you that question?"

"Then use me for a witness," said Considine recklessly.

"You been drunk for forty years," Shor dismissed him.

Once Toots's headwaiter and two of his captains *did* do a very authentic Shor impersonation. They started drinking one night in New York and moved their drinking for some reason to Chicago, from which toddling town, as Joe E. Lewis sings, they sent Shor reassuring telegrams from day to day. Ultimately, they returned home and nervously reported back to work. They waited for the diatribe to come. It didn't. Shor ignored the guilty trio. He wouldn't speak to them or even toward them.

Finally, it was too much for the headwaiter. "Aren't you even going to say something to me?" he demanded almost hysterically.

"Yeah," growled the padrone. "Why didn't you take me?"

If Shor has never gone off the deep end because of booze, it is probably to the credit of his tiny wife, Baby, who sometimes looks as though she could fit in his pocket. A call from the grapevine for

Baby brings her sudden appearance. She can cool her bull of a husband with a few words and sometimes with one steady look. Their marriage surely must be one of the most successful in Broadway's history. In their thirty-fifth year of marriage, they have four children, two grown. With all of his antics, Shor has never so much as made a burlesque pass at another woman. Indeed, he frowns upon married men who cheat. He will not come near them anywhere and ignores them in his own drinkery. At his loudest and most drunken, he is basically a prude.

For some forgotten reason, possibly because both were sometimes concerned with the same charities, Toots and Baby were dinner guests of the late Francis Cardinal Spellman at the latter's residence behind St. Patrick's Cathedral. Toward the end of the dinner, the Cardinal asked Shor how he liked the residence food.

"Not so good as mine," Toots told him frankly, "but it's cheaper."

It is remarkable how few real tensions ever developed at either of Shor's bars. There was the rumor, when the new place first opened, that Rocky Graziano had taken offense at something Jackie Gleason said or did and bowled Gleason off his stool with a straight right. There were arguments and behind-the-back insults and complaints, of course, but the only two contretemps which I ever remember being moved to the sidewalk for further physical determination both ended up in hilarity for everybody—including the original combatants.

On one occasion a TV agent took umbrage at an advertising man and both moved outside to slug it out. The TV chap remembers the final round of the no-contest and it was soon the best laugh at the bar.

"I was mad as hell and I would have taken him outside sooner," remembers this gladiator, "except that I was wearing a brand new suit. Well, once outside I took off my jacket and hung it on the door handle of a car which was parked there. I turned to do battle, circled a couple of times, and then started running up the street like a thief. Behind me the bar mob was screaming 'Yellow, yellow' or 'chicken!' or something but I kept running. There was a traffic jam up the street and I reached my goal.

"That damn car had driven off with the jacket of my new suit hanging on the door handle. I was too winded to do any further fighting."

There was an even better street "brawl" which erupted from the bar. Two regulars who shall be nameless took each other outside to settle matters. Since neither were renowned for physical strength or athletic prowess, the bar mob stayed inside, waiting for the combatants to come back in with their arms around each other and the argument resolved. When they didn't come back within a few minutes, Shor and several aides went out to halt any possible damage.

The gladiators had "fought" their way up the street as far as "21." No punches had been struck as yet, although all fists were up and the contestants were warily feinting at each other. The mediators ran up the street toward the "fighters" and then burst into raucous laughter.

It was raining lightly. Circling with the gladiators was the Shor's doorman. He carefully held over their heads his big umbrella to keep the gladiators from getting wet.

Bob Considine, probably the most experienced of the Shor biographers, remembers a time when he thought Toots himself and another important personage were about to come to blows. Bob remembers he was sitting at a table some distance away when Joseph P. Kennedy came in. Shor went to sit down with him.

As they talked, Kennedy's face got red and soon he was pounding a fist on the table. Gorge kept rising up his neck muscles. He glared at Shor and pounded the table harder. Soon he got up and left.

"What was Kennedy mad at you for?" Considine asked the padrone. Shor looked amazed.

"He wasn't mad," he explained. "He was telling me how much he likes Bobby. He was saying that if Bobby has any enemy anywhere he will go around and through anything to get him."

In recent years Shor, now in his late sixties, has not only mellowed but slowed down considerably. For one reason, his injured leg gives him long hours of pain. And he gets moody because so many of the old convivial faces are no longer on the scene. So many have moved away, or are carrying busted livers or indeed are just plain dead.

Further, New York is a different city than in the giddy old postwar days. Prize fighting, which could transform Shor's on fight night into a sort of New Year's Eve party, is struggling for a comeback and is hardly a big-time sport anymore (except for two or three big fights a year), where once it was a Friday night social event. His beloved baseball Giants have moved away and so have his despised Dodgers. His beloved Yankees at this writing are wallowing in the depths of futility after their long years of glory. So many of the new, young professional football heroes prefer those "swinging singles" hamburgeries with the pretty girls to Toots's saloon and the professional athletic talk.

"A thing that has really hurt this place," said an old-timer the other day, "are the house accounts. For years Toots wouldn't honor a credit card here. If he knew you, you signed the check. That was fine with his old friends, all of whom were doing good, and if some of them weren't he didn't worry about their debt. Now this place is full of young executives who start signing tabs, and pretty soon they owe a few hundred dollars. Then they desert the joint for somewhere else. They get in over their heads."

"I don't think he has much in common with the new customers," says another long-time student. "Remember when he used to stand at the entrance to the dining room, say hello to everyone, say goodbye to everyone, and sit down with almost anybody who asked for him? Now he doesn't want to sit down with anybody except some old pal."

"He should have franchised this place years ago," contends another historian. "He should have had a Toots Shor's in every city that has a big league baseball or football team. What the hell, he's always going to those cities for the games anyway. If he had his name on a joint in those places he would only have needed to show up for a couple of days before the big games. He could have made a real fortune."

Luncheon and the cocktail hours at Shor's are still loud and crammed but—alas—as the early diners leave, the white tableclothed tables somehow seem too numerously empty. This, of course, is not peculiar to Toots's place. There seems to be no late-night business anywhere in the Big City, as we remember late-night business.

Which recalls what is probably Toots's most historic remark. It was uttered early in World War II when a Government edict stopped all public drinking at midnight instead of the previously legal 4 A.M. Nightclubs and restaurants moaned and groaned at the heavy economic blow. Not Our Hero.

"Any bum that ain't drunk by midnight," he pronounced, "ain't trying." This classic was widely quoted and even got him an approving editorial in one of our most staid journals.

Whatever the current downbeat, the old guard remains faithful. Just the other night I dined there and at the front "important tables" were Frank Gifford, Bill Veeck, Paul Screvane (then actively working for Robert Wagner's aborted mayoralty comeback), Sonny Werblin, Kyle Rote, Wellington Mara of the football Giants, Tucker Frederickson of same, the famed jockey Eddie Arcaro, Mickey Mantle and two or three more of equal celebrity.

Such a gathering would have sent any other restaurateur in town screaming for his press agent to get the newspaper photographers there, get some publicity for God's sake! But getting publicity was the last thing on Toots's mind. You don't, after all, expect publicity because your old pals are right where they are expected to be.

DIRTY JOKE

By the time I made New York, the early giants of journalism had departed this vale, but there were, however, veterans on the copy desks of newspapers and even still at the typewriters who could relate the legends, whether factual or mythical. Horace Greeley was the publisher who was the center of most of the legends. His New York Tribune had been a stickout publication and to this day Greeley is still quoted for his "Go West, young man, go West" advice. An old hand whose name I have forgotten was working the lobster shift rewrite trick with me on the old New York Evening Post (then an eight column standardsize) and one night he told his only memory of Greeley.

It seems they were both riding either the subway or an elevated train. Greeley was always curious about who and why people read the Tribune. He watched a man reading another newspaper, got up, sat down beside the chap and began to query him on his reading habits. The reader didn't look up. He just said he read the Herald and the Sun. Didn't he ever buy the Tribune? Greeley demanded.

"Oh, I buy the Tribune," the reader said, still not bothering to look up. "I use it to wipe my ass with."

"Keep it up," Greeley told him after a moment of thought, "and pretty soon you'll have more brains in your ass than in your head."

They Also Serve

ONE MAN SERVING ANOTHER THE food and drink that sustains him is a very basic relationship indeed. It is therefore interesting to consider the perverse relationship that has prevailed, in my total memory of eating in New York, between eater and restaurant waiter—a relationship that calls for some sociological examination. If ever two humans were meant to be temporary brethren, it is the eater and the server. It has never been thus, alas. I have felt, at times, that the eater and the waiter may as well speak separate languages.

Possibly the most illustrative story about this relationship is probably the oldest one. It is supposed to have happened years ago when Lindy's was *the* late spot for the hip set. A customer asked a waiter standing nearby, "What time is it?"

The waiter looked at his watch and looked away, "I don't know," he said firmly, "this is not my table."

There is another fable that should be juxtaposed to the above. "Waiter," says an unhappy customer, "this check is so big I have exactly enough money to pay it. I will have to forget your tip."

"Let me add up the bill again, sir," offers the waiter, "and see where I am in error."

The Hatfield-McCoy relationship between waiter and customer often breaks into open feud between waiter and boss. Once Max

Asnas, a boss-type character who ran New York's famed Stage delicatessen, tried to bawl out a waiter who had firmly refused to serve a certain customer and even sent the man to a far table.

"You're lucky," sneered the waiter at Asnas, "that I only sent him to another table. I should have sent him to another delicatessen."

Sam Jaeger, a legendary waiter at the old Lindy's, considered himself a true celebrity and held tightly to his aristocracy. "I serve only celebrities," he would state with his wolfish grin. "I would rather be stiffed by an important man than get a five buck tip from a nobody."

Perhaps the sociologist could find an underlying cause for the tension between customer, waiter and boss in one of the contradictory tenets of New York City law. Under one of these regulations (at various times unsuccessful attempts to bend the law have been made), two strangers who might arrive, say, at Grand Central Terminal and both want to go say, to, Pennsylvania Station, are not allowed to share the same cab even though they have no intention of offering each other more than an aloof nod. If the same two strangers should arrive at any one of the town's delicatessens, both would doubtless be seated together at a table with two other strangers.

And, before anybody could cut the mustard, an argument or at least a heated discussion would involve them all. The argument would be refereed by a waiter who would claim expertise in all things under the sun and, very likely, the boss would appear and take one side or another.

Consider the aforementioned Asnas and the comedian named Fat Jack Leonard. A nearby diner had smeared mustard on Jack's sports coat and he gestured for the padrone. Asnas took a light view of the tragedy. He pointed out that there was a cleaner next door who would take out the spots immediately. Mr. Leonard was still concerned, as well he might have been.

"That's an expensive jacket," he told Asnas.

The former charger for the czar (he had been a boy cavalryman with the White Russian army) fixed the comedian with a cold stare. "You think I use cheap mustard?" he demanded.

Possibly because of the very perverse character they develop, waiters are very often like the clowns who yearn to play Hamlet. Waiters like to wax poetic. Delicatessen poems are often propped against the cream cheese or the hard rolls. Examples that come to mind are the epic "Try Our Schtickel for a Nickel" at the Sixth Avenue deli and the near-sonnet in the window of the huge Katz's on East Houston Street, which suggested: "Send a Salami to Your Boy in the Army."

It is quite understandable, then, why each delicatessen takes on its own personality, flavor and modus operandi. All delicatessens look alike. Yet almost any one, taken alone and examined with care, has a definite individuality. One can easily understand the "take-out" business of all delicatessens. The items need no home cooking, there is wide variety, the stuff seems invented for watching the football game or noshing while watching late TV.

The "eat-in" trade is harder to explain. There are analysts who think that the most successful delis are the ones that distill their specialties into exotic appeals that will draw a trade of faddists, who are as hooked on their ideas of true food value as fly fishermen are about their tackle or philatelists about flawed stamps. Consider, for example, a few specialty delis that have been popular for years, but for all sorts of different reasons.

The Old Denmark has one table seating four people and thus proclaims itself "the most exclusive delicatessen in the world." A place called Manganaro's will make you thirty different varieties of hero sandwiches. A place listed in the phone book simply as Greengrass, B., Sturgeon, sent regular orders to the White House through three Presidencies. In Harlem, of course, a deli not only has the basic foodstuffs but also pickled hog's maws, ears, tails, snouts and chitlins. The Scandinavian delis strung along the East Side midtown sneer at any competitor who cannot offer ninety-eight kinds of canned sardines.

Harry's deli in the show-biz sector has a warning bell for actors who may blow their cues. Before its building came down, the Toast sold hero sandwiches by the foot—a dollar a foot. Schaller and Weber's in Yorkville has eighty-seven varieties of wurst. The Sixth Avenue Deli recently named a sandwich after Israeli hero Gen. Moishe Dayan. It is called, of course, the Jewish Hero. At the other swing of the pendulum, the swank Vendome will make you a caviar sandwich "to go," and the gag is that you don't buy it, you negotiate for it. To carry elegance still further, an East Side deli that has since disappeared boasted a doorman.

Almost every day at noontime, a chauffeured limousine would

arrive at Abe Liebwohl's Second Avenue Delicatessen, downtown. The chauffeur would enter, pick up three corned beef sandwiches and three bottles of soda. He would turn the limousine and rush back to his bosses, who run a Wall Street brokerage firm. Bernstein's-on-Essex-Street serves "kosher" Chinese food twice a week.

Zabar's, which calls itself a gourmet appetizer shop, for years has featured a six-foot sandwich with caviar, pâté and other goodies. It is known as "the seagoing deli" because it does a brisk business with yachts in the nearby Hudson River marina. Some years ago a delicatessen opened that featured curries and exotic spices and called itself, of course, the New Delhi. When the musical *Hello, Dolly!* opened to smash acclaim some years ago, a nearby rendezvous changed its name to "Hello Delly!" In tune with the social trend, a place called Gaiety East opened. This is not to be confused with Gaiety West, launched by the aforementioned Asnas years ago to seat twelve customers (when it became immediately successful, it was "renovated" by Asnas to seat ten customers).

Until his death a year or so ago, Asnas was by all means the greatest character of all the deli boys. His boyhood sounded like something by Tolstoi, rewritten by Nick Carter. He had one of the thickest accents extant, but could show you proof that the last stop on his long journey to America was in Havana, where he was language interpreter for President Menocal. He made the Stage into such an institution that after his death his relatives decided to "go public" and sell stock in the place.

He would never accept a reservation from anybody. A titled Englishman, who must be nameless, tried to reserve a table for eight and kept offering bigger and bigger personal tips until Max had to refuse $50 for himself.

"Listen," Asnas closed the conversation. "Give me your address and I'll *send* you a table for eight."

He was just as firm with labor union delegates. Once when a union delegate told him that his shop had "number-one help" and scale should be higher, Asnas disagreed. "What's lower than number one?" he demanded.

He was a berserk horse player and, possibly knowing how luck can turn on anybody, was openhanded with a long string of "old brokers," as he called them, who came in nightly for a sandwich handout. One night one of these "steadies" told the counterman he was in a hurry. Max rolled a bilious eye at him.

"Are you double parked?" he asked the bum.

He had many other idiosyncrasies. Until the very last he never upped his charge for coffee. "A fast nickel is better than a slow quarter," he would explain. He was ambivalent also. His favorite customer was an eighty-six-year-old man, the favorite because "he has eaten more than anybody else I know." He had another patron who had changed five wives but "never changed his restaurant." A bad customer was one who went somewhere else.

Yet he would sometimes sigh and proclaim, "Jewish food has killed more Jews than Hitler."

Webster's big dictionary, which can get somewhat garrulous in its definitions, is amazingly succinct in defining a delicatessen. It says: "Delicatessen. Prepared foods, cooked meat, preserves, etc. Also a store where food is served."

That raps up a deli in a preserved nutshell.

Waiters in more standard restaurants are not conversational guerillas of the style of their deli brethren, but they can be abrasive or, at least, off hand with job and client. A New York veteran who had made it all the way from busboy to maître d' once told me that waiters have a long list of reasons for their distrust of customers and that many of these reasons are, indeed, authentic and justifiable.

"The average party at a good restaurant," he explained, "is four people—two men and two women. Right away things can get off to a bad start because men invariably order in a hurry and women dawdle over the menu. The waiter stands there sucking on his pencil. Nobody in the party says whether they are hungry and want to eat quickly or whether they want to linger over dinner. If the waiter brings the first course right away, he is apt to be told not to 'rush' things. If he doesn't hustle, he is often bawled out for loafing.

"Then, just as the big dish is brought to the table, all four customers will get up and dance. Or the gals are in the rest room. Or one man has found a friend and gone over to say hello. When finally some food is put in all four mouths, one of them is sure to remark, 'The food is cold. Tell that lousy waiter.' By this time the waiter has gotten up a full head of steam. But he has to hold it in."

He sighed. "Another thing, it is absolutely amazing how many people who are ready to pay important money for first-class food know nothing about how to eat it. A certain amount of cocktails or whisky can sharpen your appetite, but too much deadens your taste. The man or woman who eats two pieces of bread before the first course is not going to enjoy dinner. Likewise, the man who got there early, sat at the bar and swallowed a couple of handfuls of salted peanuts. It's idiotic to drink champagne with steak or roast beef. Beer is better.

"These are just basic rules a person should discover by experience. But any housewife-cook who's worth her kitchen salt should know that unless you can stand over a Welsh rarebit and keep stirring it slowly it won't be good. So why order one at the height of the dinner hour when every chef in the kitchen will be busy with three other things? There are so many other things that, you would think, a woman in the party would remember. But no, they order and then complain."

One thing that makes a waiter instantly calculating and suspicious is how much the host of the dinner party plans to tip. What percentage of the bill? The customer, who long ago made up his own tipping scale, does know. The waiter is thus at a disadvantage, never a condition making for mutual affection. Over the years, however, veteran waiters have pooled their professional diagnoses and come to a few rules of thumb:

1. Doctors are the worst tippers in the world
2. Musicians are almost as bad
3. Actors are a fast-closing third
4. The louder the customer's mouth, the smaller the tip

Perversely, a waiter will often shape up and try extra hard when confronted with a party of out-of-towners who immediately give every indication that they rarely eat in a public place and have no idea what their financial responsibility is regarding the ultimate gratuities.

Often, waiters have long since discovered, such visiting firemen are so embarrassed and ill at ease that "they pay their way out" with a tip far more handsome than will be given by the wordly party at the next table. And, adversely, the veteran restaurant patron is apt to be somewhere between suspicious and certain that the waiter (1) isn't listening to him, (2) doesn't care how he wants his food and (3) is just going through the motions until he can stare him, the sophisticated diner, out of a bigger tip than lackadaiscal service deserves.

The waiters' pool today is an exact science. When he goes off duty, the head day bartender can often be seen separating the dollars, halves, quarters and dimes in separate piles, counting same, and writing notations. He is often so concerned in being right with his figures that he hasn't time to serve you a drink. But in a restaurant pool where there are two and even three shifts of public help, the contributions and the divisions must be carefully accounted for and audited. Indeed, in the great days of the Stork Club, the help hired their own accountant to weekly audit and divide the pooled tips.

Tips are not always in money and, believe it or not, some of the noncash tips are sought most eagerly. There was, for instance, the man in the restaurant at Newark Airport.

He had his breakfast one day and told the waitress that he would give her a special tip, a sort of tip tip. He told her to bet two horses in the daily double. She was at first annoyed, but since all restaurant employees seem to be compulsive horse players, she spread the news around. She played the double and so did the staff. It won nicely. Next day same customer and same "tip." Another double won nicely. Ditto the third morning. On the fourth day the staff refused to let their benefactor even pay for his meal. They chipped in and paid the tab themselves.

Both ends of this double went down. The horse tipper has never been back.

One veteran headwaiter has spotlighted another common type tipper, the big-guy-with-the-girls. "He has a loud mouth, he complains about his food, and then he tips like a miser. On his way out, though, he gets his hat and coat back from the pretty hatcheck girl. He gives her a ten-dollar bill. The sucker doesn't even know she has to put it in a locked box and hand it over to the concessionaire who leases the hatcheck room."

Some years ago a steady customer at a Polynesian restaurant retrieved his hat and coat and offered the girl a sealed envelope as her tip. He said it was a one-way ticket to Honolulu. Only condition was, he was flying there, too, on another ticket. Offer refused.

It is a fact that any horse tout or stock market hustler finds a fertile field among waiters. They are invariably gamblers. Some years ago a TV producer who had a regular table at Toots Shor's discovered his regular waiter was more deeply in the stock market than he, the customer, was. He even started taking the waiter's stock market advice.

"He was having his dinner in a fine restaurant near me the other night," recalled the TV chap, "and I must admit he's a bigger tipper than I am."

Some years ago, also, a promoter of oil wells talked practically an entire eatery staff into buying shares. He let them buy in at below market prices and warned them to hold tight. Ultimately the oil tycoon's lawyer called him down and told him the Internal Revenue boys were breathing hotly on his neck. The first thing to do, the lawyer advised, was to drill some real wells. Anywhere.

The promoter dipped into his safety deposit boxes, leased equipment and crew, and started drilling. Almost right away, a well produced oil. What did our benefactor do? He went back to the restaurant staff and moaned that his operations were failing. He nearly cried. But, he said, he wouldn't let his own mistakes cost his friends their money. He bought all the stock back at full price. It was weeks before the sad facts of life in the oil fields were brought home to the restaurant help. The promoter found other places to eat.

Like the Big Butter and Egg Man, the Big Tipper has disappeared from the scene, together, in this day of high-protein diets, with the Big Eater. Today hardly a restaurant waiter can remember a tip of $100 or over. Nobody takes over an entire restaurant for a private party anymore. It has been a generation since a millionaire hired a favorite chef or waiter to go into his personal domestic employ at a lifetime salary and a bequest in the will. The high cost of merely living and the snowfall of annual tax forms have outmoded such pleasures.

Such dread words as "heart attack" and "blood pressure"

and "overweight" and "cholesterol" have scared the old-time gluttons into thinking about their stomachs instead of overworking same.

The last of the big Broadway eaters, and one who could have challenged Diamond Jim Brady in certain areas, was a press agent named Kenneth McSarin. He was known simply as the Belly, and he was partial to eggs and hot dogs as a specialty. On the day President Truman issued the Food Proclamation, McSarin ate only thirty-two eggs, twelve slices of toast and ten malted drinks.

"I'm as patriotic as anybody," was his answer to criticism. "After all, I only ate two meals today."

Once he was offered a TV appearance if he would eat seventy-five hot dogs in a single sitting. The producer, however, wanted McSarin to prove his ability by eating another seventy-five at rehearsal. McSarin firmly refused for business reasons.

It wasn't that he was afraid to double what, to him, was a snack. He merely wanted to be paid for rehearsal, too. He lost only one eating bet in his career—and that through treachery. His "managers" would bet the unwary that he could eat ten omelets and wash down each one with a double malted. This one time, the Belly couldn't make the finish line. It was learned later that his opponent, backed by other sportsmen, had bribed the counterman to make outsize omelets and double malteds. So much for the last of the big eaters.

Next to the often misunderstood question of the tip, the biggest common beef in restaurants is overcharging. There were many clip joints of old and possibly here and there a waiter, in contrivance with a food checker and a cashier, has found a way to falsify a check. But in this modern day of computers and management systems and consultants and tax investigations, a restaurant has to be pretty much on the square.

"How do you know your waiters are honest?" I asked a successful restaurant owner years ago.

"Because they've all been here five years," was the answer. "If they don't steal enough to open their own joint in five years, then they're honest."

The only New York eating establishment that ever combined the quality and service of a fine restaurant, plus the added features of a delicatessen, was Lindy's, in the great days when Leo Lindemann was at the wheel. Possibly it was the delicatessen overtone that made Lindy's such an inexhaustible source of anecdotes and comedy. Consider:

It was the only restaurant that started as a gag and lasted to serve 50,000,000 people. . . . It was the only place in town that served breakfast *after* lunch. . . . It was the only eating place that got its first impetus from Al Jolson and was later saved by Eugene O'Neill. . . . It was the only place of employment where the man who made the pickled herrings arrived for work wearing spats and carrying a cane. . . . It was a place where Mrs. Eleanor Roosevelt insisted on serving herself and where Margaret Truman insisted on standing in line for a table. . . .

Lindemann and his wife, Clara, had worked German restaurants as waiter and cashier when he was tapped by two haberdashery men and a lingerie manufacturer, to be headwaiter at Gertner's in Times Square. The owners eventually harked to Lindy's food advice and knowledge and made him a partner in the first Lindy's, across the street from the much bigger one that was to come to Broadway and 51st Street. The original partners told everybody that their new Lindy's was just "an $8,000 gag."

Another delicatessen on Broadway caused no big stir until Al Jolson, a next-door Winter Garden standout star, dropped in. Soon Jolson, from the stage, was commanding his audiences to "follow me down the street to Lindy's." The place was in. Overnight, people such as Harpo Marx were dropping in for oddities—Marx's was cooked spinach with a dab of ice cream on it.

Once the restaurant was home, the inevitable quarrels were commonplace between the four partners. Lindy and partner Jack Kramer bought out the other two. Soon Lindy and Kramer were at odds. Kramer kept the small place until the building came down and Lindemann moved catercorner across the street into L-shaped corner premises.

The new "store" was to cost $100,000, but construction soon boomed the investment to over $170,000. In the Depression year of 1930 it seemed impossible to carry such a financial burden. Then came Eugene O'Neill—in spirit if not in person. Around the corner, O'Neill's five-hour drama *Mourning Becomes Electra* opened. At seven o'clock the audience was turned out to partake of some nourishment. Audience, actors and stage crew would hustle to the corner Lindy's. Word-of-mouth advertising soon turned the tide. The "big store" was in, too.

In the days before waiters' unions and other groups could countermand a tough boss, no small detail missed Lindy's sharp eye. "If he saw a waiter touch his hand to his hair," an old employee remembers, "he would immediately send the culprit to the men's room to wash his hands. He would never let us twist a napkin or dust a table with it. The napkins had to be fresh and pure."

Sam Jaeger, the celebrity waiter previously referred to, was a tall, gaunt man who served a nightly attendant, Damon Runyon. Many of Runyon's famous short stories are set in "Mindy's," and the writer made national literary heroes of South Street Benny, Nathan Detroit, Nicely-Nicely, Cheese Cake Ike and Vrooked Dollar Moishe. Runyon's pastiches were read by almost everybody, including a little old lady who came in one night and told Jaeger she wanted to see a real gangster.

Jaeger dutifully introduced her to Morris the Schnook, the famous horse race fixer. The Schnook was polite but abstracted. Actually he was Abe Lyman, then a top orchestra leader. Like most of his confreres in the place, Jaeger could, however, return insult with insult. Once a troublesome lady forgot her manners and demanded, "Why aren't you in the Army." "For the same reason, madam," said Jaeger, "that you aren't in the *Ziegfeld Follies.*"

Erroll Flynn often tried to entice Jaeger to spend some time on his yacht in the tropics. "Bring it to Sheepshead Bay," responded Jaeger, "and Jaeger will visit you if he has time." Nor did he ever succumb to the dozens of invitations from Hollywood stars to visit them in the Hollywood fairyland. "Jaeger reserves the right to choose his own swimming pool," was his stock answer. Once a stage producer gave him a script to read and submit an opinion. "So many nightclubs have flopped this year," Jaeger told the producer, "that a play about them is sure to be a turkey." It was.

A regular was Moe Snyder, known to Broadway and Chicago as Colonel Gimp or the Gimp because of his limp, an infirmity caused by receiving too many bullets in early Chicago days. For some reason the Gimp demanded only female lobsters and made a big fuss when he analyzed the sex of a proffered langosta as male. Married to the then top singer Ruth Etting, the Gimp one night shot her pianist, causing mild wounds. Miss Etting was in the process of divorcing the Gimp to marry her pianist. The Gimp was promptly placed in durance vile.

This caused much comment in Lindy's. It was argued whether or not the Gimp could make the warden serve him female lobsters. Wires were sent to the jailed Gimp from Lindy's, offering help and suggestions. The Gimp promptly named the Lindy regulars his "Eastern Defense Committee."

This fascinated Chuck Green, a pal of Runyon's who was a jewelry salesman known as the Doorway Tiffany. Green was further delighted when the Gimp wrote suggesting that a big Madison Square Rally should be thrown by his Broadway pals.

"The Gimp," decided Green, "must think he's Sacco and Vanzetti."

Through this maze of nonsense moved Lindy, hands folded on his stomach, eyes darting this way and that. His original planning had been just as meticulous. "I will not have a table in this place," he told the architects, "that is more than twenty steps from the kitchen. This, putting the kitchen right in the action (if enclosed), caused the room to have a front and three sides, a sort of square U. The sections soon had their own titles.

There was the Pressure Chamber, located between a bar end and the 51st Street window, a magnet for comics and gagwriters. For some reason, a row of booths along the north wall was always referred to as Oshkosh. The Damon Runyon Corner was up front, below an oil portrait of Runyon showing him holding a lighted cigarette. The cigarette actually glows, since its coal is a small electric bulb. The sector immediately inside the front doors was Hollywood and Vine. The far side of 51st Street was Dixie, too far "south" for any regular. A main sector was the Boiler Factory, and some quiet booths in the back were Palm Springs.

Possibly feeling that his store needed an added touch, Lindy became a collector of art. The north wall of the place was hung with large oil paintings that depicted sheep-grazing, peacocks strutting, fruit arrayed on a table, musicians at harpsichords, frail ladies gazing out of high windows, and other pastoral scenes. One painting is obviously the original of a magazine cover. It was generally accepted that the art display was worthy of one of the better museums.

Lindy did, in fact, have the advice of an art expert. His art connoisseur was one Ernest Rotchi. He came to work for Lindy the first month the place opened, and until recently he was still there—and still a waiter.

The place seated 344, and it was not unusual to "turn over" (repeat capacity) as many as ten times a day. Oddly, little liquor was served there, although the small Lindy bar was stocked with nothing but the finest of brands. "I would rather sell milk to a child," Lindy would say, "than booze to an adult."

Because it was so favored by the late-rising Broadway mob, a breakfast was always available after the lunchers had largely departed. These sleepyheads never appeared until long after J. Edgar Hoover had lunched and left. Lindy devised Hoover's favorite sandwich—raw chopped meat with condiments, a variation of Tartar steak. It is still on the bill of fare as a G-Man Sandwich. When things were slow, or he felt depressed, Lindy might allow himself some small entertainment. He would take Hoover or Marlene Dietrich or Doris Day or Jerry Lewis to the arcade next door. There he would play a few sets of Ping-Pong.

Meanwhile, cheesecakes and salamis and herrings were being rushed off to the White House, the Hollywood studios and to almost any famous person who found himself somewhere in Europe with nothing fit to eat. The Franciscan Fathers in Buffalo were particularly interested in Lindy blintzes and were sent the recipe. A jar of Lindy pickles sent to a bandleader who was in Moscow was confiscated on the theory that it had to contain something dangerous.

The accepted theory is that a great restaurant dies with the personality who founded and operated it. Lindy's lasted several years after the boss's death. It was run by his nephew Albert Abend and then, also successfully, by Jack Kramer, son of an original partner. Then the long lease was up. Kramer was faced with a new landlord. No agreement.

The landlord, a wholesale butcher, ran the place according to his own rules. To say that it was not Lindy's of old is probably redundant. A new owner and a new name are there now.

The Great Goofs

GOOFING, AS IT HAS COME TO BE known, is now a word familiar to almost all of us. Over the years, a newspaperman hears of many a great goof. Only a few years ago, for instance, the New York Racing Association decided that the late Frank Lloyd Wright, the architect who was so far out he sometimes disappeared from normal comprehension, was just the man to design a truly modern racetrack. Wright was given the assignment. He drew up an eye-shattering beauty.

There was only one thing wrong. Wright's ultramodern racetrack had no place for any betting windows.

Such things seem to be commonplace. When the original Ebbets Field was being built for the original baseball Dodgers, there were four daily newspapers being published in Brooklyn. The builders asked the sports editor of each newspaper to suggest anything and everything that might help Ebbets Field be the greatest of the new ball parks. The sports editors were full of ideas about where to put the hot dog stands, the comfort stations, the ticket windows, the visiting benches and whatever.

So Ebbets Field opened with everything in place. Only one thing was wrong—the sportswriters had forgotten to tell the builders they needed a press box.

There was some further confusion that day. The rotunda at the main gate was, in the eyes of brewer and owner Charles Ebbets, a thing of great beauty. There was a special, very social party planned just for the first look at the rotunda and all its marble. The celebrities gathered. Mr. Ebbets arrived. The great moment was at hand. Nobody had a key to open the rotunda. They had to break in.

I remember attending the official opening of the Morgan Annex of the post office on New York's Ninth Avenue. There were speeches and more speeches. Everybody toured the new building and oohed and aahed. Next day it was discovered that our fair city had a new post office building with no mail chutes or any provision for routing mail. The builders had to come in and rip it apart.

And in case you may think that a Government learns its lessons quickly, even as this is being written the biggest and newest post office building, constructed on a carefully chosen site to speed up the operations of mail trucks, is being partly torn apart—the doors just don't happen to be big enough to let the trucks in and out.

The theatre, of course, offers a natural ambiance for goofing. The Forrest Theatre in Philadelphia was built without a box office and so was the Hanna Theatre in Cleveland. Anthony Farrell bought the Hollywood Theatre on Broadway only to discover that he hadn't bought the lobby, which was being rented from a shoe store. He had to cut an entrance in from West 51st Street.

And then there was the time Bob Hope made the big-time in vaudeville and hurried around to buy a new comedy act worthy of his sudden new success. In those days it was an accepted custom for a writer of comedy acts to do a new routine for a famous big-time comic and, under mutual understanding, also give the routine to some small-timer who was playing out in the sticks. Hope, out in the sticks but already booked for the fabled mecca of variety, the Palace, bought a new act, brought it to Broadway and had instant success.

Two weeks later Jack Benny arrived from a tour of the big-time road and also played the Palace. He died all through his first show. Bob Hope had been on the same stage with Benny's act a couple of weeks previously.

The architect for one of Miami Beach's most gaudy hotels was responsible for a fine goof. Not being a card player himself, he built a card room that was virtually lined with mirrors, including the ceiling. Anybody sitting anywhere could look in one or more mirrors and plainly see what cards everybody else was holding.

Addison Mizner goofed pretty well in Palm Beach when he built a mansion that had no stairs in it. Mizner recouped by adding stairs *outside* the building, thus starting a fad for outer-wall stairways. They can still be seen on some old Palm Beach houses. The Senate subway that hit an empty lot instead of the Capitol was a fairly fine goof, and the time a promoter went to a Caribbean island with all the machinery to build an ice cream plant and make a fortune from the perspiring natives was another fine example. After the ice cream machinery was unloaded, it was discovered there was no milk on the island, and no way to get milk except by impossibly expensive importation.

My own research indicates that the word "goof" was first used by jazz musicians. A definition of a goof is hard to make, but an old tale of jazz musicians explains it well enough. As this legend has it, a busload of jazzmen were on the road late at night and the bus crashed into a heavy truck. The musicians were thrown out and lay around the road like scattered tenpins. Broken instruments were everywhere. A saxophone player and a trumpet man came back to consciousness at the same time.

"What happened?" asked the sax man.

"Somebody goofed," explained the trumpet.

MOONLIGHT

Even before the blight of Prohibition was lifted from the land, the restaurant that can be called "21" or Jack and Charlie's or the Iron Gate—with equal correctness—was one of the finest oases in the country. It remains so, bigger and better and richer, to this day. When it was smaller and devoted largely to society and the famous, the legend was that you couldn't get through the door unless you were known, sponsored and favored. This embittered many a social climber and fostered many historical footnotes that usually had snide overtones.

The original partners were the late Jack Kriendler and Charlie Berns. The original Berns is very much around and so are other Bernses. Three original Kriendlers—Mack, Pete and Bob—are still active, and so is a second generation of Kriendlers. It's that kind of a steady success. But back to its critics. In the old days "21" had a neighbor that shouldered it on the west side. This was a raucous and for a long time successful nightclub called Leon and Eddie's. It was Leon and Eddie's. As we shall see, it was the fountainhead for one of the best snide legends about the exclusivity and charged arrogance of Jack and Charlie's.

On the night in question, goes the story, a woman somehow got past the doorman unescorted and somehow was seated before the restaurant brass could explain why unescorted ladies were not admitted. She got a small table next to the swinging doors to the kitchen. She was flanked on one side by a serving table loaded with butter and ice buckets, on the other side by a table piled with salad bowls and warming lamps. Both Jack and Charlie watched her nervously. Who could predict what a woman unaccompanied might do to the aura of the staid place?

The lady was only midway through her dinner when a captain of waiters arrived at the bosses' table and said they had made a big mistake. "She must be *somebody*!" said the captain. "She ordered just the right dinner and the best, appropriate wines. You better talk to her."

So Charlie Berns is supposed to have gone over and asked

madam if her table was satisfactory. Perfectly, was the answer. Was service all right? Just ideal, said the lady. Well, said the padrone, was there anything at all the management could do for her? Just one little thing, admitted the lady. Just a small point of information. Of course, she was assured.

"Which are you?" asked the lady, sipping her wine. "Leon or Eddie?"

In Our Garden

THERE HAVE BEEN FIVE MADISON Square Gardens, reaching back in time to P. T. Barnum, and within their walls were written long chapters in the political, social and sports history of America for more than 150 years. It would take a shelf of books to detail the highlights of the Gardens that started in 1837 are still very much a part of New York life with the newest, biggest, shiniest and most current exhibit in the procession of Madison Square Gardens.

There hasn't been a Madison Square Garden on Madison Square since 1924. The original was launched in a railroad freight shed near the Madison Square site by the circus man Phineas Taylor Barnum. This was revised in 1879 and lasted ten years. Then, in 1890, a new one on the same site was designed by the famed architect Stanford White (who was to be shot to death in his own monument by the socialite Harry K. Thaw) and this one survived until 1924. And then, in 1925, the fourth Madison Square Garden came into being at Eighth Avenue and 50th Street. It was in business until 1968, when the bright and modern new multiple arena opened over the railroad tracks on Eighth Avenue between 31st and 33d Streets.

But because its time span roughly parallels those of us about whom I write, it was the Garden at Eighth Avenue and 50th Street that was "our" Garden. Its original guiding light was the fight promotor Tex Rickard. He was always proud of his partners, invariably referring to them as "the 600 *rich* millionaires."

Looking back, it sometimes seems as if *everything* happened at our Garden. Franklin D. Roosevelt climaxed his first Presidential campaign there. . . . Marilyn Monroe rode a circus elephant there. . . . It was there that the flamboyant producer Michael Todd threw a $410,000 party with his bride, Elizabeth Taylor. . . . Jimmy Walker, Mayor of New York, sat in a ringside seat and "rode" with the punches in the ring. . . . The place was once draped with Nazi flags for a Bund rally. . . . There Joe Louis made his wartime speech "Because we are on God's side.". . . The historic list of prize fighters reads from Jack Dempsey to Cassius Clay. . . . And of other athletes from Paavo Nurmi to Jim Ryun. . . . And so many more.

The crowds covered such a wonderfully wide spectrum, too. They ranged from the jeweled and draped socialites for the annual horse show and dog show to the overcoat thieves of the six-day bike races; from the polite gatherings for social or dance events to the rude and raucous at the Friday night fights.

When Sol Hurok first brought the Russian Bolshoi ballet to America, he admitted, "We were able to create a new public by using the Garden." His public did not, of course, include the Friday night fight regular who, when an important politician arrived with a lady not his wife, bawled so all could hear, "Who's the broad?"

This essay, however, must be kept to my own memories of our Garden and must not attempt any overall history. And, sitting here, it is suddenly apparent how tricky memory is. Ask me what I remember about our Garden and I will say the six-day bike races and the weekly prizefights. And not even the fighters themselves— more importantly the nicknames of the long departed pugilists.

But first the bike races. There were several types. A bike rider would ride up behind a motorcycle that had a swivel bar attached to its rear end. The motorcycle would take off, the bike rider pedaling furiously to keep his front wheel stuck to the motorcycle's revolving rear bar. As long as the bike rider stuck in there, he could make amazing speeds, largely because the vacuum held him in behind the motorcyclist's air-splitting body. But if the bike rider slipped back, he caught a blast of slipstream air that seemed to physically punch him yards back. The motorcycle had to slow down. The biker had to catch up. Precious seconds were lost.

Don't ask me why motor-paced bike racing had all those loud fans. It just did.

But the six-day race was the big event of the bicycle year. First, let us examine its modus operandi. Several two-man teams were entered. Around the infield were little curtained sheds with a cot inside. When one member of the team was out there pedaling, the other was resting or sleeping. For twenty-four hours a day and for six days hard running, one of the team members was on the track.

However, there was no assurance that the relaxing partner would get a good rest. After plodding around a few turns at minimum speed, somebody would start a "jam" and try to steal a lap. If somebody could circle the field, it was stealing a lap. Points were alloted and eventually toted up to determine the winner.

When this happened, alarms were sounded in the tents and all team partners came tumbling out to mount their bikes. After the teammate on the track had "jammed" until tired or successful, the mounted teammate, steadied by a trainer, would be pushed on the track and given an extra hard shove by the approaching, speeding racer (somewhat in the manner of foot relays). Off he would go to uphold the team's honor.

With twelve or fourteen bike racers strung around an oval track, this one passing that one, another falling back as he accomplished his goal, riders tumbling on to the track to replace their partners and everybody pedaling like hell, one was more or less forced to wonder how Frank Chapman, the old bike champ of another era, and now a referee, could possibly (not to say honestly) keep any kind of a score or point system accurately. Nonetheless, every day the leaders were announced and all the "stolen" laps properly listed.

This week of madness had many other entertaining and even dangerous features. Before radio and TV practically took over the music business, the six-day race was the mecca for every old-time song plugger in the business. No sooner was a jam finished and the maniacal shouting of the fans quieted, than some silver-throated minstrel would push his piano toward one side of the Garden and start belting out Irving Berlin's, or somebody's, new song. As he

sang it, the wheeled piano and its player would be pushed around
to follow the balladeer as he gave each side, end and angle of the
crowd a head-on treatment of his musical epic.

And then there were the extra "purses" offered, when things
were dull for too long, by any celebrity or near celebrity in the
audience who wanted his name and presence brought to the
crowd's attention. For this, the announcer would raise his gravel
voice and announce: "Mr. James Barton, famous comedian now
headlining at the Palace Theatre, has offered a purse of $200 for
the winner of a one o'clock three-lap jam." Or: "Joe Regan, the
silver-voiced tenor starring in the musical *Varieties* offers a purse of
$100 for the first rider to steal a lap after 11:30."

These awards were for real, as was basically understood, and the
racers rode like hell to win them. Certain rules were also
understood. A celebrity did not, for instance, offer a purse for a
stolen lap immediately after the teams down on the track had
ridden themselves breathless stealing laps just a moment ago. The
celebrity waited until things were quiet and possibly a little
dull—he got more attention that way, and it was best for
everybody.

The phenomenon of the six-day race was explained by many
people in many ways. Paul Gallico, then a sportswriter and now a
distinguished fictioneer, once noted that there was never any more
excitement, or much bigger crowds, for the sixth-night finish than
there were at the start and throughout the grind. Gallico concluded
that the attraction was "the continuance," not the terminus of the
race. He decided that the six days of nonstop wheeling had an
hypnotic effect and that its victims just couldn't miss any of it.

There were other explanations. Old New Jerseyites, particularly,
pointed to the almost frenzied preoccupation with bike rides and
bike racing on New Jersey roads early in the century.

"We had velodromes and racing strips for years after the
automobiles got popular," a veteran Jerseyite told me. And,
indeed, Jersey newspapers in Sunday-feature "yesterday" specials
still print pictures of bicycles that would carry ten or twelve riders,
bikes almost as long as a hook-and-ladder fire engine. And to this
day there is a group of aging Jersey bike racers who regularly have
dinner together and talk about the great days of two-wheeled
speed.

A bike was the same status symbol with a kid in the days when I was a kid as the sports car is today. So in the 1930s there was still a big reminiscent audience for men who could ride bikes at breakneck speed. However, as the six-day race took hold, it was obvious that there was a more solid reason.

Even to this day, road bicycle racing is a big sport in many parts of Europe. And the six-day races I remember were always liberally sprinkled with champions from France, Italy, Germany and even Australia. New York's foreign and ethnic groups could hardly wait for these annual home-country heroes. Any true American's patriotism came to a boil when Alf Letourneur of France or Gerard Debaets of Belgium or Maurice Brocco of Italy tried to steal a lap on our Reggie McNamara or Torchy Peden.

Oh, that Brocco of Italy. The New York Italians took him to heart, and the Garden would ring with that sustained, harmonized shout of "brrrrr-ah-ah-co-co-co!" He was a little before my time, but his legends would not die.

There was the time, for instance, that Brocco stole a lap when, under some common riders' agreement, no laps were to be stolen. Brocco took off and stole one with ease. He was to pay for it dearly. During a later jam, about six riders closed on him, forced him up the slanting track and *rode him right over the wall*. He landed in the laps of two spectators.

Spills and pileups were common, of course, even when unintentional. The greatest hazard to a bike racer, naturally, was splinters from the wooden track. Doctors and attendants spent much of their time removing wood slivers from the bodies of the heroes. It was also inevitable that during the grind at least one or two, sometimes more, racers would be put out with more serious injuries. When this happened the remaining partner merely teamed up with a racer whose own partner had been injured. Some adjustment was made in their scores and things ground along as usual.

One jam remains in old-timers' memories, although unfortunately I was not there to see it. The charge started and all resting partners were alerted. The hero of this jam, whose name is lost to memory, tumbled out of his bunk, relieved his tired partner and stole a lap. It was doubtless the only lap ever stolen by a rider who was naked except for his colored jersey. He had forgotten his pants. We knew our bike racers by their colors, back then. Numbers and names on jerseys came with a less dedicated generation.

The dangerous part of the six-day madness was the compulsion of a certain type of fan to steal your overcoat. At the grind, everybody sat on his overcoat, for some reason. But when a jam came, most people got up to holler and watch. Too often, when you sat down again, your overcoat was gone from the chair. Don't ask me how and why an overcoat thief existed. Perhaps nailing somebody's overcoat was, to the thief, his own status symbol.

The thing that had helped make our Garden a place for civilized folk, as against the hoodlum cutpurses and footpads who were the main attendants at the old sports palaces, was the Garden's insistence that a person who bought a ticket got the seat to which he was entitled. If there was a tough mug in the seat that belonged to somebody else, it was only necessary to bring this to the attention of a couple of much tougher Garden cops. This police force included some of New York City's toughest detectives. They were early moonlighters.

Pilfering was so frowned upon by Rickard's 600 rich millionaires that it led to a peculiar agreement between the New York City police and the nation's pickpockets and petty thieves. The word was passed that any "bump" man or "hook" who was caught with a hand in a citizen's pocket would be taken to a little room somewhere in the Garden and sternly dealt with by Garden cops. In turn, word came back that the Pickpockets Union, or whatever, had voluntarily put the Garden off limits during working hours. But they asked for a concession.

It was a well-known unwritten law, said the pickpockets, that even if they were caught in a crowded area, without any jostling in mind, they were automatically picked up on suspicion and, if they had a record, almost as automatically convicted. If they promised on their scout's honor that word would go out to every pickpocket to keep his hands in his own pockets only, could they use Madison Square Garden as their one and only crowded place of enjoyment?

The cops mulled it over and gave the entente a try. Capt. Dan Campion, in charge of the New York Pickpocket Squad for years, told me late in life that his squad hadn't had a Garden pickpocket complaint from the day of the agreement, many years before, until the wreckers tore down the building.

The last six-day bike race at the Garden, in 1961 after a lapse of twenty-two years, was a disaster. The newly and hurriedly built track didn't fit and caused a delayed opening that fouled up ticket sales and publicity. The riders were strange. The crowds sparse. Even the fanatical New Jerseyites were apparently too old to cross the river. I went one night and picked out a seat behind about six enthusiasts. To my surprise, they were not only young but amazingly conversant with the riders and riding. And then I realized that they were all former GI's who had spent time in Europe and watched bike racing there.

One would think there would be enough ex-GI's to support almost anything, today. Apparently not.

Although prizefighting is looked upon by many as a brutal and degrading sport, the regular Friday night fights at our Garden were almost social events. It was chic to arrive not much before the main bout, lingering in the lobby, shaking hands and greeting old friends who hadn't been seen since the previous Friday night. Socialites mixed with politicians, gamblers spoke softly with cops, sportswriters chatted with established figures in the game, wives and sweethearts were introduced around.

Ringside always had its goodly share of women. Film stars in town always sat well up front. And afterward everybody repaired to some restaurant such as Toots Shor's or Moore's or Gallagher's and fought the whole fight over again. I remember those nights so well. The few great fights stick out in my mind, and now and then something will come up to recall a lesser bout. But by some quirk of mentality, what I remember most vividly are the nicknames.

Paul Berlenbach was the Astoria Assassin, Billy Petrolle was the Fargo Express, Jack Delaney was the Rapier of the North, Luis Firpo was the Wild Bull of the Pampas and Jack Dempsey, of course, was the Manassa Mauler. Sid Terris was the Ghost of the Ghetto, Mickey Walker was the Toy Bulldog and Georges Carpentier the Orchid Man. Tom Heeney was the Hard Rock from Down Under, the Deacon was Tiger Flowers, and Lou Kaplan was the Hartford Windmill.

Joe Louis was the Brown Bomber, the almost forgotten Sam Langford was the Boston Tar Baby and, even farther back but still in the annals, John L. Sullivan was remembered as the Boston

Strong Boy. To keep to the color scheme, Max Schmeling was the Black Uhlan. Phil Scott was derisively spoken of as Phainting Phil. But the one I remember with most amusement was a lightweight named Joe Glick, who at one point in his youth had worked for a tailor. And so, of course, he was known as the Brownsville Buttonhole Maker.

I wouldn't attempt, in this short piece, to even list the other great Garden events—the heart-stopping track and field events, the popular ice revues, the great hockey stars and teams, the annual event that was the circus and the other annual event that was the bone-breaking rodeo. But one event does deserve brief mention, since it very well may have been the biggest personal party thrown since Nero's times.

It was on Oct. 17, 1957, that Mike Todd celebrated the first birthday of his smash movie hit, *Around the World in 80 days.* Never one for understatement, Mike invited just "a few personal friends," or enough to fill the Garden. There were to be prizes ranging from fur coats to motorcycles to an airplane. Free champagne for everybody. Mrs. Todd, the glamorous Elizabeth Taylor, was of course the hostess. TV would broadcast the great affair.

Mr. Todd's "personal friends" jammed the huge arena and soon began to take advantage of friendship. Thousands thundered down from reserved and unreserved seats to attack a birthday cake that had taken twenty days to bake. Ushers, turning themselves into waiters, were soon selling the champagne Mr. Todd had ordered for his personal friends. The fur coats were swiped quickly. Things went from bad to worse. The "crashers" grabbed the motorcycle door prizes and roared out onto Eighth Avenue. A mob of drunks, possibly mistaking the displayed airplane for a set of goal posts, climbed up on the wings and played seesaw until the wings broke off.

Everything liftable disappeared, including all the prizes. Duke Ellington bravely played *The Star-Spangled Banner*, but everybody was already standing up. It was bedlam. Mr. and Mrs. Todd went home. Next morning Mr. Todd's lawyer and accountant appeared as he was breakfasting.

"Just give me the bottom line," said Mr. Todd.

236

"The bottom line," was the accountant's answer, "is that your personal friends cost you $410,000."

The new Madison Square Garden is, of course, an improvement over the old building. It is modernly scientific and designed to house more and diverse attractions. It is always sterile and never stuffy. It is no doubt a big improvement.

A big improvement over everything but the memories of Our Garden.

The Hard Guys

IN AN ERA WHEN THE MAFIA BAD Guy is painted in dark colors indeed, it is often hard to remember and understand that, until sometime after the repeal of Prohibition, the gangster was a highly colorful fellow and, more or less, an object of admiration. If a chap picked up a girl in a speakeasy, for instance, her inevitable query would be, "Do you work for a living or are you a racket boy?" Far too often, answering yes to the last part of the question moved you forward on your way to the boudoir much faster than you moved if you started to detail your dull but honest job.

The hard guys all looked or acted like Clark Gable. Indeed, Gable and other film heroes of thirty years ago gained their earliest renown portraying hoodlums. In my business I have met and known scores of them, from Owney Madden (peaceful death in bed), through Waxey Gordon (death in jail), through Frank Costello (still a senior citizen in the movement, respected and accepted almost everywhere) through Chink Sherman and Tony (Accacio) Bender, both of whom disappeared from the face of the earth without leaving a trace.

And there are many of them still busy at their chosen trade, such as the members of that sinister if often sanctimonious outfit called the Syndicate or the Cosa Nostra (nobody ever heard it so called in my day) or the Mafia or the Combination. I never knew the late and unlamented Ben (Bugsy) Segal, but he was accepted as a hot flash with the girls and a personality boy all the way through. He must have been the only one. I never met a professional hoodlum who was a wit, a good conversationalist, showed a likable personality or gave any evidence of having brains enough to do anything worthwhile.

Once my casual saloon acquaintance with a hoodlum called Nutsy came close to being lethal. In hoodlum circles of the day, names like Nutsy or the Bug or Bugsy didn't mean that the bearers of such titles were idiots. The nicknames identified them as desperadoes who would go up against any proposition no matter what the odds. My Nutsy decided one night that all of us at his bar would take a ride up to Harlem "to drop a few" dollars in a new saloon that an old friend was opening.

We were dropping a few and downing a few when who should come through the door, backed by his personal entourage, but the late Dutch Schultz. I don't remember the exact beef, but it was soon evident the Dutchman—who insisted that he be called by his right name, Arthur Flegenheimer—and Nutsy had some old, personal vendetta. In a flash we were all lined up against the side wall with our little hands high above our heads. In front of us stood the Dutchman and his lieutenants, all holding guns in one hand.

"Listen, Arthur," said the infuriated Nutsy, "you know this is just a thing between you and me. A personal thing. So let's you and me go out in the street and settle it."

The Dutchman sneered. "I wouldn't waste my time on you."

Then this wild man had a thought that seemed to intrigue him. "Tell you what," he advised Nutsy. "We'll have some fun. I'll pick one of my guys and you pick one of yours. They go out in the street and take their best holds. Whoever loses takes his guy and goes home safe. A contest, like."

"A deal," agreed Nutsy. The Dutchman looked over his troops and picked out the hardest looking specimen. Nutsy looked over his guests and picked one.

He picked ME!

I seem to remember almost fainting but, in times of danger, they say your brain works overfast. I looked the Dutchman straight in the eye and told him I would first have to make a phone call. After two frantic calls I found the circulation manager of our newspaper. I told him my position and problem. He laughed fit to die, probably laughing at the idea of my going up against one of the Dutchman's hard guys. Then he stopped laughing and told me to "put that maniac on the phone."

I went out and motioned Mr. Flegenheimer to the phone. At first he was inclined to ignore me or maybe give me a disciplinary belt in the mouth. "You'd better talk to this man," I said as airily as I could. "Otherwise, it might be your ass." In a few minutes he came out of the booth, collected his minions and stalked out into the night. My circulation manager later told me he had advised the Dutchman to "get lost."

I saw Nutsy for some years afterward. We never mentioned the incident. To this day I wonder why he chose me. Did he figure I might go out and get slaughtered, and his ancient enemy would have to face the heat that always followed when a square guy got hurted? Did he think Schultz would back off? Did he think I had wit enough to save myself, himself and our group? I still don't know what he thought. I never asked.

In gangster terms, a "hitter" is a fellow who does heavy work, like killing people. I have known a few of these, but the only one I ever knew who had any personal philosphy or reasons for his actions was (and is) a chap we will call Tappy. He is still extant and healthy, although God knows how or why. Not long ago I visited him in a hospital. He had gone there to have a couple of bullets dug out of his carcass. He caught the bullets many a long year ago, but one of them had started to "walk"—move about in his bloodstream—and the doctors decided to carve out both the pellets. Tappy was in excellent spirits.

"After all these years," he said from his cranked-up hospital bed, "my conscience is clear." It was the first time I had heard him admit that he had a conscience, clear or clouded. He obviously wanted to tell me the story, and I sat there and listened to it, as follows:

"It was about forty years ago," he began, "and I took my wife and small kids to have dinner with an Italian friend who lived on Mulberry Street on the first floor. His wife had cooked a big Italian dinner and all of his kids were there, too. How did I know

240

that the Unione Sicilione had a hard on for him? And anyway it was Sunday. I never believed any wops would cause trouble on a religious holiday.

"But right in the middle of that Sunday afternoon [Tappy's voice took on remembered outrage] here come two of these dago belters with two of them sawed-off shotguns. There they are with those goddamn sprayers and my four kids are there and four or five kids of my friend to say nothing of innocent wives. I saw my host go pale and I knew it was serious, so I stepped right in front of those sprayers.

"I shoved my belly right into one of them and looked the belters right in the eyes and I called them various names and said who I was and who I worked for and pointed out that if they shot those things off with all those kids and women there they would have to kill me first and I said I hoped they knew what kind of a feud that would start. To say nothing of the heat from the law.

"Well, we talked back and forth, and meanwhile in the confusion my host makes it to a window and goes through the window and gets away for that day. I collect my own wife and kids and we go home without dinner. I didn't accomplish much, I guess, because they caught my host a couple of days later and hit him good and final."

Tappy permitted himself a small in memoriam smile.

"The Unione must have talked it over and decided I had purposely helped my friend escape. I guess they figured I had caused them to lose face, like the Chinese say. They probably had a convention and decisioned I needed some discipline. Anyway, this night a few weeks later I came home late to my house in the Bronx and I start up the porch stairs to my house and all of a sudden these bullets begin coming at me from a car parked at the curb."

Again Tappy sighed a little, remembering.

"I had the key in my door," he continued, "and I wasn't hit yet so why I didn't push the door open and run through I do not know. Shock, maybe. So instead I turn around and start running toward the car. I am going down the steps and they are still blasting at me. I was mad enough to tear them bums apart with my bare hands."

The first slug that reached him, as Tappy remembers, hit him in the chest but strangely didn't knock him down. The second bullet hit him in the hip, and that one knocked him all the way down. At the hospital, in due course, the doctors probed and sewed him up and advised him not to have the bullets removed because of their positions in his body. By a freak of luck, both slugs were lodged where, in the normal course of his lifetime, they shouldn't cause him any more trouble than the extra weight they gave him to carry. On his feet again, Tappy decided on vengeance. It was not hard for him to identify his assailants.

"I hit them both personally," he told me from his bed of pain. "I belted them both out. Single-handed. No help needed. I found one and then I tracked down the other. They were the same guys who had those shotguns that Sunday afternoon. I hit them both. It gave me a lot of personal satisfaction at the time."

But soon thereafter, he admitted, satisfaction began to pale. Tappy knew both gunmen and their reputations. One of them was a well-established wrongo. But the other was just a sort of stooge and general helper. Tappy brooded over the fact that perhaps the stooge, on hire, had merely driven the car and had not, indeed, fired at him. Perhaps Tappy had hit him back without sufficient reason. Such things can be worrisome, if you live by Tappy's code of ethics. It began to hurt his conscience, Tappy told me.

So the years rolled by and Tappy's conscience continued to give him an occasional twinge. Then a few months ago he began to suffer from some strange pains. A new set of doctors took X-rays of his chest and hip. They discovered that the bullet in his chest was "peaceable" but the one in his hip started to "walk" and was now endangering his heart. It should be removed and, for safety's sake, so should the other one. So Tappy submitted to the anesthetic and the scalpel while the croakers removed his excess baggage.

It cleared his conscience completely, Tappy related happily.

Why? How?

Because one slug was a .36 calibre and the other was a .32 calibre. Obviously from two different pistols.

"Now I know," Tappy said in righteous conclusion, "that I did right in hitting both them bums. They both must of belted me. I didn't do nothing wrong. My conscience is clear."

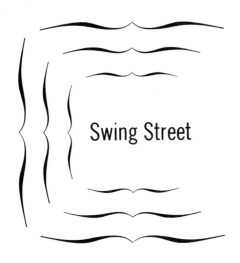

Swing Street

THERE REMAIN, INCREDIBLY, TWO battered, deserted brownstones and one tottering graystone in the block of West 52d Street between Fifth and Sixth avenues. They are on the north side where the elegant "21" and the second edition of the raucous Toots Shor's stand shoulder to shoulder. Otherwise the north side of this block consists of the side rises of two enormous skyscrapers, a garage, and a fancy store or two. The south side of the block climbs in one solid line of skyscrapers. A row of banks crowd each other at sidewalk level. Banks take in money.

So did the buildings they replaced.

This single block, more than any other, was probably the very hub of night life in New York through two different eras and two dissimiliar phases. Previously the block had had an even different aura. It was a block of brownstone and graystone buildings never more than five stories high. They were the town houses of the rich and the celebrated. A town house was *the* residence from the early 1900s through the early 1930s. By the early 1930s, however, the town house had become an economic anachronism.

First, the town houses had deteriorated into genteel boarding houses or were cut up into small one-floor apartments. Later, most of them further deteriorated into unfashionable rooming houses, although one or two old families grimly held on. Oddly, the deathblow finally came to the town houses as residences when the "class" speakeasies took over the ground and basement floors during the later years of Prohibition. Laughter and gaiety and drunken roughhousing filled the nights with sound and fury. The few brownstones that still existed as living quarters found it imperative to put small white-on-blue metal signs on their entrances. These signs said, uniformly and tiredly: "This Is a Private Residence. Do Not Ring Bell."

It was during this period that an Ivy League student, in town for some weekend high-life, wandered from room to room in one of these smart nightclubs wearing a puzzled frown. He finally called the manager and asked the exact address of the place. When told, he allowed himself a satisfied sigh.

"I knew I recognized this house," he said. "I was born in this room."

The original Leon and Eddie's, later to move across the street and transform itself into a noisy cabaret, was a rather elegant intimate speakeasy that utilized all the room of what had once been the home of the socialite Sailing Baruch. As more time passed, Baruch's old home, where many a robber baron had swung many a deal and before which horse carriages had once waited, became Jack White's Club 18, an almost demented operation that never opened until everything else was closed.

With the rosy dawn of Repeal, the smart speaks faded from the West 52d Street scene. The Peronas and Billingsleys, Salvins, Moriaritys and LeMazes moved eastward to open more glamorous and surely more legal oases. No longer did the Yacht Club Boys or Dwight Fiske sing ditties that brought a blush to the cheek in that more innocent age. No longer did Tony and Renee DeMarco dance their gliding ballroom routines on a floor the size of a large handkerchief. Gone were Helen Morgan and Arthur Brown and Harry Richman and Vincent Lopez, the last-named going legit to the Taft Hotel Grill. And all the others.

Even the dumbest drinkers saw no reason to drink in illegal dens when they could do it cheaper and better in the new, clean, popular restaurants and clubs. The West 52d Street brownstones seemed to settle deeper and more dejectedly. They leaned against each other in grimy exhaustion. The parlor windows showed crookedly hung "For Rent" signs. The upper windows were filthy; nobody would live on these unmaintained warrens. It was a street of memories, outmoded; an alley of shuttered gopher holes and rats' nests. It was also a time called the Depression. Nobody had any money to risk on new construction for which there would, most probably, be no tenants looking for space.

During the winter of 1935 a chap named Jack Colt, who had to be on the street daily for business visits to the nearby Musicians Union offices, found himself feeling nostalgic for the nights when the street furnished work for many musicians. Colt was the manager of musician Lenny Hayton, later wed to Lena Horne, and others in the popular music and jazz fields. Swing music was taking its first clef-hold on the popular fancy. Among musicians, the hip attitude was becoming evident. Further, musicians have always been clannish. Why not, Colt wondered, at least have one intimate little hangout all of their own? A place where a few fellows who knew a riff from a rideout could gather, lift a few glasses and discuss problems peculiar to their own intellectual world? The project fascinated Colt more and more.

He and Hayton put in $2,000. Then they started lapel-grabbing musicians who were of their own thought and ilk. After some effort, Colt banded together eight musicians, each of whom actually had $100 to spare.

These daring financiers were the late Glenn Miller, the late Jimmy Dorsey, Jerry Colonna of radio and film renown, Gordon Jenkins of *Manhattan Towers* fame, Jack Jenney, James Lanin, Artie Bernstein and Henry Bluestone. They took a lease on a closet-sized cellar at 35 West 52d Street. With a hard shove, the place would seat fifty-five persons.

Thus did $2,800 launch one of the wildest and most memorable chapters in the history of night life. Thus was Swing Street born. And, to an extent, thus also was jazz music first taken seriously by critics and cultists and pundits and the general public.

Colt called his club the Famous Door because the only contract signed by the partners was when they all scrawled their names on the door. The $2,800 investment was exhausted the very moment the club opened for business. The bar price for whisky was fifty cents a drink. A bottle of beer brought thirty-five cents. A family-type nightclub for musicians only was ready for its opening chorus.

This early evening debut of the new rendezvous was anything but auspicious. On the stand an unknown cornet player from New Orleans named Louis Prima tried out various ideas with his combo. A single bartender leaned back and bit his knuckles. Two waiters huddled in a corner and cursed their union for even suggesting such a job. No musicians came to drink and talk. Nor did any listeners come to hear the music. By eleven o'clock things were unchanged. Colt got his hat from the office and discouragedly walked out into the night air.

He walked all the way to Central Park and into its sheltering darkness. This was a time before muggers, but the way Colt was feeling a sudden, hard blow to the back of his head would have been welcomed. He walked for almost two hours and then headed back to his dream-turned-nightmare. He had to face the music—not the New Orleans music of Louis Prima, but the sour financial notes of the cash register. At the corner of 6th Avenue he halted. For a moment, he remembers, he contemplated flight.

"I figured there must be some sort of drunken riot in the joint," he recollects.

He braced himself and shouldered his way inside. A waiter known to Colt from other cafes, but never hired by Colt for the Door, had some quick advice. "Jack," he shouted through the noise, "the sucker who owns this trap has disappeared. We sent down the block to borrow whisky. I'll pass you a few bottles and we'll sell them later."

Still in shock, Colt remembered that the bar supply when he had left for his walk had totaled two bottles each of scotch, rye, bourbon and gin. Why had the place needed two whole cases of extra booze? What had happened, anyway?

What had happened, it soon dawned on the bewildered Colt, was that he himself had overlooked the basic theme of his whole idea. It was to be a club for musicians. Musicians worked until midnight at least. Once through work, musicians had descended on the rendezvous en masse. The Famous Door caught on the first night. The unexpected customers somehow found it too. It was an overnight must for Broadway, for society, for everybody who stayed out late at night.

The Door has a well-deserved niche in any musical hall of fame. It brought to early fame such musicians and singers as Billie

Holiday, the Ink Spots, Bunny Berigan, Red Norvo, Max Kaminsky, Teddy Wilson, Bobby Hackett, Wingy Manone, Joe Marsala and many others. Further, it soon spawned a long list of imitation saloons.

Since imitation, while flattery, is also the curse of so many show business entrepreneurs, the deserted and unwanted brownstone caves in the block soon blazed with new lights and new sounds. Clubs called the Downbeat, the Three Deuces, Jimmy Ryan's, the Troc, the Swing, and a dozen more transformed the grimy cellars. Many of them expired quickly. Many others lasted for years. The Famous Door had spawned Swing Street.

Several of the old Swing Street operators are still alive and active and their memories coincide remarkably. All the jazz clubs that followed the Door were in almost identical buildings and were confined to almost identical small space. Yet with a seating capacity of fifty-five and whisky going for a half buck a copy, Colt took a $1,000 weekly profit for himself as long as the club was on an upbeat. The successes among the imitations probably did the same. A thousand dollars a week was very solid money indeed in an era when the Great Depression still had its heavy foot on show business.

Possibly it was the mood of the time, but Swing Street drew as its stars and attractions a Coxey's army of characters who were not only to leave their impress on music but were also to make additions to our language that are now accepted as commonplace by the most erudite dictionaries. Such words as "hip" and "square" and "solid" and "cool" and "bread" were a part of our language when today's hippies were unborn.

This tidal wave of jazzmen simply washed up on the small, friendly beach. They had no leader but they did have a highly articulate spokesman named Albert Edward (Eddie) Condon. It was Condon who, more than anyone else, was to take jazz music and, by sheer force of personality and stubbornness, move it from the cellar and the saloon to the concert halls and theatres, and to serious consideration of and acceptance by the critics and musical pundits.

Condon had come out of Chicago sometime previously with his own idea of a guitar under his arm. He had been a tough sergeant in the legendary Austin High School band, musical revolutionaries who numbered such names as Benny Goodman, Gene Krupa,

Frankie Trumbauer, Jimmy McPartland, Wild Bill Davison, Joe Sullivan, Bud Freeman, Davey Tough and assorted others. Chicago wunderkind or no, he found himself unsung and unwanted in New York in an era of popular radio bands with their meticulous and often overarranged music.

Condon the Inconoclast had his first brush with the System in a radio studio. He insisted on playing his own idea of a guitar break, digressing from the written arrangement.

"Can't you read it?" the studio band leader finally screamed at him.

"I can read it," Eddie admitted, "but I can't divide it." Dismissed.

His next contretemps with the Establishment as it then was came when he reported to play with a Broadway stage orchestra. He had spent a delightful night hither and yon, from lower Greenwich Village to Upper Harlem, and he arrived for the morning show at the theatre wearing one black shoe and one brown one. The leader was understandably furious.

"What's the difference?" shrugged Our Hero. "Playing guitar I keep one foot under the chair anyway, don't I?" Fired again.

Now in his sixties, he is possibly the only man in the history of medical science who has three times beaten acute pancreatitis, an ailment which, when he had his first bout with it, was inevitably fatal. As long as he can remember, his diet has included strong fortifications of alcoholic liquids; doctors over the years are convinced he is made of concrete. He had a close call with his first pancreatitis engagement, so close that at one time he was fed rectally. He awoke, found himself on his stomach and asked the medico what he was getting.

"Never mind," said that worthy. "It's better than whisky."

"See what the boys in the back ward will have," Eddie ordered groggily.

Swing Street, of course, might have been invented for him. He was soon a regular attraction with his own bands and combos and his own highly individualistic ideas on anything under the moon. Jazz music had always been held in higher esteem in Europe than at home, and the Swing Street revival of jazz brought almost immediate attention from the European critics. The French authority, Hugues Panassie, was one of the first to cross the ocean to study the Restoration. Panassie, in his subsequent books and treatises, has always been highly complimentary of Condon's style and musical taste. Nonetheless, Condon has always been highly unimpressed by foreign critics. On Panassie, he delivered one of his classics.

"Why should that frog come here and criticize our jazz?" he demanded. "I wouldn't think of going to France and telling him how to jump on a grape."

A bantamweight in size, he backed up for nobody. Once he was on the bandstand when a girl about town, in those days always mentioned in the columns as "prominent in café society," had a table argument with her escort and threw a heavy bottle of perfume at him. The bottle missed the escort's head but crashed into Condon's guitar. Eddie got up and walked straight to her table.

"I'd call you a two-dollar whore," he said furiously, "but I know you haven't got brains enough to change a five-dollar bill."

Such outbursts were rare, even in his younger days. With maturity he began to build the same sort of reputation for immediate, ad lib wit also earned by Dorothy Parker and Joe Frisco.

It was natural, no doubt, that an iconoclastic character such as Condon should, like a magnet, draw to his pilgrim's progress other oddballs and determined personalities. One of these was the great clarinetist Charles Pee Wee Russell, who at this writing is still winning jazz poll awards. Russell and other Condon employees always seemed to be operating under a compulsion that they must drink more whisky than the boss. On the rare occasions when Condon wasn't being fired for back talk or backroom booze, one or more of his musical stalwarts usually was. Playing the Onyx club one time, Mr. Russell was not behaving even up to the Condon musical standard, so Eddie made arrangements for Pee Wee to prevent him from sampling the neighboring delicacies during work hours.

"Be here," a hard-faced type ordered Pee Wee, "or be dead."

This frightened Russell into a night or two of perfect attendance, but he soon devised a counter gambit.

The Onyx had a men's room, and the men's room had a window. Across a narrow alley was the back door to Reilly's saloon, a musician's hangout. The elongated Pee Wee would wait until somebody in the band started his solo. Then, as now, ad lib jazz solos go for three or four choruses. With the first note of, say, the cornet solo, Russell would slip off the bandstand and into the men's room. Thence through the window and across the alley to Reilly's back door. There, clarinet under his arm, he would have a fast pickup.

He never talked to anybody. He couldn't. While he was drinking he kept beating time with his hand so that he'd know when the cornet solo should be almost over. Then he would scurry back through alley, window and men's room and pop up on the bandstand just in time to join the group musicale.

Such antics put an overwork load on Russell's liver, and some time later also put him in the hospital. He came within a riff or two of perishing. Condon was delighted when his man took a turn for the better and survived.

"Pee Wee almost died from too much living," he told friends.

Eddie had daily reports on Russell's progress. "Pee Wee gained two pounds," he reported one day. "One under each eye."

The late Jimmy Ryan, of the jazz saloon of the same name, was one of Eddie's close friends on Swing Street. Ryan's was the last jazz spot to survive the wreckage of the Street, losing to the huge CBS building several years ago. It opened in September 1940, and on opening night lost little time in furnishing an incident that established its character. Things were rough in show business then, and Ryan set his prices accordingly. He featured a twenty-five cent martini and had a big sidewalk sign outside featuring the drink.

Opening night a harsh windstorm swept the block and carried the martini sign some distance to the east. It lodged in the iron grillwork of the exclusive, determinedly expensive restaurant "21." It gave the "21" owners quite a start when they arrived to open for lunch next day.

Soon after Ryan's opened, the Metropolitan Opera also got under way for the season. After the opera a man in tails and a lady in mink and jewels climbed out of a cab and came into Ryan's. Henry "Red" Allen was blasting a cornet on Ryan's bandstand, drunks were arguing at the bar and the smoke was so thick nobody could identify his own brother. Ryan is convinced that the classy couple had meant to take their trade to Tony's West Side, the only decent dining-and-soft-music boîte on the block, which shouldered Ryan's to the west.

Whatever the reason for their presence, Ryan heard the lady sigh and reprove her companion with: "I told you the West Side would be dreadful."

The admixture, planned or accidental, of jazz musicians and society folk in those days spawned some amusing footnotes to the town's social history. There was the time, for instance, when a young East Side matron had a dozen jazz musicians in for a sit-down dinner. After dinner another twenty or more musicians arrived for some hot licks and a jam session. For dessert the hostess had bought a dozen squashy rum cakes that were to be spooned from small crockery pots. A jazz guitarist, finished with his dessert, studied the little pot with concentration.

He picked up one of his hostess' silver forks, dug a small hole on one side of the pot, dug another across from it, inserted a marijuana cigarette in one hole, turned the pot around and drew the smoke through the empty pot and into his lungs. The approved smoking of marijuana requires that it be taken into the lungs with a large chaser of air. The guitarist took several drags.

"Man," he announced, "this is the greatest."

Every dinner guest grabbed a fork and started digging holes. There were only twelve pots, and meanwhile the after-dinner guests had started to arrive. The demand was greatly in excess of the pot supply.

"Where did you buy this stuff?" a musician demanded of the hostess. She said it had been purchased from a small specialty delicatessen around the corner. A collection was taken up and four musicians were dispatched forthwith. The delicatessen owner found that he had two dozen potted rum cakes left. The musical patrol bought the entire stock. They brought them back to the party and everybody immediately set to the task of spooning out the rum cake, flushing it down the toilet and making the pots into air pipes. It was a great party from everybody's standpoint—except possibly the hostess.

"A few days later," a veteran jazzman who was a guest remembered recently, "was the first time our mob got to referring to marijuana as pot. First time I ever heard it. I always think of that party when I hear some kid talking about *pot* as if his generation had discovered it."

"There was a funny epilogue to the party," another jazzman related some time after the affair. "I was in the same neighborhood a few weeks after the ball and I saw the delicatessen window was loaded with those potted rum cakes. They were stacked up like in a supermarket. I went in and bought some little thing and started a conversation with the owner. I asked if he sold a lot of rum cake. He seemed bitter and disillusioned.

"He told me he couldn't understand the vagaries of his business. Seems only a little while ago he had stocked a couple of dozen of the things and they had all been snapped up that first night. He shook his head sadly.

"'I figured I had found a terrific neighborhood item,' he told me. 'So I practically bought out the wholesaler. I haven't sold three of the goddamned things since.'"

But the best laughs and the best talk and the best action was on the Street. At home. It was at the aforementioned Ryan's one afternoon that Eddie Condon, of all males, was awed by another drinker. Eddie stood talking to Matty, the Ryan barman, when a stranger came in off the street, demanded a bottle of White Horse Scotch whisky and a beer glass. He filled the glass almost full and downed the whisky as though it were lemonade. Condon and the bartender watched the action with proper reverence.

"What will you have for a chaser?" the bartender finally asked. Condon stared at the picture of the white horse on the bottle.

"Give him a whip," he suggested.

Another legendary Swing Streeter was Wingy Manone, the one-armed New Orleans cornetist who is still extant and still sassy. When Wingy was a boy he was a New Orleans Western Union messenger. His messenger opposite number was one-legged. Both delivered communications on bicycles.

"I could pedal faster than the other cat," Wingy still says proudly."

Once, when World War II was young, some clown asked Wingy why he wasn't fighting for his country.

"You can't work all night," said Wingy patiently, "and fight all day."

Wingy did contribute to the war effort, however. He wrote a song titled "Stop That War! Them Cats Is Killing Themselves!" It sometimes seems a shame he could never find a publisher. Playing at Ryan's during one stretch, Wingy asked Ryan if the latter thought his music was sufficiently solid. Ryan said it was solid as Gibraltar. For three days Wingy regarded Ryan with suspicion and seemed to avoid him. Then one day both met in the corner drugstore. Manone was still being remote. At last his eye found the Prudential Insurance calendar behind the fountain. He stared at the picture of Gibraltar and he suddenly warmed.

"Man!" he told Ryan apologetically, "that *is* solid!"

On a later occasion, the bop trumpeter Dizzy Gillespie was having a vogue on the Street. In front of his club were posters advising: "Come in and Hear Dizzy." Manone attended and listened. He went back to Ryan's and posted his own sidewalk sign. It read: "Come in and Hear the Truth!"

The Manone orchestra changed personnel almost as rapidly as Condon's. Wingy had just outfitted his mob with brand new uniforms when he lost a saxophone player to another group. He walked over to the Musicians Union with an empty uniform coat on his arm and waited until he saw a musician carrying a saxophone in its case. Wingy approached the stranger.

"Try this coat on," he ordered. The sax player did. It fit.

"You're hired," Wingy stated authoritatively. The sax player was to become a Manone veteran.

If the denizens of Swing Street had one common characteristic, it was probably their wondrous and childlike ability to ignore all troubles or trials that did not directly affect their own mode of life. In this they resembled the little rich girl of legend who, when told by the Millerites that the end of the world would come next Tuesday, said it didn't concern her since she was going away to boarding school before then. A typical example of Swing Street ambiance happened when the team of Riley and Farley were at the Onyx Club.

Riley and Farley had recently introduced a novelty song called "The Music Goes Round and Round—Ooh Hoo Hoo—And It Comes Out Here." The song swept the country, brought song pluggers from all over and even got the small club its own radio "wire," which meant Riley and Farley had their own broadcast every night. In those days these broadcasts were called "remotes" from the main studio, and if a piece of important news broke, the studio engineer would simply cut out the music and the news would be announced from the home studio. These occasions were called breaks and were uncommon but occasional.

253

One night Riley and Farley went out for some air after their broadcast session and were accosted by a song plugger who seemed distraught.

"You had a break during the broadcast," he said in funereal tones. "Something about a big airplane crash."

"Was it bad?" asked Farley, interested.

"Nah," said the music man, "only forty seconds."

A highly successful and long-lived jazz spot wasn't on Swing Street proper but backed into it. This was Kelly's Stables, operated by Ralph Watkins, who is still on the jazz scene. It started in 1938 and went for years. To this day Watkins cannot remember why he chose the name.

"It worked out well, though," he recalls. "Everybody in the joint was renamed Kelly, so when anybody asked for Kelly he got the nearest employee."

The Stables later moved to Swing Street proper, but in its first location it was purely a sawdust joint. It cost Watkins only $1,500 to open the original and $2,500 to launch the sequel. Show business economy was different in those dear, dead days. Watkins remembers he paid $16 a case for rye whisky and $31 for Scotch. His top price for a drink was sixty cents, and there was no cover charge. Yet Watkins, also, took down a thousand a week for himself.

Of course, it was a different world, moneywise. At the Stables the late Nat King Cole got a weekly salary of $140, Billy Daniels sang for $90 and the to-be-legendary Billie Holiday was paid an unbelievable $75 to sing every night of the week. The six song-and-dance men who made up the then-popular Harlem Highlanders got a staggering $300, and Hazel Scott worked at the relief piano sessions for $50. Yet the place drew everybody from East Side debs to Broadway stars and Harlem headliners.

"About my only problem," remembers Watkins, "was a clip joint next door. It would drug and roll a customer and toss him into the mutual alley. The guy would come alive, charge into my place and demand his money back. They were hard to convince."

Swing Street, like all phases and fads in entertainment, would have doubtless faded in its own way in its own time. But many veterans believe two unforeseen influences hurried its demise. After World War II came the influx of the new bop and modern music and, with it, the appearance of the drug problem. Arrests and raids hardly help nightclub business of any sort. Jazz and jazzmen were turning in new directions.

Also, amazingly late, the hoodlums discovered that there was money in music. In those days hoodlums retained some of their glamour and all of their muscle. They began to move in and, moving in, proved once again that if there is one thing a hood does not understand, it is any form of show business. Swing Street began to lose most of its spontaneity and all of its fun.

The Famous Door itself came to a sour end. A hood moved in on Jack Colt when Colt had to have protection from a smaller but more vicious hood. Soon the major hood moved Colt out completely. That was the monotonous formula, in those days. Then the hood, as new owner and show biz celebrity, began to give himself airs. He had brought in his sweetie as hatcheck girl, originally, but with his newfound glamour he involved himself with a half-baked half-society gal. Revenge was soon being plotted in the hatcheck room.

By this time the narcotics traffic and the arrogance and ignorance of hoods in Swing Street had begun to annoy the police. The hatchick planted cocaine and heroin in the checkroom and anonymously tipped the Narcotics Squad. Several innocent people almost went to jail, and a couple of people who belonged there went. The original Famous Door lost its license.

It has been several years since the first of the sky-reaching new buildings obliterated some of the old rat-hole brownstones that housed the music clubs. As the wrecker's big ball continued to pound away at the old musical landmarks, Eddie Condon one day stood on the sidewalk in front of Jimmy Ryan's, the last old soldier of the jazz ranks, and made a prediction.

"In a couple of years," said Eddie, "there will be only three filling stations on this block—"21," Toots Shor's and the Esso building." Eddie was right. He knew he would be.

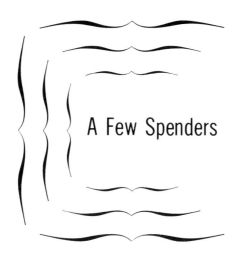

A Few Spenders

ANY RESTAURANT OWNER CAN tell you today that the big spender, the credit card customer, the man who is doing "business entertainment" is the backbone of the trade. True enough. If you can't sign with the waiter's pencil (naming the business firm where the monthly bill is to be sent) or if you haven't got a pocket wallet full of credit cards that can also be charged against and "laid off" to strictly business, you had better keep out of public dining rooms, especially after dark. However, there was a time when the big spender was the backbone of the night business. That time was, of course, before Uncle Sam discovered that a war was the ideal excuse to establish tough new taxes and find an excuse to keep same long after the war was settled.

In another and more distant day, the nightclub owner who saw Seymour Weiss, partner in business with Huey Long, come through the door, knew that he had no further financial worries for the rest of the week. Weiss always arrived with ten or more guests. His first gesture was to send champagne bottles to everybody, including the musicians, and his last gesture usually was to take all the musicians, entertainers and bosses back to his hotel apartment and hand out $100 bills to keep the jollity rampant. A Detroit advertising man, Louis Maxon, who had the Ford account, was a comparable blessing to any joint.

Jack Kearns, the prizefight manager, was a fast and big spender, and so were many racetrack bookmakers in the days when a horse book was legal on the racetracks. A Pittsburgh zillionaire and a Philadelphian of bluest blood were also sights for the sore eyes of imminently indigent nightclub operators. Tommy Manville, the marryin' man, was known as a Great Big Good Party. And so, indeed, were three Canadian brothers named McMartin—Duncan, Alan and Jack—whose family mines in Canada somehow managed to produce more money than the boys could spend on their frequent trips to the New York scene.

There is a railroad tycoon alive today, but so aged and slowed down that we refrain from embarassing him with memories of his earlier years, who could spend $1,500 in one spot and then call up the next day to make sure he had been openhanded enough with all the help. On one occasion, possibly suffering more than usual from his own odd guilt complex, he called the owner of a nothing-type club and asked for the amount of rent the owner paid, the rent paid by every employee and the landlord for all. This took some research, but the nightclub manager put his back to it, you may be sure.

So a month later when Christmas arrived, the nightclub impresario was delighted to learn that his railroad customer had paid the rent for an entire year on the joint. Also on his Christmas list was every employee of the club, all of whom lived a solid rent-free year from the same source.

Jack McMartin, one of the three Canadian merry miners, was also very partial to any nightclub that offered the aforementioned stuttering comedian, Joe Frisco. Joe's partner in clubs was an absolute beauty named Loretta McDermott, and Mr. Martin could not resist watching her any more than all of the rest of us could. This was one champion chick for looks. And a great foil for Joe Frisco, even.

Anyway, Jack McMartin bankrolled a series of Frisco-McDermott clubs, all of which had brief popularity spans. It is possible that one or all would have been lasting successes if only McMartin's business interests hadn't kept him away from his usual table so much. He was always his own best customer.

One night, shortly after Frisco and Loretta had folded their newest venture, McMartin came to town to find his hangout padlocked. He looked up Frisco and took him out on a tour of the town. The tour finished at dawn, and soon thereafter both were in McMartin's hotel suite.

"How much money do you need to get going again?" demanded the Canadian mine owner.

"Only $1,500," said Frisco. And, indeed, that was about all it took to open a cellar joint in the Depression days.

McMartin picked up the hotel phone and called the cashier.

"Send me up $1,500," he ordered.

In a moment the phone rang and it was the cashier. "I have only $900 in the safe," he apologized.

"Send to the bank for the rest," ordered McMartin.

Joe Frisco used to shake his head sadly, remembering the incident.

"That G-G-George Washington is down in the records as the m-m-most honest g-g-guy in the country and the father of our c-c-country," he would say. "But n-n-nevertheless he s-s-screwed me out of $600."

Other welcome customers at any and all nightclubs in those days were known as "the Big Wolves from Wall Street." One of the best of these was a man named Russell Ryder. His stock market manipulations put him behind bars for a while, a constricting experience that failed to dampen his extravagance. A showgirl at one night spot caught his eye. The next day a fur coat arrived at her apartment. The following day a brand new automobile arrived, also anonymously. The next thirty days brought, each afternoon, a piece of jewelry or some expensive gift. Always anonymously. After that Ryder delivered himself.

"And the gal would have nothing to do with him," remembers Nicky Blair, a nightclub operator from way back who has forsaken Broadway for Las Vegas and the Caribbean. "She insisted on giving everything back. Ryder refused to take anything back. He never contacted the girl again. He acted like he had been betrayed."

On another occasion, in one of Texas Guinan's many joints, Ryder paid no attention to the beauty he had at his table, but he could not take his eyes off a gal in the show.

"He found out who she was," Blair remembers, "by giving one of the musicians $1,000." The musician delightedly introduced the playboy to the girl, and Ryder was in another short romance.

"He could have accomplished the same thing," recalls Blair, "by just giving the dame twenty dollars. That's all the guys in the band ever gave her."

To this day Mickey Walker, the great middleweight champion of the era, blames Texas Guinan and Jimmy Durante for a faux pas that cost him a coveted belt. Mickey had to attend a boxing writers' dinner to receive the belt he had just won as new champion. Instead of performing this duty, he sent Jack Kearns and Jimmy Durante to the dinner to collect the belt while he himself repaired to Texas' latest nightclub.

Kearns and Durante got the belt and Jimmy insisted on wearing it to go and meet Walker. On the sidewalk in front of Texas' an argument developed with a stranger over who bumped into whom. Kearns, ever ready for a fight or a frolic, started swinging fists. Durante went down. Some scoundrel made off with the loose championship belt. "Watch what you're doing," Durante told the cop who hurried over. "I'm the world's middleweight champeen." He opened his coat to prove same. The belt was gone.

The boxing writers were so disgusted with Walker's indifference that it was several years before they forgave him and handed him a duplicate. This second belt Walker made sure he wore home in person.

Texas Guinan was a shrewd, homely old gal who somehow became the darling of the Mob and lasted through all sorts of adversity until the Mob got mad at her about something or other. Then they started putting small bombs in her place, wherever the new place happened to be. She was a darling of the Broadway columnists and always identified as "the Queen of the Nightclubs."

On one occasion a Guinan waiter found a tablecloth covered with intricate designs. This was in an era when stock market experts would often mark something down on a tablecloth that a waiter could use as valuable investment advice. But nobody could figure out the new design on this cloth. Ultimately a society architect was appealed to. He took a look and explained that it was the Pythagorean proposition of triangulation worked out in detail.

And on another occasion a famous athlete who is alive and must be nameless walked out on the floor with a borrowed cane. He put his head on the crookhandle of the cane and, bending over it, circled the cane several times, then straightened and went up and shook hands with the orchestra leader.

"I'll give anybody $50 who can do it," he offered. Everybody wanted to try. People were reeling and falling down all over the floor. It looked like the violent ward at Bellevue.

"In those days," remembers Blair, an original Guinan customer, "it cost us just about $800 to open a joint and we often got it back from one good party on the opening night."

The aforementioned Nicky Blair remembers a story about a big spender—in reverse. The spender was Owney Madden, at that time boss of the New York rackets. Owney had a fight with his girl, took Nicky to Atlantic City to keep him amused, wouldn't let Nicky spend a dime and wound up spreading $1,300 around the Atlantic City dives.

The boys returned to New York. Madden opened a place on West 54th Street, which was a flop. Blair opened a place down the street with the fabled Helen Morgan as star. Blair did turnaway business. Madden's was empty.

"One night in comes Owney from his empty joint," Blair recalls, "and he stands at the bar and glowers at the mob in my place. I asked if there was something I could do for him.

"'I spent $1,300 bucks on that jaunt to Atlantic City,' he tells me. 'Your share is $650. Just give it to me now.' Well, you can bet I went right to the damper and gave him my guest debt."

Them days, as the old burlesque gag had it, is gone forever.

DIRTY JOKE

Since Jack White, Pat Harrington, Frankie Hyers and the other outrageous clowns who worked the Club 18 were the earliest comedians to make a living insulting or at least ridiculing their best customers—and thus becoming a legend on the night club beat—it was probably inevitable that every once in a while, and when least expected, the tide would turn. The tide was given a good strong turn one night by one of the club's favorite customers.

This was a chap who almost singlehandedly handled the advertising and promotion for one of the great auto manufacturers. He would come to town once a month or so and, as soon as it was properly dark, he would head for the Club 18. There White & Co. would immediately start abusing him. They would order him to send champagne to the entire orchestra (which he would do cheerfully) and they would otherwise abuse him to the Favored Customer's obvious delight and appreciation.

Sometime after midnight, with the first show on, White & Accomplices started playing their version of the old "Knock Knock!" gags. By this time Favored Customer was drunk and asleep at a corner table. As White hollered out his "Knock Knock!" to the audience, Favored Customer raised his head from the table.

"Who's there?" dutifully yelled somebody in the audience.

The response came not from White, on the floor, but from Favored Customer at the corner table:

"Cohen," he shouted.

"Cohen who?" sang back White.

"Cohen fuck yourself," yelled Favorite Customer.

Favored Customer was given a sedative in his next drink and dropped off to sleep again. He did not awaken again until almost four A.M., during the second show, when as fate would have it the "Knock Knock!" lunacy was having its second go-round. Exactly the same formula was repeated. White hollered "Knock Knock!", and somebody demanded "Who's there?" and Favored Customer raised his head again and this time yelled:

"Gallagher."

On the floor, Jack White heaved a sigh of relief. Gallagher, it was obvious, was no Cohen.

"Gallagher who?" demanded White.

"Gallagher fuck yourself," answered Favored Customer, lowering his head and returning to slumberland.

The Chosen Children

SOCIETY—WHATEVER THAT IS and whatever eligibility rules, if any, are required—has had many subdivisions over the years. There have been international society, the old guard, the current beautiful people and, most idiotic of all, the spin-off known for years as café society. If café society has any claim to social history, it must be that it was the only "social" stepchild that was invented. And invented by outsiders, at that.

The nightclub and saloon operators invented the café society of the 1930s and early 1940s. They needed names, important people to be regulars and furnish publicity photos and news for their boîtes. Unfortunately, there were never enough important people who wanted to waste long evenings boozing it up in fancy saloons. So the bistro operators had to dream some up. And they had to pay off their creations, pay off with free food and drink and, too often, hard cash for some emergency that had to be faced by one or another "rich and social" hang-arounders.

"If there aren't enough rich and social types to fill my place," one of the most successful nightclub owners said confidentially during the great years, "then I'll make as many as I need."

It was funny, if you were on the inside. The bankrupt first cousin of a good family became "the café society playboy" if he were just lucky enough to bear the good name that went back to his paternal grandfather. The daughter of a Broadway ticket broker was widely hailed as "café society's wittiest and most independent charmer." Soon, however, the café owners realized that their best bet was the kids. Kids are better looking than old folk and get their pictures in the newspapers more easily. They have romances, they marry, they divorce, they have had good educational backgrounds and they can talk the English language.

The kids were in—the chosen kids, that is—and the newspapers of the day went right along with the promotion. It was hardly possible to pick up a newspaper of that era without seeing several pictures of good-looking "rich young socialites," sitting at a nightclub table with the house ashtray between them distinctly identifying the joint by its white-on-black coat of arms.

To the nightclub operator of the time, any kid who was in a good college was proper prey. Both Billingsley and Perona, plus a handful of other veterans, already had the ingredients for their own prescription. They had been carefully building the "college kids" who had been appearing and spending the "due bills" that the cabaret men had given (instead of cash) for advertisements in college and school papers, most of which were happy to get any kind of advertising.

Ultimately, these gents even dispensed with the formality of the due bill. The kids just kept coming. Free. Everything free. Make the place your second home. No charge. Why, if you happen to come in a dinner jacket and your girl has on a nice gown, the house photographer will take your picture and give you each a set of prints. No charge for that, either. You might even be lucky enough to have your picture printed in a newspaper.

To the day of his death, Billingsley always insisted that the college kids who early came to his Stork Club did not drink then, never became drunks, went on to fine jobs and even executive positions, and to the very end were still loyal customers who didn't drink much. He was doubtless honest about some of this trade. But he also ignored the long list of yesterday's "kids" who are today worthless, cadging bores, to say nothing of those who have lived on the fringes of the criminal world where, in more than a few cases, some of them fell afoul of the law and now go through life with well-tarnished reputations.

Example: Not long ago an aging character who once was "high in the bright sky of café society, was bodily thrown out of a midtown restaurant. He had been drinking at the bar and was caught red-handed picking up other drinkers' change. He was tossed out, possibly with gusto, by the owner who had once been the headwaiter in a society nightclub and had to treat the young playboy with all deference, even though the socialite found it beneath him to tip anybody.

There was one undisputed queen of the young café society and she retired her tiara early to marry and take to the quiet life. She was (and is) Brenda Diana Duff Frazier, who did have substantial social background and, with her mother, had *some* income. The others were mostly fraudulent Dauphins and excommunicated ladies-in-waiting from the financial temples.

In the Depression of the 1930s these children had (1) little or (2) absolutely no spending money. This was true when they were still in school and it stayed true, in too many cases, when they came out. They couldn't hold a job or earn a salary during the day because they were up boozing all night. It was at night they got all their attention and adulation. Nobody gave them much time when they started at the bottom of the ladder in whatever job they were soon to be fired from. At night they were fawned on by headwaiters, quoted by newspaper columnists. Life was a whirl, life was free. It was all too easy.

And, all too soon, most of them were spoiled rotten. They didn't know it, but their own place in life was in an already fading economic variant of life—the nightclubs. But the glamour was still there. A well-publiced young café society gallant was usually clothed free by some tailor, shoed and hatted. Some of the best designers draped the "debutantes" with their newest models as long as the debs would promise to talk loud and long about how her clothes designer was the gem of them all.

Meanwhile, the saloon owners were faced with the problem of supply. New young faces had to be found each year to be promoted as "likeliest nominee as debutante of the year" or "most popular college athlete at Yale." Near debutantes and rollicking young playboys who didn't catch the fancy of the society editors soon found their welcomes getting thin and even—horrors!—now and then handed a check to teach them their place. Those weeded out by the cabaret men were often shocked to arrive at their nightly corral to be told, for no reason at all, that they had been "barred."

Trouble was beginning to rear its ugly head.

Things were otherwise tense. A war was on the horizon. But the children had no intention of surrendering to a tougher, rougher life. They began to hang out with the more solid friends they had made over the years. They began to angle for dinner parties and yacht trips and vacations as guests. They were rubbing shoulders with the authentic rich, as they always had, but they were still empty of pocket. What was going to happen was predictable.

One of the first things that happened—one of the first of the scandals—occurred when a café society male butterfly attended a weekend party on a big Long Island estate, made off with the hostess' jewel box and was caught as he clumsily started to fence the gems. More sinister accusations were soon to be made.

New York detectives, who can analyze a modus operandi as quickly and thoroughly as anybody, soon began to have a few definite ideas. They noted that every time a real socialite's home or apartment was robbed of jewelry or other valuables, the socialite was, at the time, out on the town with a few graduate children of café society. They made inquiries of the victims and had their ideas endorsed.

Almost invariably, the victim would report, a café society kid of doubtful finances had been invited to the party. The kid—sometimes a he, sometimes a she—had invariably called the day of the party to ask what the hostess was going to wear. Would she wear "all her wonderful jewelry" or would dress be more informal, or what? It was when the hostesses had explained that they planned to wear only the second best ice, or even the imitation or costume stuff, that a house or apartment was burgled. The good stuff was known to be back home.

It was obvious enough. Some of the café society kids were now "fingering" victims for professional thieves, in return for the standard fingerman's cut. These cases weren't ended until the police began to haul the kids over to the precinct, question and harass them, and threaten them no matter who Daddy was or how rich Uncle might be.

Parents who still had some control over their offspring began to haul their kids in off the night beat. Some of the children remained stubborn. More trouble to come, of course.

Some of the kids, old enough now to know better but, then again, knowing nothing but the free-loading that had been their life, became steerers for phony stock brokers. Anyone who remembers the Mickey Jelke shenanigans knows that booking a stable of girls was not beneath the talents of some of the former saloon heroes—and pimping isn't hard labor, either.

The girls went down the ladder, rung by rung, in the usual way. They married a fairly solid citizen, then a less solid citizen, then a musician or actor, then a hustler and then some poor slob who, as a bartender or headwaiter, manages to make enough money to keep them both under shelter and in sufficient alcohol.

The great days were over. But some, possibly by now punch-drunk in the losing battle, still hung on. I remember one late night when one of the former chosen male children collared the owner of a fancy saloon in the men's room, where I was sheltered in a booth.

"Lend me fifty dollars?" he asked casually.

"No."

"Then let me have five bucks for cab fare to take my girl home."

"No." Long pause.

"Then give me a dime," was the final request, "so I can call a rental limousine. I can charge that."

On still another occasion an aging playboy approached the established men's tailor Pat Caruso with a familiar proposition. The business deal was that Pat should clothe him for free for a year in return for which he would tell "all his rich and important friends" that Caruso was his personal and favorite tailor. Caruso sighed and declined the offer.

"The only friends you have," he told the potential clothes horse sadly, "are guys who come in here every day making me the same offer you just made."

"I think the day of the kids was over," one veteran saloon keeper recalled some years ago, "when I decided on a new deal for them. I made them pay a basic $2 fee per person. I don't know why I did it, for there was no profit in it. I guess I was just trying to do some handwriting on the wall for them."

It soon became evident that even a meager two bucks a head was beyond the reach of these young "celebrities." Indeed, one lad who must have had his picture in the papers a hundred times as "the grandson of the famous financier," arrived at a class cabaret to be informed by the headwaiter that his party of four must furnish eight dollars to get through the door. The young celebrity loudly berated the headwaiter and the owner of the place for whom he "had done so much." He swiveled to stalk out with his party.

Before he could make his indignant exit, however, he had to retrieve his hat and coat from the checkroom girl. He presented his check. The gal brought his hat and coat. The grandson of the famed financier searched through his pockets. He came up with three pennies. With a noble gesture, he dumped the three pennies on the counter. Then he and his party swept out.

As he left he made way for one of the new "pencil celebrities"—a man who lived on a company expense account. It was the new nobility replacing an earlier royalty.

By and large, probably, the Chosen Children were more exploited than exploiting. We shall never know whether, left alone and not overcompensated, they would have minded their own business, gone to work and even made a success of their lives. Or did most of them have the seed of spoiled bums in them from the moment they knew what they might have inherited or to whom they were actually related?

It is noticeable that such café and class saloon owners who are still working at their lasts get a little uneasy and apologetic when the subject comes up in conversation.

MOONLIGHT

Just the other day I passed the building that had housed so many nightclubs in its cellar, over the years and, to my surprise, they were tearing it down. i was surprised only because they apparently had to knock it down. I thought it had fallen down years ago, after a nightclub operator called Footsy made his own alterations on the structure.

Footsy was scarcely unique as a speakeasy hard guy turned "honest" nightclub operator. He tried not to pay anybody, he was quick with a threat, he had a loud mouth, he padded checks, he was ignorant of almost everything that had anything to do with talent or taste, and with all his big talk he couldn't make any money—or if he made it he couldn't keep it.

One of the last nightclubs Footsy tried to run was in the cellar of this just-off-Broadway building. Footsy had a small band in there, a series of bad comedians and a string of chorus girls. And right in the center of the floor, he had a big vertical steel beam that a previous owner, with standard nightclub imagination, had wound with phony bark and fronds to make it look like a palm tree.

Sitting around glaring at his empty joint one night, Footsy came to a conclusion: The big beam tree was the cause of his no business. The girls had to dance around it. The band had to play through it. The comedian wasn't seen by one section of the room no matter how he stood near the tree. It was all the tree's fault. It had to come out.

So Footsy took himself down to the Buildings Department and had a man help him look up the plans of the five-story building where he had his place of business. He told the man what he wanted to do—he wanted to tear out his beam tree.

"Are you mad?" demanded the city employee. "That is the central stem of the whole structure. You tear that out and the whole building will fall down into your cellar."

Footsy went back to his cellar trap. He sat for a few nights and glared at the beam tree. He uttered curses. Business got worse.

That goddamn tree was to blame. Something had to be done. Footsy did something.

Early one morning after his employees had all gone home, Footsy brought in some friends who were construction workers. They brought tools. In no time at all they cut the beam tree right out of the cellar and filled up the holes. Now all customers could see everything on the floor. No beam tree to spoil things.

Sad to say, no added customers appeared and Footsy eventually had to abandon his latest club de société. That was to be expected. What a lot of people suspected was something else—they suspected that any minute the whole building would collapse right into the cellar. No such thing happened. A whole string of other nightclub entrepreneurs operated the place in years to come. Nothing fell in.

As I say, just a little while ago I walked by and they were having the usual hard time *knocking down* a building that, theoretically, had no central beam to hold it up.

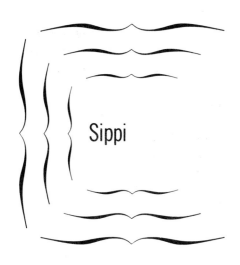

Sippi

IF YOU ASKED HIM WHAT HIS NAME was he would tell you it was Mississippi. Just call him Sippi, which is what we all called him. He was an ageless Negro, a taller and even thinner version of the Uncle Tom image. He drove a spavined horse and a battered carriage, like the ones that roll slowly through Central Park, but we never saw him in the Park. We always saw him sitting in a doorway or asleep in his carriage on some Broadway corner, the horse nodding, head down in the traces.

His trademark was the most battered high silk hat you can imagine, and there was even a legend about that. It was told that Ted Lewis, the early jazz clarinetist, had given Sippi his first battered hat. And it was also told that Ted had bought one of Sippi's toppers and used it for all of his long career as the Lewis trademark. Whatever, Sippi was never without it.

He would go on occasional rather lengthy drunks, and when he reappeared on the Broadway scene it was always on foot. He had hocked both wagon and horse. I should remember the horse's name, but that item has escaped memory's feeble mesh. Afoot, and abject, Sippi would make the rounds of his customers and friends. The producer Earl Carroll got Sippi's horse and vehicle out of hock several times. Horse-playing comedians such as Willie Howard or Harry Richmond and "Doc" Stein, the druggist at whose curb the carriage was often parked, were a few who were intermittently good for the rather smallish sum for which Sippi hocked his business assets. There were others. Somebody always came to the rescue.

Coming to Sippi's rescue was not altogether altruism. There could be no doubt that he knew as much about racehorses and bloodlines, equine faults and flaws, as anybody in town. From his talk, or from the places and names he dropped in his talk, it was clear that he had once been closely connected with great racing stables and great racehorses. Horseplayers sought his advice, and when it was good, as it often was, they paid for his tips and information. A true horseplayer always pays off in such matters. Not out of honor, but out of fear that if he doesn't he'll break his luck.

Sippi seemed to need virtually no sleep because frequently he could be found at the racetrack, backtrack or hanging over the rail, watching the horses train. I do not remember ever seeing him on the lawn or in the grandstand afternoons when the racing was on, and I do not know whether or not he even bet horses in his later days. Why he had left horses and the track as a way of life was unknown, but some indication of the trouble he may have brought on himself was contained in the story a veteran bookmaker told.

This story had it that when Sippi was a handler for a big, rich stable owned by a prominent socialite, the owner had somehow or other given some sort of orders to run a horse in the wrong race or the wrong way or when the horse was not well.

Sippi had been at the finish line when the jockey brought the horse back after the race, blood pouring from its nostrils. Sippi had looked the rich and famous stable-owner straight in the eye and said, merely: "Trash."

One early morning I climbed high up into the grandstand to sit in a patch of early morning warm sunlight, and who was sitting there also but Sippi. He was dressed in his usual uniform: an old pair of drill pants, a dark flannel shirt tightly buttoned at wrists and throat, woolen socks and high, buttoned shoes. No battered silk topper. That was for work. Things must have been good for him at the moment, for in the shirt pocket were five cellophane-wrapped cheap cigars.

His hazel eyes flicked briefly over the racing form under my arm.

"Read me the news, Mr. Bob," he said. "I left my glasses to home."

I didn't laugh because we had all heard the statement many times. Nobody had ever seen Sippi with glasses on, but it didn't cost anything to humor an old colored man who could or could not read. Anyway, he didn't have to read about racehorses. He looked and he listened and that was all the knowledge he needed. I sprawled out beside him and read off the claims and the private sales and the breeding notes. I told him another trainer "had severed connections" with Elizabeth Arden, and I read other mundane notes.

Sippi shook his head. "Must be suthin' else," he said. "I got a feelin' like suthin' happened."

"Well," I told him, turning the pages, "here's a jockey got killed. Some hardboot track up in Canada. Horse crossed its legs and went down and three more went down over it. Boy and horse killed instantly. Nobody else hurt bad. Boy's name Frankie Ryan."

"That's it," Sippi nodded. "Frankie Ryan. You remember him?"

I didn't.

"I had him," Sippi said slowly. "I had him when I was with the Mr. Keith J. Rollings stable. Not so many years ago, either, although Frankie was a pretty old boy to be riding today. He come to us the year Lawrin win the Derby, a little redhair boy stubborn as a mule. We thought for a while he would make out to be the best one ever. Dead, eh?"

"Dead," I confirmed.

I lit one of my own cigars and offered Sippi an addition to his own pocketful. He took it and rolled it around in his lips, the faraway look on his face. If he had a story to tell, I knew he would tell it in his own way on his own time, and I had all day. After a while he started talking softly and slowly in his musical voice, his eyes still on the horses moving around the course.

"A jock," Sippi started, "has got to learn to treat a hawse like a machine. You can't get yourself smitten with a hawse. You gotta treat it with care and see the parts are all oiled, and like that, but when a jock gets personal smitten with an animal it ain't any good. Like he thinks twice before he takes the hawse through a small hole. Or he takes back when he hadn't oughten or he gets out front and tries to win by half the track because he's so proud of the hawse. That's the way Frankie Ryan was with First Love.

"He was an apprentice when he first came to us. Mister Keith J.

Rollings bought his contract from one of the Christmas boys and I took him in hand. I liked him real good. He was a little slim kid, but he was willing and a good worker and he had the guts of a burglar. He laughed all the time and putty soon all of us around the barn were laughing all the time.

"Mister Rollings was just enlarging his stable then, and a course you know by now he's a smart man. That time he come up with Pulpwood, that I had a hand in bringing around, and that one win five stakes, and also we got four or five useful geldings that did nicely. We didn't have no stickout hawse, but the stable is doing good and Mister Rollings is happy. So was all of us.

"So up in Saratoga that year Mister Rollings makes several buys at the yearling sales and one of these is a chestnut filly by Original out of Romance by Conquistador. He names this filly First Love.

"Next Spring Frankie breaks her to saddle and we start to put the pressure on her and after a couple of weeks we are hopping up and down. We was sure we had a real flyer. And just about this time Frankie meets Cookie Rollings, Mr. Keith's daughter. You know Cookie, a course. Or anyway you read about her. I heard she got married again the other day. Mr. Keith J. Rollings' daughter.

"Like I say, Frankie met her and from then on it seemed like she was around the barns all the time, all day, all hours. The whole thing sort of caught fire all at once. Frankie in love with her and her stuck on him and both of them plumb crazy about that filly. They couldn't keep away from each other and neither of them could keep away from that hawse. Neither of them wanted the filly to have any discipline at all. The first real argument we had around the barn was when Frankie spoke real mad to Big Ed Botterud, the trainer, over the way Big Ed was training her out of the gate. All the time I saw Frankie up on that filly I never saw him use the bat once. He couldn't even bear to sting her with the whip.

"She sure was a pretty little filly, at that. The sun on her coat made it shine like gold, and she had a nice, easy way of moving. I couldn't fault her nowheres and I guess I began to believe, like Frankie and Cookie, we had a champeen on our hands. And maybe we would have except for one thing—she was just plain unlucky, like I'm going to tell you about.

"As for Frankie and Cookie getting stuck on each other, a jock and a daybewtonty, that worried us at first but it come out all right. Mr. Keith J. Rollings is a self-made man and like I said he's smart. He watched Frankie for a while and I guess he made up his mind. Cause one day there was a message that Frankie should go downtown to the big office there. I took the message and when I told the boy he got kinda white under his frackles.

"'Maybe this is it,' he says to me. 'So let him fire me. But he can't break me and Cookie up. And I tell you something more,' he says, sticking out that jaw, 'if he drives Cookie and me away from here we take First Love with us. One way or another. Any way.'

"But when he come back he is chipper as a yearling. I don't know what him and Mister Rollings say to each other but like I told you, Mr. Rollings is a smart man and a smart man prolly figures that a hardworking, honest boy is what a father should want for his daughter. I guess he knew enough about the other kinds, at that.

"So everythin' is pure, shinin' happy around our barn. Cookie hung over the rail mornings and clapped her hands and hollered when Frankie galloped the filly. She got underfoot when I was trying to rub the animal down and she and Frankie had a lot of advice for the vet and for Big Ed and me and everybody else. You'd a thought the filly was their first baby.

"Well, we got the little hawse ready and Big Ed drops her in a special weights at Belmont. And from then on there was no more laughin' around the barn because Frankie and Cookie were so nervous and tighted up that we were all stretched to breaking. You'd a thought the filly was on trial for her life instead of entered in a little ole nursery sprint which it makes no difference if she wins by a mile or finishes up the racetrack. That kid and that girl fussed and fretted until we were all half crazy. Big Ed finally threatened to put another boy on her, but a course he wouldn't a dared.

"It comes race time, and George Mothorn has an Equipoise filly in, and he thinks he's got somethin' real special and is going to run off from evvybody else. Genaro is up on this filly, I remember, and when they break Genaro charges out of the gate and slams into First Love and almost knocks her down. It sounds funny but that was the start of all the bad luck that came. I was thinking only the other day that if Genaro hadn't slammed First Love, things might of been different.

"Anyway, like I told you, Frankie is a redhead and he's got the temper to go with it. He just simply blew. Right then, at that start, he stops thinking about winning and he starts thinking about catching Genaro. He wants to catch Genaro so he can kill him.

"First Love settled into stride and began to eat up that lost ground and they halfways to the wirc, right in front of everybody in the stands, they come alongside and Frankie takes two swipes with the butt end of his whip at Genaro's head. He misses both so he lugs out and kicks Genaro's filly so hard she slides halfway across the track. Meantime two other fillies come up inside and they go through a hole as big as a barn. Frankie gets his hot head back on business and starts after them. He catches them a couple of yards from home and wins by an inch, but none of us bother to cash our tickets.

"We're not wondering about First Love being disqualified. That's a sure shot. We're wondering how long Mr. Frankie Ryan is going to get set down for.

"He's so mad he's crying tears when they get him up before the stewards, and when they bring Genaro up Frankie tries to get at him with his hands and they have to be pulled apart. There is considerable excitement, as you might understand, but Frankie's got a nice clean record and Genaro ain't. So Frankie only gets set down thirty days."

Sippi made a sound between a grunt and a sigh and relit his cigar.

"Well," he continued through the smoke, "that was the start of it. Next Frankie and Big Ed had an argument and Big Ed was not the kind of trainer who held that jockeys should speak back to him, not with his years in the business and a course his record, too. Then Frankie speaks back to Mr. Rollings himself, and when Cookie tries to cool him out he jumps on her too and now we have a lovers' quarrel on our hands, together with all the other grief. For the next weeks Frankie spends all his time with the filly. He'd of slept in the stall if I would of let him.

"Also, nobody is doing any laughing atall around Mr. Keith J. Rollings barn now.

"So that's how it started," Sippi continued, after remembering some more, "and that's the way it kept going, only worse. Ed entered First Love in another race a week or so later and brought in Joe Haight to ride her. Frankie acted like he was crazy.

276

"'He can't handle my horse,' he screamed. 'He's got hands like a butcher. You know what a soft mouth she's got!'

"The best Haight could do with the hawse was a bad fourth, and a course the arguments started all over again with Frankie accusing everybody of trying to ruin the filly. Big Ed was getting madder and madder, and Mr. Keith J. Rollings was beginning to narrow his eyes every time he saw Frankie coming at him. I knew how the kid felt and had a talk with Big Ed. So the next time he started the filly he put Herbie O'Malley on her. Herbie was going real good, then.

"First Love threw him off in the gate and even tried to trample him.

"That's the way it was going, like I say. You know how luck is around the racetrack. It's contagious like. Sure enough, Pulpwood gets to coughing and scares us half to death, and all of a sudden the useful claimers can't get out of their own way, much less win, and pretty soon we somehow started looking at First Love like she was an omen, or something, and was bringing us all this grief.

"We give her another chance with Blackie Sands up, I think it was, and she run a very dull race, never really trying, and Big Ed starts to talk about getting rid of her. I talked to him real hard and finally he grunted and said he'd wait a while. I argued real hard because I see things are beginning to come between Frankie and Cookie and I figure that if First Love will only get herself a nice win everybody will be happy and laughing all over again.

"I dunno how much good I did, in the long run. I was sitting in the dark against the stall one night and they come up to the gate. The filly come and nuzzled Frankie and Frankie tells Cookie how great she's going to be. Cookie tried to change the subject, innocent enough, and all of a sudden they was in an argument.

"Pretty soon she was crying and then she was gone and there was the boy alone, just whispering to a hawse. Maybe his mind was a little unsettled, I doan know. Doc George M. Gaylord was our vet and a real doc, too, and he told me a funny thing. He said First Love was a symbol to Frankie. He called it something like transference, I think, that the filly meant everything to Frankie that he really loved—his life on the track, Cookie, horses, riding, winning, everything.

"I told Big Ed what Doc had said and Ed said maybe and maybe also things might change when we got to Saratoga and Frankie's suspension was lifted. He said he hoped things would change, because he said if things didn't change he was going to change them hisself. The way things was, we was snapping and snarling at each other like a pack of ugly dogs.

"We shipped to Saratoga and Frankie's set down was over and we begin thinking about the Champagne, I think it was. Frankie was to ride the filly again. She was working real good and things were easier, and I guess we all begin to get excited again. The day of the race I boosted Frankie up on the filly and he turned to speak down to me and he was laughing for the first time in weeks.

"'Sippi,' he said, 'this is the day we redeem ourselves. Both of us.' I knew what he meant. He was always at heart an honest, willing boy.

"First Love ran dead last that day. She pulled up lame, too. She never did have any luck.

"It was right after the races, in Ed's office in the barn, that the end come that day. Ed told Mr. Rollings to sell First Love and Mr. Rollings said all right, go ahead and sell her.

"Frankie was still in his silks and he was white as a sheet. He tried to buy the filly himself, but a course he didn't have the money, not enough. Then he cursed us all and ranted like mad, and when Cookie tried to cool him out he turned on her like a wild man.

"'You're as bad as the rest of them,' he screamed at her. 'First Love is our horse and you know it. If you'd desert her when she needs us so bad, you'd desert anybody you say you love. You're deserting me. When the chips are down you go with them and leave me to fight this thing alone.'

"I won't tell you about the long wrangle. Nobody changed his mind. In the morning Frankie was gone. First Love was soon gone, too. Ed sold her to Frank Boardman, who had pretty good luck patching up cripples and making them earn their keep. We heard about her once in a while on the bush tracks. She never did do much. Unlucky.

"What we heard once in a while about Frankie wasn't good, either. He was set down out West for some scramble, and people who moved around told us nobody could get along with him and he was always in trouble. He didn't write Cookie, either. Cookie is from fighting stock, too, and she just stuck out her jaw and tried to look natural and we didn't see her around the barns anymore. After a while I begin to notice her around with one of the Tripp boys, I forget which one. They all got money, and in about a year she married him. It didn't last too long. They told me the other day she married a third man, some Englishman.

"After a while I went to Big Ed and told him I was quitting. He asked me what was wrong and I said nuthin' wrong, I just wanted to get away from the big time and take things easy in the country or somewhere. Ed was looking out the window and he said a funny thing.

"'Sippi,' he said, 'a guy in our business has gotta make a barrel of mistakes. Most of them you can lay off on one excuse or another, but I made a mistake I'm sorry about. I'm sorry about that filly the kids were so set on. She wasn't a bad little thing, she was just unlucky. Maybe if I'd had a little more faith in her, things would have worked out the way they promised.'

"Funny," said Sippi, grinding out his cigar butt, "but I was thinking about Frankie just yesterday. What race did you say he got killed in?"

I said the fourth. He asked me the name of the horse. It was a horse we had never heard of.

"I suppose it should have been First Love," Sippi murmured. "They should of gone together. But First Love went a long time ago. Now they're both through that Big Gate. Maybe they'll have some luck where they are."

I got to my feet and asked Sippi if I could make a bet for him. He named a horse in the sixth that he liked, and when the time came I bet a tenner for him and another for myself. Sure enough, the horse had a lot of bad luck, plus a bad ride, and got beat.

Not that it mattered. Sippi and I had been beat at the races before and would be again. But somehow I had to wonder if old Sippi had made up the story to lead me into a bet or whether it was for real. But, what the hell, twenty bucks was a small price for that kind of a racetrack story.

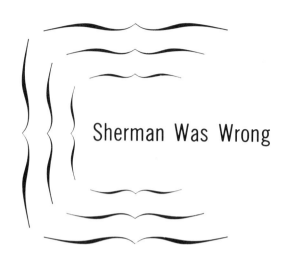

Sherman Was Wrong

"War is hell"—William Tecumseh Sherman, 1864
"Like hell it was"—Robert McPhierson Sylvester, 1946

In common with many shore-bred ignorami, I could never find anything very colorful, amusing or even descriptive about hardline Navy talk during the four years I spent helping to save the world with World War II. Looking back on the Great Unpleasantness, now three wars back in history, I wondered why, if a stairway must be called a ladder and eating is chow, etc., why should the officer's quarters aboard a ship be referred to as officers' country? Sitting here now, I can remember only two ethnic, authentic Old Salt sayings that ever made me smile. One was the standard advice to anybody who was bitching about his lot in life: "Tell your troubles to Jesus, the chaplain's gone ashore."

The other was a sort of au revoir one old-timer would give another: "Call me if the wind shifts and I'll take her through the straits."

For some reason these two gems amused my addled mind. However, my war, as I like to think of it, furnished many a memory I can still laugh at. For instance, there was the time the all-star sports aggregation came to a Pacific Island to raise our morale.

They were under the direction of Jack White, a former Manhattan College star athlete who went on to become a prominent figure in professional football. Jack had under his wing thirty big-league baseball stars including Pee Wee Reese, Johnny Vander Meer, Johnny Mize and two dozen more. Also along were tennis champ Bobby Riggs, light heavyweight and middleweight boxing champs Fred Apostoli and Georgie Abrams and assorted famous muscle types.

The main chore of these heroes was to play a baseball game, give boxing exhibitions and lessons, tennis advice and so forth. However, the Navy did not want real fighting men or real sailors to be able to sneer at a bunch of sissies who didn't have to do anything but play games. So each day, wherever they were, the athletes had to turn to and do one manual chore in plain sight of the common seadogs. On this island, on this occasion, the thirty-odd baseball players and other sports-page heroes were assigned to fertilize the grass outfield of the base athletic field. They dutifully climbed off big trucks loaded with chemical fertilizer and set to spreading, shoveling, raking and grading. The fertilizer rose in clouds, knee high. There was much coughing and cursing.

"I never thought I'd see it," said Jack White, shaking his head in amazement.

"See what?" asked a nearby former hero of Ebbets Field.

"A million dollars worth of manure," Jack told him.

In Pearl Harbor when I was there, the confusion on the docks and in the shipyards was such that nobody knew where anything was when it was wanted. The shipyard had a little newspaper of its own, and I remember one rather hysterical ad which started: "Lost or STOLEN! One airplane carrier anchor. 16,000 pounds. If found please notify dockmaster's office." There was probably a minimum of professional thievery, but the amateurs did some brilliant things indeed. As everywhere else where GI's collected, it was a foolish jeep driver who didn't take the distributor cap with him whenever he left his trusted vehicle. The more cautious jeep shepherds were known to carry away the entire carburetor when leaving the vehicle out of sight for any length of time.

However, there was a legend in Pearl Harbor repeated so often that there had to be some basis to it. The tale had it that the crew of an outgoing submarine calmly dismantled an entire jeep, stored the piece belowdecks and sailed off for their advanced base where they reassembled the treasure and used it to envious advantage. Having seen jeeps assembled in their home factory, I believe this wonderful feat was entirely possible.

One twilight I found myself on the beautiful Hawaiian island of Maui. I climbed a winding road up a mountain and, halfway up, was a tiny native store. I started in for a cold beer, and near the door I could hear the sounds of the familiarly unfamiliar and discordant Japanese music as it was hammered out on a small stringed instrument on the floor.

Inside, in the semidarkness, an old Japanese sat cross-legged playing his native music. He was wearing a T-shirt. The T-shirt had a printed motto on it.

"Remember Pearl Harbor," it read.

Everytime I see a regatta or sailing races I must think back and wonder what ever happened to the Drop Tank Yacht Club of Saipan. This club came into being when the B-29 bombers, returning from visits to Tokyo, dropped their empty portable gas tanks in the ocean as they neared home. Some quirk of the tides inevitably brought the light pontoon tanks washing ashore at Saipan. By cutting a hole in the top of the tank, adding an outrigger for balance and hoisting a small canvas sail, the drop tanks made a very satisfactory smaller-than-Star-class sailboat.

Races, as in many smart yacht clubs, were usually held on Sundays. Some Sundays you could hardly tell the difference between Saipan and Larchmont.

If it is true that generals die in bed, then I would make a fairly stiff wager that they die in very comfortable beds wherever the beds may be, in or out of war. When I reached Hollandia, New Guinea, Gen. Douglas MacArthur had just vacated his bed and country home atop a small mountain. I didn't see the bed, but I saw the home, which was an outsize Quonset hut, and I saw the road leading up to it, which had been specially built up the steep rise.

The Pacific's maximum leader had ordered a home built in a hurry and he wanted one high up, where it would be cool. The engineers and the Seabees went to work on the road. They graded and leveled, and all heavy construction equipment was put to work. In those spots where no fill was available, anything at hand was used for fill. So crated jeeps were used for fill. Hundreds of crates of canned foods were used for fill. Drums full of oil were used for fill. Everything was used for fill except the sacred cases of officers' club whisky.

The road was finished in the nick of time. General MacArthur took up quarters in his new home.

He lived there seven days and seven nights and then moved on.

On another island another general with mining experience let his mind wander from the Japanese problem momentarily to instruct his own mining engineers to make tests on his private road and the land on which his hut stood, for any worthwhile mineral deposits. After the tests the general was wont to tell any visiting fellow officer or VIP that his "property" assayed at seven dollars worth of gold per ton.

When a Pacific admiral's yeoman, running through the classification cards of new personnel, found that a famous college swimming champ had been landed on his island, the admiral lost no time in taking the aquatic speedster away from Recreation.

He assigned him to building a swimming pool fit for an admiral.

In Dutch New Guinea, also, I spent some time watching the "headhunters." These were tall, strong natives who actually took off every once in a while and also took some heads from enemies. We all learned that to a headhunter anybody is an enemy unless he is a blood relative. By the time I made their domain, the head-hunters had fallen desperately in love with American cigarettes and with Chlorox. They would take a bottle of the latter and dump it over their heads. In a reasonable period of time their thick, wiry hair would turn a sort of orangy red. To us heroes they were referred to, with some reason, as Fuzzy Wuzzies.

But before I learned all this salient knowledge there, I was on a jungle road and here came a Fuzzy Wuzzy walking toward me. His hair was a wild red, he had a small bone in his nose, his joints were swollen with whatever native disease the locals were suffering at the time. He walked straight at me. I thought that it was my last moment on earth.

"Hi, buddy," he said with his toothless smile. He asked for a cigarette. I gave it to him as fast as I could.

It was on this same island that we went to the village school to hear the local school kids in concert. I wanted to hear the ancient native chants. What I heard instead was "Pistol Packin' Mama" and "You Are My Sunshine." Don't tell me that aboriginals don't learn fast.

Things became liberated very quickly in the Pacific, I found. Everything got Americanized, including the language. Instances:

Mog Mog Island almost immediately became Egg Nog Island. The Okinawa Japs in my day were the Okies. The area of Tacloban in the Philippines was quickly translated as Tacklebaum and, of course, the dreaded dengue fever was always referred to, with respect, as dungaree fever.

It was on one of these rocks, I forget just which, where our British cousins came to learn some modern warfare. Our Navy and Marines had had some fine success with specially trained units for underwater demolition. These strong swimmers, carrying a hefty load of tools, would swim in at night and wreck the underwater mines and obstacles in harbors and off-islands that were targets. This naturally came to the attention of the British, a nation long famed for its seamen. So Britain scanned its Navy records and picked out some two hundred of the bravest, strongest, youngest heroes they had. These selectees were shipped to the Pacific to learn how to handle underwater traps.

It developed that there was only one thing wrong with the new group—most of them couldn't swim at all, and the others could only swim a little bit.

With such action at the highest levels, it is little wonder that widespread confusion was the order of the day in the lower ranks. The traffic in phony "souvenirs," in fact, was such that toward the end of My War the Red Cross was actually giving expert advice on items, like a pawnbroker. It was a rather valuable service since by war's end some GI's in the Pacific were operating what amounted to souvenir factories.

Indeed, the visiting crews of merchant marine supply ships came to be known as "the tourist trade." It did not take the natives too long to catch on. In Tacloban I once saw a visiting GI haggle for all of ten minutes over a red, transparent bracelet worn by a native. In the end he surrendered a khaki shirt and two packs of cigarettes for this objet d'art. It wasn't until he gave it close inspection that he discovered that the bracelet was made from an ordinary plastic American toothbrush handle.

If there is anything of which there is more than a sufficiency in the Pacific, it is coral. Coral comes in two classes, live coral and dead coral. The island of Tinian, like most of its neighbors, is entirely coral. Yet when the Americans got really launched on their construction spree there, using coral as the building material for everything, there simply wasn't enough to go around. It was found necessary to put priorities on the stuff and even mount armed guards over the coral stockpiles.

One of the first chores of the American Military Government, when it liberated a territory, was to see that the natives got work and wages, but also to see that they didn't take undue advantages. With the liberation of Leyte, the natives had the laundry business under control long before the American military could move in modern machinery. In its usual style, the AMG then made out a long and involved list of prices for every imaginable item that might need washing.

The busy native launderers studied the long price lists, sighed, shook their heads and decided they'd set their own prices. It was simpler that way. Their prices?

"Big bundle two pesos. Small bundle one peso."

It was on Leyte, too, that the control tower repeatedly complained about one pilot who always approached the field from the wrong altitude. Eventually he was called in for questioning and had a ready answer. It was all his monkey's fault, he explained. It developed that he had bought a pet monkey, and the little devil was so much fun he took it along on all his missions. But everytime the plane got above 5,000 feet the monk became groggy and drowsed off. He was no fun when asleep, so the fun-loving pilot had taken to flying his plane closer to the ground all the time.

We didn't have too many Negro companies or GI's in my part of the Pacific, but those we did have got along very well with the native girls. The natives were at first inclined to be confused with black Americans among white Americans, but the blacks soon found a ready explanation.

"We're American night fighters," they would tell the gals.

I don't know whether they make fly boys these days the way they made them in My War. Once in Australia an American pilot and an Aussie got into a saloon argument over their respective fighter planes. We all repaired to the Aussie air field.

The Australian was contending that he could do a complete loop in his plane starting the loop from the ground. It was soon seen that the Aussie plane would only seat *one* pilot. This was really no problem. The American pilot *sat in the lap* of the Aussie while the latter did his loop.

Gene Tunney, the former heavyweight champ and student of Shakespeare and Shaw, was titular boss of the Navy's physical fitness program. I was walking with him once when he stopped a street brawl in Sydney, Australia. The combatants all took to their heels except one American who turned out to be in Tunney's own program. He explained that he had been returning from teaching his judo class when he had been unfairly set upon by the bad guys. He explained he made good use of his fists.

"Why didn't you use judo?" demanded Tunney.

"Judo!" said the expert, looking superior. "Not for a case like this!"

We had all sorts of entertainment out there, ranging from famous stars to the touring groups of earnest if small-time musicians, singers and dancers. Most of the entertainers who came to cheer us up were very fine folk indeed, but every now and then we would get some kind of a slob. A movie actor who, these many years later, does not get many roles but was then a hot shot, gave everybody a bad time.

His tour finished, he was told he had been booked to take a very comfortable ship back home. He refused. He wanted to go by plane. Special Services rushed around and finally told him that he was lucky, they had found a plane for him. It was going direct to San Francisco.

"Nothing doing," said the ham. "I want the Los Angeles plane."

We also enjoyed good, healthy outdoor sports. Or some of us, like a chief petty officer named Duke, did. Duke was on a ship that had a real rear admiral, and the admiral was an enthusiastic duck shooter. So Duke scouted around and found out that if he could scrounge a jeep and went so many miles this way and then so many miles that way, he would come upon a shallow pond loaded with ducks.

Duke and his admiral got up before dawn and took off. Sure enough, there was the pond and there they could hear the ducks. They settled in the reeds and waited for dawn. With first light they stood up and started blasting. Ducks began falling down dead all over the water.

Also over and through the water, from the far side, came an Old Chinese running toward them. He splashed up in front of them, literally quivering with rage.

"American horse cock sons of bitch," he screamed. "No fly-fly duck! Walk-walk duck!"

Duke and his admiral packed their guns and left the duck farm.

In conclusion, I have often been surprised that American industry did not learn a couple of lessons from My War. For instance:

There is no way to chill beer faster or with less effort than throwing the cans into a drum of high-test aviation gasoline. And nothing approaches fire-extinguisher fluid for washing dirty clothes in a hurry.

Of course, these methods are expensive. But what isn't, these days? "Especially in a war!"

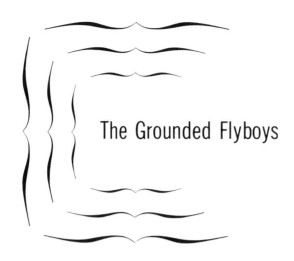

The Grounded Flyboys

WE WERE JUST BARELY IN WORLD War II when Irving Berlin, even then no youngster, dredged what talent he could from our earliest soldiers and produced on Broadway "This Is the Army." Possibly because of everybody's emotional involvement, I would say that this revue had the most exciting opening night in my forty years of theatre memories. Of course, the Air Force could not be outdone. So, no less than Moss Hart, then and until his death a top drawer playwright and director, got together a syndicate of Broadway managers and backers and produced, in 1943, an Air Force musical called "Winged Victory."

"Winged Victory" will not be remembered either on Broadway or on the farflung forward areas where "This Is the Army" spent a couple years touring. However, it is at least arguable that because of "Winged Victory," the Air Force should be collecting agency commissions from at least a score of then unknowns who came out of the show to go on to fame in films, theatre, nightclubs, radio, and television. Hark to a partial list:

The cast included Edmond O'Brien, Red Buttons, Lee J. Cobb, Peter Lind Hayes, Karl Malden, Kevin McCarthy, Gary Merrill, Danny Scholl, Keith Andes, Donald Richards, Alan Baxter, John Tyers, Ray MacDonald, Tony Ross, Philip Bourneuf, Alfred Ryder,

Barry Nelson, Tommy Farrell, Eugene Conley, Zeke Manners, Henry and Jack Slate, Archie Robbins, Donald Beddoe, Jack Powell Jr. and Grant Richards, among others.

An enormous orchestra was led by David Rose ("Holiday for Strings" and other musical hits) and had as a sort of special pianist a chap named Joe Bushkin, of whom more later. Much more. From the military standpoint (if that is the correct description) the show was commanded by Col. John Dunham. The cast had two convictions about Col. Dunham: 1) He was the brother-in-law of Air Force General Hap Arnold. 2) He was given the command because he knew something about show biz from having been a church organist in Texas.

"Winged Victory" opened at the 44th Street Theatre on November 22, 1943, and hilarity was the keynote even before the favorable critical reviews. First, newspaper criticism during rehearsals accused the cast and management of "living in luxury" at the New York Athletic Club. Actually, the heroes were sleeping on army cots in the NYAC gym and dormitory. But the Air Force bowed to the public mood, moved the actor-airmen off their cots and installed them on real beds in New York hotels.

With an actual head count of 84 actors and entertainers on stage for any given performance, it was obvious that there was not a lot of acting, singing or dancing for any single cast member to do. No star roles. No big parts. Just a little bit for everybody. But it was far better than being at an Air Force station on some rock and nobody wanted to be transferred, especially since "Winged Victory" was next door to Sardi's restaurant. It behooved cast members to make themselves useful.

"I flew 187 missions to the Gaiety Delicatessen," Red Buttons remembers. "Henry Slate was tail gunner on the Broadway IRT Express."

Joe Bushkin, finding a more classical musician on the piano stool, convinced Col. Dunham that what the orchestra needed was "a jazz piano."

"I spent five weeks pretending to look for one," remembers Joe, "before management decided to help me. They kept bringing in old uprights. I would play a few chords, shake my head and say no, it wasn't a proper jazz piano."

And so, for 212 performances, life went merrily on in what

Bushkin and his friends always referred to as "The Silver Foxhole." Ultimately, it became time to go on tour. Then the fun started for real.

"On the day we left Broadway, "Bushkin recalls, "we fell in, real military-like, in front of Sardi's. I was to lead the march because I had been assigned to make an arrangement for the whole cast of that Air Force song—you know, the one about the wild blue yonder. I did it up real nice with tenor and counterpoint for those who could sing. For those who couldn't sing but could whistle pretty good, I had the whistlers for a background. For the other slobs I made them hum. We did a staggering left face and started off for the unknown.

"What a march down Eighth Avenue! I swear to you people stood along the curb and actually cried. The hearts of the populace bled for us, such a fine body of young men going off to possible death. They cried and they cheered. They didn't know where we were going. I knew where we were going. We were going to Penn Station to take a train for a tour that would take us to Hollywood where we were to make a silly movie."

On the road, however, there were some wartime rigors. One night a new buck private who was assigned to the box office couldn't make the night's gross come out right. No matter how many times he counted up, he came out $270 short. The big brass arrived and sternly lent a hand. Nobody could find the $270. In due course everybody was weary and the brass was hinting at disciplinary action, possibly a life sentence in the stockade.

"Oh, the hell with it," said the new buck private. "I'll make up the difference myself." He reached in his pocket, came up with a bundle and counted off the $270.

"This youth," remembers Bushkin, "just happened to be the heir to one of America's big fortunes. No show ever had such a capable box office treasurer."

Inevitably, "Winged Victory" ran out of the bigger cities and took to the sticks. Nat Hiken, then a radio writer, and Ade Kahn, still a Broadway press agent, had roomed together for the long tour. One morning, Nat remembered, he woke up in a small hotel in some place in Montana. Outside the snow had piled halfway up the walls. The show was now on one-night stands. Nat yawned and looked around.

Across the room, in a rickety chair with his portable typewriter on his knees, Ade Kahn was maintaining his ties with home and business career. He was writing jokes to send to Walter Winchell. He looked around at the wakening Nat, who didn't know what hotel he was in, which city or town it was, or, for that matter, what his own name might be. Ade stared at him for a moment.

"Got any gags?" Ade demanded.

Things got no better. Ultimately the commanding officer called together his troops.

"I know that audiences have been very poor," he told them. "I know you must be quite discouraged. But I have some good news for you. I have restudied our route and I find that from now on we will be playing smaller theatres."

It wasn't until the cast was settled at a Hollywood film studio, however, that military discipline cracked all the way down. A stage manager was called in by a member of higher brass and informed that he was now a part of Air Force intelligence. He was to keep a sharp eye on any infractions of civilian rules such as black marketing or breaking rationing rules.

"Even if you see a cast member taking an extra chip of butter in the commissary," the new intelligence agent was told, "I want you to report him to me immediately."

After the rigors of Hollywood, "Winged Victory" was broken up into small units and sent through the Pacific.

"It wasn't so bad out there," a veteran of one of the groups remembers. "One of the guys in our group had a sister who worked in a cannery back home and she would send us canned whisky with standard canned fruit labels on it. And one of the musicians had a girl friend who was a good cook. She sent us loaves of homemade bread. In the middle, wrapped in tinfoil, was a nice filling of marijuana."

All of which may or may not prove that a wasted youth is a requisite for success in any form of show business.

Where Did It Go?

WHAT BECAME OF THE OLD ATMO-sphere of the biggest and most sophisticated city in the world— when I say atmosphere I probably mean *ambiance,* which is today's "in" word—has concerned deeper scholars than your irreverent author. The one word, *economics,* probably was the most villainous factor in the end of night life in New York as we knew it until just a few years ago. As this is written, there is only *one* nightclub—the Copacabana—as my age group came to think of nightclubs. A few hotel rooms here, a boîte here and there, the discotheques and the rock joints can hardly be considered nightclubs as we grew to recognize same.

It is completely understandable that back in the boom 1920s night life and booze joints should have flourished. Yet why did they come to full flower in the Great Depression of the 1930s, which was when New York night life and general metropolitan color was at its most colorful? And why did World War II, with all its hot-spending factory workers and a new financial boom at hand, injure rather than solidify the fun town we all knew? Veteran saloon owners, when they are not giving you figures on the cost of labor and supplies, believe that the wartime midnight curfew was one of many fatal blows.

"A bum who ain't drunk by midnight," said the sage Toots Shor when the midnight curfew was implemented, "ain't really trying."

Mr. Shor can be complimented for his patriotic attitude, but it is likely that, once the curfew was lifted, his bar business was one of the first to suffer. People just got out of the habit of staying up all night. It is unlikely that Jack White's Club 18, which never got really under way until two in the morning, could draw a handful of customers today.

"The streets aren't even safe anymore," is the excuse you hear both from saloon owners and saloon goers.

Then, of course, there is the cost of an evening out in the big town. It has been detailed so often. The cost of baby sitter, cab to dinner, price of dinner, price of theatre tickets, price of after-theatre snacks or drinks, cost of transportation home.

"I cannot see," says a veteran rounder, "how a man can take his wife out to dinner, to a show, to a few drinks after the show without ruining an even hundred dollars."

Whatever and whichever, prices have knocked out most of the many delightful small restaurants and cafés where, once upon a time, we could hear a first-rate pianist or guitarist or singer (or all three) without going to our cash reserve for more than six or eight bucks. The complicated and graduating taxes in the Big Town these days can alone be enough to discourage the vast army of medium spenders.

It is also at least possible that night life, as we knew it, was just an anachronism that outlived itself. Maybe the general public caught up to the economic frailties of cut booze, steaks that called for a hacksaw, indifferent or insulting waiters and hatcheck girls, the undanceable dance floor, the bad music and the owner's idiotic assumption that everybody who came through the door to leave some money was a born sucker.

But the city changed greatly overall in just a few years, and attitudes changed with it. Broadway, Times Square and other items formerly glorified in song and story, almost overnight became depressing, dismal and too often dangerous. The mass information media—the press, TV, radio—dropped the old favorite subject of Broadway, its bright lights and its bright stories.

The files of the city and state regulatory agencies furnish the hard facts, if not the hard reasons. Each year there are fewer cabarets and places to have fun after dark. Indeed, Broadway and New York are no longer the great entertainment capital of the world and have not been such for many years. Las Vegas and

Miami Beach, to name two centers, boast more big-time night life and far more action for the tourist.

As to changing economics, perhaps the subject was best illustrated by John Bruno, whose Pen and Pencil steakhouse was first drawer for over thirty years.

"I served steaks for $1.95 when I opened in the early 1930s," John once remembered. "And I made more money then, than I can make today with a steak for which I've got to charge you seven dollars."

From a purely personal point of view, the Big Town lost much of its color when it lost so many of its newspapers so quickly. The city is still there and we can see it by just looking. But reading about it in varied versions was always entertaining and informative. It is, of course, quite possible that newspapers as a medium of information are as outmoded as two-a-day vaudeville. We can watch it and hear all about it on the Magic TV Box virtually as soon as it happens and hours before we can buy a newspaper and read about it, whatever *it* was.

But another factor entered strongly into the death of so many once great newspapers—the newspapermen who founded them died and the business office took over. Today there is scarcely a newspaper in the country that is not "edited" by what is known to the editorial hirelings as "the Cash Register Cornballs." Does the paper make money? It does? Then the business office is a great editor. Who the hell were Pulitzer and Hearst, Greeley and Bennett? Did they ever establish the advertising income any business office can bring in today? And if what's to read in the paper stinks, who cares? Look at the bank balance.

I have worked for the same newspaper for thirty-four years and will offer just one example of how newspapers are "edited" today. Almost every year a union called the Newspaper Guild argues with the business office over pay raises, grievances, fringe benefits and sundry tiresome matters. Many of us are often asked to sit in on these dreary arguments. We are asked to sit in and keep our mouths shut.

In the years I have sat in, now and then, on these negotiations, I have never seen *any single news editor* allowed to have a say on any item under dispute. Negotiations between management and editorial employees are strictly a *business* matter—for the business office to handle.

"If those jerks would just ask my advice," a former managing editor once admitted to me over a freshener-upper drink, "I could tell them how to give in, surrender on certain subjects, and save the whole newspaper money. There are times when what the union is fighting for would be good for the paper. But, of course, if the union is fighting for it, those jerks upstairs figure it's got to be wrong."

Nobody ever asked this man, who was running the entire news operations of the biggest newspaper in America, for any advice on *any* editorial subject. The money changers in the upstairs temple know it all. Or so they think. They keep thinking it until all of a sudden the year's figures are in red ink instead of black. That's when the yoonowot hits the fan.

But more important than such relatively minor matters is the fact that the Great City simply decided to strangle itself to death. Once a normal midtown square block would be, perhaps, three stories high, be occupied by a couple of saloons, a dry cleaner, a shoemaker, an upstairs dentist, a what-not store and two drugstores. The whole block might have employed a couple of hundred live bodies. Down it came under the big wrecker's ball and up went a forty-story skyscraper.

What was the difference? Well, the difference was that the new skyscraper was built right to the sidewalk building line and it housed thousands of employees, the mail trucks, the toilet paper trucks, the spring water trucks, the salesmen in cabs and the bosses in limousines, who began choking the street at each corner. All progress, no doubt about it, nothing lost but those rickety old buildings that held the old tailor and that old man who ran the haberdashery and never could find what you needed.

But what else was lost? Things that were lost included those funny, impractical apartments that were one flight up or two flights up and where a couple of ballet dancers or aspiring actors or struggling young business employees could live within their income and, while doing so, have themselves one hell of a fine time in the Big City. Mostly at night.

Today, aside from a few downtown areas and the absurdly overpriced apartments on the East Side where the "swingle" saloons are, and where four to five girls must share the rent, or two or three junior business executives, just to raise the rent in New York City is beyond the average person's ability.

Of course, nobody thinks about the Old Home Town anymore. Our thoughts are on the Red Threat or the Racial Problem or the Urban Crisis or whatever is on the other side of the fence. We listen to the voices of doom on television and read the same dire prognostications in what is left of the daily press. We hear and read about "community" action, but such action, when studied, always has to do with race or minority. The Big Town itself is no community, as it once was.

It is, of course, silly and even senile to wish for the good old days. Nothing stays put, and change is essential to life itself. The fun days and nights of my era will not and cannot ever return. Maybe they weren't as much fun as memory paints them. Maybe it just *seems* that an earlier era was better.

Wanna bet?

Index